MEXICO

A Global Studies Handbook

GLOBAL STUDIES: LATIN AMERICA & THE CARIBBEAN

MEXICO

A Global Studies Handbook

James D. Huck, Jr.

A B C  C L I O

Santa Barbara, California   •   Denver, Colorado   •   Oxford, England

Library of Congress Cataloging-in-Publication Data
Huck, James D., Jr.
    Mexico : a global studies handbook / James D. Huck, Jr.
        p. cm. — (Global studies. Latin America & the Caribbean)
    Includes bibliographical references and index.
    ISBN 978-1-85109-982-5 (hard copy : alk. paper)
    ISBN 978-1-85109-983-2 (ebook : alk. paper)
    1. Mexico—Handbooks, manuals, etc.   I. Title.

    F1229.H83 2008
    972—dc22

                                              2008016624

12   11   10   09   08   1   2   3   4   5   6   7   8   9   10

Production Editor: Anna A. Moore
Production Manager: Don Schmidt
Media Editor: Ellen Rasmussen
Media Resources Coordinator: Ellen Brenna Dougherty
Media Resources Manager: Caroline Price
File Management Coordinator: Paula Gerard

ABC-CLIO, Inc.
130 Cremona Drive, P.O. Box 1911
Santa Barbara, California 93116-1911

This book is also available on the World Wide Web as an ebook.
Visit www.abc-clio.com for details.

This book is printed on acid-free paper ∞

Manufactured in the United States of America

Contents

Series Editor's Foreword

In a world in which borders are blurring and cultures are blending at a dizzying pace, becoming more globally aware and knowledgeable is imperative. This is especially true regarding one's immediate neighbors, where the links are most intense and most profound. For this pragmatic reason, knowing more about Latin America is especially relevant to people living in the United States.

Beyond such a practical consideration, Latin America is a fascinating region of the world on its own terms, and it is worth the time and energy to get to know the region better simply as a matter of intellectual curiosity. By providing a readable and engaging introduction to a representative selection of the region's countries, this series hopes to engage readers and nurture their curiosity in the region and its peoples.

One point that this series will make abundantly clear is that Latin America is not a homogeneous region. For example, its population is remarkably diverse. Indigenous peoples are spread throughout the region, constituting the majority of the population in countries where the largest of the region's magnificent pre-Columbian civilizations were centered. Descendants of the Iberian European colonizers continue to dominate the region's political and economic landscape, though recently arrived immigrant populations from Europe and Asia have made significant inroads into the economic, political, and cultural aspects of these countries. The Atlantic slave trade network brought hundreds of thousands of Africans to Latin America to labor in the plantation economy. The African cultural legacy is particularly relevant to modern Brazil and the Gulf-Caribbean countries. And the process of racial mixture, or miscegenation, that occurred freely and consistently over the past 500 years of the region's history has created a unique mestizo identity that many modern Latin Americans embrace as their own.

Obviously, therefore, one characteristic of the region that makes it so intriguing is that it is so vastly different from one country to the next and yet, at the same time, the countries of the region bear striking similarities. In addition to sharing a physical continent and space in the Western Hemisphere, the countries of Latin America also share a basic, common history that stretches from the colonial period through the present day. And the region is also bound together in many ways by language and culture.

In terms of its geography, Latin America is a vast region, encompassing more than one-half of the entire Western Hemisphere. Further, its natural environment is one of the more diverse in the world, from the deserts in northern Chile to the lush and ecologically diverse rain forests of the Amazon River basin. It is also a region rich in natural resources, providing the world with many of its foodstuffs, energy and mineral resources, and other commodities.

A few basic statistics can help to illuminate the importance of learning more about the region. Latin Americans constitute approximately 12 percent of the world's total population, and Latin American countries make up approximately 6.5 percent of the world's landmass. By some estimates, the Spanish language is the most spoken language in the Western world and is second only to Mandarin Chinese among all linguistic groups worldwide. The vast majority of Spanish speakers reside in Latin America. Portuguese, the native language of Brazil, is among the world's 10 most spoken languages.

Among the regions of the developing world, Latin America ranks consistently at the top in terms of most economic and social indicators in aggregate terms, but the region still struggles with chronic poverty and suffers from highly skewed patterns of income distribution. A consequence of this income gap has been growing out-migration, with more and more

Latin Americans each year making their way to better opportunities in wealthier and more economically developed countries. Recent efforts to promote greater economic integration by way of regional free trade agreements throughout the Western Hemisphere also illustrate the growing importance of a greater knowledge and awareness of Latin America.

In terms of politics and governments, Latin America finds itself squarely in the traditions of Western liberal democracy. Most Latin Americans embrace the values of individual freedom and liberty and expect their political systems to reflect these values. While these political aspirations have not always been the reality for Latin American countries, as of late democracy has been the norm. In fact, all of the countries of Latin America today, with the exception of Cuba, have democratically elected governments, and all are actively engaged globally.

The specific volumes in this series introduce Mexico, Brazil, Costa Rica, Cuba, and Argentina. They represent all of the different subregions in Latin America, and they range from the smallest countries to the largest in terms of population, landmass, and economic wealth. The countries included in the series vary in terms of their ethnic and class composition, with Cuba and Brazil containing large Afro–Latin American populations and with Mexico representing a society shaped by a rich and vibrant indigenous culture. The inclusion of Cuba, which remains the region's stalwart socialist experiment, offers ideological variation within the series. Argentina, Brazil, and Mexico represent the region's top three economic regional powerhouses, whose places in the global economy are well established. These three countries are also the region's most influential actors in the international arena, serving not only as leaders within the Latin American region itself but also exercising influence in the world's premier international bodies. On the other hand, Costa Rica and Cuba demonstrate the challenges of and possibilities for the region's many less influential global actors and smaller economies.

Finally, it should be noted that Latin American culture is seeping much more into the mainstream of U.S. culture. People in the United States enjoy the foods, music, and popular culture of Latin America because they are all more readily available in and appealing to the U.S. population. In fact, one might argue that the United States itself is becoming more Latin. Evidence indicates as much, as the numbers of those who identify themselves as Hispanic or Latino in the United States are growing rapidly and disproportionately to other ethnic or racial groups. According to the 2000 U.S. Census, the Hispanic population in the United States constitutes about 12.5 percent of the total U.S. population and is now the country's largest ethnic minority group. Even more striking is the incredible growth rate of the Hispanic population in the United States relative to the total population. In just 20 years, the Hispanic population more than doubled, and if this trend continues, Hispanics will constitute a majority of the U.S. population in about 50 years. The fact that Hispanics in the United States maintain strong ties to their countries of origin and retain an affinity for the culture and lifestyles common to the region makes Latin America all the more relevant to understand.

The volumes in this series provide a basic introduction to some of the countries and peoples of Latin America. In addition to a survey of the country's history, politics, economy, and culture, each volume includes an extensive reference section to help point readers to resources that will be useful in learning more about the countries and even in planning to visit them. But above all, the hope for this series is that readers will come to a better appreciation for Latin America as a region, will want to learn more about it, and will eventually experience the richness that is Latin America.

—*James D. Huck, Jr.*
Series Editor

Preface

Mexico is a country of great contrasts and complexities. It is also a country of great achievements and abundant resources. And, in many respects, it is a country that is misunderstood. Mexico cannot escape the reality that it borders one of world's most developed economies and one of the world's modern military superpowers. For all practical purposes, this means that many will see Mexico not on its own merits but in the reflective shadow of its northern neighbor, the United States. But Mexico itself is a country with a rich history, a vibrant economy, and a reserve of power that appears in its resilience in the face of foreign influences and that is projected through its magnificently rich history and culture.

The intent of this volume is to extract Mexico from this shadow of defensive obscurity as much as possible and to allow Mexico to stand on its own with regard to a profession of its unique history and identity. It is a country that has struggled and continues to struggle mightily for its independence in the face of overwhelming forces of assimilation and integration into a world that can be alien and hostile to the value of its uniqueness.

Chapter 1 places Mexico in its geographical and historical context. In this chapter, Mexico's unique demographic features, as well as its natural landscape and physical environment, are sketched out. The chapter then gives a broad-brush presentation of Mexico's extensive and fascinating history, highlighting just a few of the most important and essential events and moments in the evolution of the country. What I hope will become clear to the reader is that Mexico's physical and human geography shape and condition its history, its political life, and its economy.

Chapter 2 focuses on Mexico's economic and business environment. Here, the reader should come away with an appreciation of Mexico's complex economic structure and what it means for Mexico to be a country whose economic potential is great, but whose efforts to convert this potential into a global economic force have been part of an up-and-down struggle of successes and failures. Mexico's geographical location on the border of one of the world's most developed economies exacerbates the conditions of Mexico's economy, not to mention its business environment, as a dependent, developing economy.

Chapter 3 takes a look at Mexico's political system, some of its most important public institutions, and its relationship with the world. The discussion centers on the structure and functioning of Mexico's unique postrevolutionary governing apparatus. This includes a review of the various different branches of government; the relationships among federal, state, and local political actors; the election process; and the various avenues of public participation in the political life of the country. Unlike any other country in the Western Hemisphere, Mexico has managed to put in place a system of government that has maintained social stability and civilian control of government, creatively incorporated mass public participation in the political process, and effected a successful and relatively peaceful generational transfer of power. Because Mexico shares an extensive border and a contentious historical relationship with the United States, chapter 3 also goes into some detail about Mexico's foreign policy and international relations. The chapter also explores concepts of revolutionary nationalism and corporatism, as well as the relationship between democracy and authoritarianism.

Chapter 4 moves beyond the realms of history, economics, and politics and journeys through Mexico's social and cultural landscape. How Mexicans construct an identity, how Mexicans value and understand marriage and family, how gender determines behavior in Mexico, and how different ethnic groups interact are some of the themes touched on in the chapter. Beyond these social characteristics of Mexico, chapter 4 also explores Mexico's rich visual and performing arts traditions, as well as its literary production and its recreational life.

The second part of the book, which includes a chronology and several reference sections, offers a brief series of reference points that any reader can use for quick, practical guidance on the country and that can assist further learning and study of the country. It contains a succinct timeline of important events in Mexican history, a list of Mexico's national holidays, and a description of the food and language customs of the country. Additionally, the chapter includes brief summaries of important people, places, and events, as well as a bibliographic essay that points readers to additional sources for learning about the country, its people, and its customs in greater detail. Finally, this section contains a brief description of some civic, business, and government organizations as well as their contact information and websites.

I would also like to take this opportunity to acknowledge the many individuals who have guided me in some way through the conception and creation of this text. Professors Richard E. Greenleaf and Roderic Ai Camp first awakened in me a deep appreciation of Mexico and a fondness for its people and culture. They also were instrumental in encouraging and nurturing my scholarly interest in Mexico. The Stone Center for Latin American Studies at Tulane University has made it possible for me to pursue this project, and the many students and colleagues with whom I have had the pleasure to discuss all things Latin American over the years have played no small role in shaping my understanding of Mexico and the broader Latin American region. Any wonderful insights I attribute to them, and any errors are all my own.

I would also like to thank the editorial team at ABC-CLIO for their incredible patience, encouragement, and flexibility in working with me both on this volume and on the entire series. Alicia Merritt was instrumental in approaching me initially and explaining the project, and I thank her for her early work on the project and for placing her confidence in me to see it through to completion. Alex Mikaberidze deserves special recognition and thanks for patiently bearing with me through the writing process and for finding ways to nudge me along when things slowed down or stalled. Anna Moore, Ellen Rasmussen, and the rest of the copyediting staff have my undying gratitude for making sure that the volume reads well and is visually appealing. Finally, I would like to acknowledge the support of my wife Michele, who constantly encouraged me in the endeavor. It is to her and to my daughters that I dedicate this volume.

PART ONE
NARRATIVE SECTION

CHAPTER ONE

Geography and History

MEXICO'S GEOGRAPHY

Mexico is a country of sharp contrasts, ranging from its physical terrain to the spread and character of its population. In terms of its physical geography, Mexico's total landmass is about 764,000 square miles. This ranks Mexico as the third largest country in the Latin American and Caribbean region, following only Brazil and Argentina. Mexico shares borders with three other independent countries: the United States, Guatemala, and Belize. Its relatively open border with the United States stretches over 1,950 miles and is a major symbol of the country's independent history.

Mexico also has an extensive western coastline on the Pacific Ocean and an eastern coastline on the Gulf of Mexico. Mexico's terrain features two peninsulas, an isthmus, and two principal mountain ranges. The Baja Peninsula is located at the northwestern part of the country and extends some 400 miles directly south from the U.S.-Mexican border. The Yucatan Peninsula is located at the other, southeastern extreme of the country. The Isthmus of Tehuantepec, once considered a possible location for a transoceanic canal, lies in the southern part of the country and stretches approximately 200 miles from the Gulf of Mexico coastline to the Pacific coastline.

The two distinct and impressive Sierra Madre mountain ranges stretch from north to south and converge around the Isthmus of Tehuantepec. The Sierra Madre Occidental separates the Pacific Coast from the central valley plateaus, and the Sierra Madre Oriental separates the Gulf Coast lowlands from the central valley plateaus. The desert terrain and dry, arid climate characterize a significant portion of northern Mexico. In contrast, the central part of Mexico, which includes the country's capital, Mexico City, is mountainous and mostly temperate; however, this region is also subject to destructive earthquakes and regular volcanic activity. For its part, the southern region of Mexico, which includes the Yucatan Peninsula, is relatively flat and home to lush vegetation.

Perhaps one of the more interesting and noteworthy aspects of Mexico's physical geography is its lack of any major river systems, lakes, or cross-country waterways. The absence of unifying waterways and the geographical divisions of the country made by the Sierra Madre mountain ranges have encouraged the development of isolated and semi-independent communities, strengthening the regionalist impulses that have historically defined the country and that have led some to speak not of a single, unified Mexico but of "many Mexicos" (Simpson 1959).

The economic geography of the country reinforces the regionalism conditioned by Mexico's physical geography. Northern Mexico—particularly the borderland region, because of its access to the markets of the United States—is commonly recognized as the industrial and manufacturing center of the country's economy. In addition, most of the country's mineral resources are located in the northern region. For these reasons, the northern region of Mexico tends to be more economically oriented toward the United States, has higher per capita incomes, and measures higher on economic development indices than other regions of the country. Central Mexico, the political center of the country and where most Mexican citizens reside, is the locus of decision making and centralized authority. It is the urban, industrial, and financial capital of the country and demonstrates the extremes of both wealth and poverty. Southern Mexico, by contrast, is the most rural and agrarian region of Mexico. The economic geography of this region is defined by traditional, labor-intensive agriculture, and the economic and human development indices for this region are not comparable to the northern and central regions of the country.

Mexico's human geography parallels the physical and economic geographies of these different regions. Overall, with a total citizenry of approximately 106 million, Mexico is the second most populous country in the Latin American and Caribbean region. Mexico is also an ethnically diverse country: 60 percent of the Mexican population identifies itself as mestizo, characterized by a mix of Spanish and Amerindian heritage. However, a full 30 percent of Mexico's population identifies itself as Amerindian or predominantly Amerindian. The majority of Mexico's Amerindian population live in the most economically underdeveloped and agrarian southern region of the country and are among the poorest and most disenfranchised citizens of the country.

MEXICO'S HISTORY

Mexico is a land where differing peoples, ideologies, and cultures constantly collide. Its history is a reflection of this collision. It has been a land of opportunity, but also of seemingly insurmountable obstacles to success. Its history is marked by the existence of great empires, magnificent accomplishments in the arts and sciences, and inspiring leaders. But Mexico's history is also that of a society sharply divided along ethnic and class lines; rampant corruption and oppressive underdevelopment; and abusive, self-serving autocrats. But for a country of coalescences and collisions, its history is also one of adaptation and survival, out of which emerges a strong sense of nationalism and pride.

Ancient Mexico

The area of the Western Hemisphere where modern Mexico is situated, often termed Mesoamerica, has been a central locus of human social and political organization for thousands of years. Although the history of the region's earliest inhabitants is a matter of constant and changing debate among scholars, the archaeological record dates the presence of human life in Mexico to at least 25,000 years ago. These early peoples were, by and large, hunters and gatherers, and life for these ancient Mexicans was nomadic and oriented almost exclusively toward survival. It was not until around 5000 BC that sedentary cultures, sustained by domesticated agriculture, began to emerge in the region. By 2000 BC, which marks the beginning of what archaeologists have termed the formative or preclassic period, an agriculturally based system of social organization was firmly established in the region.

As the early Mexican peoples of the formative period settled into their routine, cyclical lifestyles characteristic of sedentary, agricultural societies and patterns of social, economic, cultural, and political complexity emerged, albeit in very rudimentary and basic ways. Religious rituals and deities developed in connection with explanations for natural phenomena, as well as the agricultural and life cycles. Social organization became more stratified and concentrated in specific centers, and hierarchies of power, control, and authority began to assert themselves among these emerging societies. Agricultural and economic systems also became more complex, with advancing technologies and markets making it possible for surplus production and the creation of a leisure class. For instance, it is during the late formative period when evidence of the use of *chinampas* first manifests itself. *Chinampas* are the floating gardens unique to Mexico in which rich and fertile lake bed mud is placed on manmade rafts and subsequently used as agricultural fields. These *chinampas* were very efficient and high-yielding sources of agricultural production, given the high fertility of the lake bed mud and the guaranteed source of irrigation. Even today, it is possible to visit the Floating Gardens of

Depiction of the floating gardens (chinampas) *of Tenochtitlán. (Gianni Dagli Orti/Corbis)*

Xochimilco in the southern part of Mexico City, a present-day reminder of this ancient agricultural method.

The Olmecs and Teotihuacanos

One of the most important and developed civilizations to emerge in Mexico during the formative period was the Olmec civilization. Located in Gulf Coast lowland areas of Mexico, in what is currently the state of Veracruz, Olmec civilization flourished during the years ca. 1100 BC to ca. 400 BC. The Olmecs are perhaps best known for their massive stone head sculptures, but many consider the Olmec culture and its nascent complex sociopolitical structures to be the root source and primogenitor for all subsequent Mexican civilizations.

Teotihuacán, located about 30 miles east of present-day Mexico City, was the largest and most important city in Mexico prior to the dominance of the Aztecs. With a population of about 150,000 at its peak (about AD 400–600), the city comprised thousands of apartments, as well as temples, plazas, and palaces. (Corel)

By the end of the formative period and the beginning of what is known as the classic period (ca. AD 200), the more important civilizations to emerge, building upon the legacies of the Olmecs, included the Teotihuacanos in the central valley region, the Zapotecs at Monte Alban in the southwestern highlands, and the Maya in the Yucatan. Scholars of Mexico's pre-Columbian history consider the classical period to be the zenith of cultural florescence. During this time, urban centers of religious and commercial activity blossomed, and social and political structures took on more defined and complex characteristics. The impressive ruins of the urban centers of the classic-period civilizations, such as the pyramids of the Sun and the Moon at Teotihuacan, the *ollama* ball courts of Monte Alban, and the temples at the Mayan city centers of Palenque and Copan, attest to the architectural sophistication and the rich social, religious, and political traditions of these peoples. In general, the archaeological record indicates that social and political structures in these classic-period civilizations were organized according to hierarchical divisions between nobility and commoners, supplemented by a well-defined and integrated religious and political elite. Patterns of imperial expansion and conquest, and their concordant emphasis on warfare, also characterized these civilizations. Evidence is also emerging that the practice of human sacrifice, for both political and religious purposes, formed an integral part of the lives of the people in these communities. However, perhaps the most celebrated aspect of classic-period civilizations in Mexico's history is the astounding achievements in science during this time, especially in the study of astronomy and mathematics. For reasons still not clearly understood, these vibrant and accomplished civilizations gradually dissolved and the great urban centers were abandoned. After a period of a couple hundred years, a period that may be called Mexico's dark ages, new areas of centralizing authority began to emerge.

The resulting social and political order established in these new centers during what is known as the postclassic period did not advance the artistic and technological innovations of the classic-period civilizations. Instead, the civilizations of the postclassic period built upon the nascent militarism of the classic period and created a world in which warfare, imperial expansion, human sacrifice, a disciplined and rigid social structure, and the fusion of religion with a militarized state were of paramount importance. It is during the latter part of this phase of Mexico's pre-Columbian history that the Aztec empire would rise to the prominence and power that the Spanish conquerors would encounter in the early 16th century. However, it was the Toltec civilization that formed the historical bridge between the dark ages following the demise of classic-period civilizations and the ascendancy of the Aztec empire; further, Toltec mythology would play a significant role not only in providing the Aztecs with the basis for their social and political order but also in encouraging the paranoid fatalism that would ultimately play into the hands of the Spanish conquerors and result in the sudden and dramatic collapse of the great Aztec empire.

The Toltecs

During the postclassic period, the central valley of Mexico definitively assumed its prominent role as the most important locus of authority and power throughout the larger geographic region that constitutes modern-day Mexico. Following the decline of Teotihuacan and the subsequent creation of a power vacuum in the region, some groups of the nomadic peoples of the more arid northern regions worked their way into the central valley. These nomadic peoples, known collectively as the Chichimecs, were fierce fighters and less culturally sophisticated than the settled urban communities of the great classic-period civilizations. One such group of nomadic peoples was the Toltecs; it was the Toltecs who eventually came to dominate the central valley region, establishing a resplendent city center known as Tula and incorporating its traditions of warfare, conquest, and imperial expansion into the area's pre-Columbian cultural history.

The Toltec dynasty, and its most important actors and legends, became the foundational mythology that legitimized and undergirded the subsequent Aztec empire and its cultural, political, and religious traditions. Central among these actors and legends is the great Toltec leader, Topiltzin-Quetzalcoatl, known for his vast knowledge and his intimate association with the Feathered-Serpent God of Wisdom (Quetzalcoatl) as this God's high priest. The association of Topiltzin-Quetzalcoatl with the God of Wisdom contrasted with a competing militant Toltec faction allied to the more terrifying deity Tezcatlipoca, who, according to legend, required the sacrificial offering of human hearts. Part of the legend of the Toltec period includes the ascendance to power of the supporters of Tezcatlipoca and the forced exile of Topiltzin-Quetzalcoatl.

The story of Topiltzin-Quetzalcoatl's exile from Tula, and the prophesy of his eventual return, became a powerful tool in the Spanish Conquest of Mexico and the stunning collapse of the Aztec empire. Further, the ascendance of the adherents to the cult of Tezcatlipoca to positions of power in the Toltec empire ushered in the practices of massive human sacrifice and ruthless military conquest of neighboring peoples, traditions that would survive beyond the early 11th century and the partly famine-induced collapse of the Toltec empire. The end of the Toltec period created a power vacuum in the central valley region, which once again encouraged other militant nomadic peoples from the northern regions to migrate south and to compete for power against one another within the region. It was out of this environment that the mercenary Aztecs (sometimes referred to as the Mexica), latecomers to the central valley, rose to predominance in the early 15th century and had the inauspicious fortune to be the imperial power of Mexico at the time the Spaniards, led by Hernán Cortés, arrived on the scene.

The Aztecs

Because the modern history of Mexico is wrapped so much in the Spanish conquest of the region, students of Mexican history spend an extraordinary amount of time and effort learning about the Aztec empire, which was magnificent, impressive, and awe inspiring for its time. In fact, one of the early Spanish chroniclers of the Conquest of Mexico, Bernal Díaz del Castillo, describes the capital city of the Aztec empire, Tenochtitlán, as more impressive than the most exotic and dynamic cities in Europe and the Middle East. It is the contact

Illustration of Tenochtitlán. In Georg Braun and Francis Hogenberg Civitates Orbis Terrarum, *Cologne, 1612–1618. (Library of Congress)*

between the European Spaniards and the Aztec peoples of Mesoamerica, more than any other pre-Columbian civilization in the region's history, that contributed so much to the shape and identity of the modern Mexican nation.

The characters and events that are part of the Aztec history of Mexico are legendary, not only in Mexico but throughout the world. This colorful story begins in the 12th century, when a nomadic tribe from the north sought a home in the central valley.

Leaving their mythical birthplace of Aztlan, the Aztecs gradually worked their way down to the central valley region of Mexico, where they could contend for access to power and greater wealth. As latecomers to a region already highly stratified and politically divided, the Aztecs found themselves relegated to the periphery of the sociopolitical environment. Consequently, the Aztecs were forced to establish their community on a seemingly inhospitable place in the middle of Lake Texcoco and served as mercenaries to the other dominant tribes of the central valley at the time.

Gradually, the Aztecs, by virtue primarily of their valor and success on the battlefield, expanded their social and political influence in the region, eventually coming to dominate and subjugate the various tribes of the central valley that they had previously served. Along with this social and political expansion came the physical expansion of the famous capital city of the Aztecs known as Tenochtitlán.

In addition to their superiority in battle, the Aztecs are known for their rampant practice of human sacrifice and the vengeful nature of their more important deities. There is no question as to the truth of this practice and its widespread use in Aztec culture. Nevertheless, while it is certainly true that Aztec practices of human sacrifice are gruesome and inhumane to the modern observer, it is important to realize that such practices existed in a context of a highly ritualistic and militaristic environment and cultural milieu in which human sacrifice was an important and accepted part of the culture.

In any event, the Aztecs came to be a formidable dynasty whose control expanded into the far reaches of what is currently modern Mexico and Central America. And it is this vast empire, ruled by a religious and political nobility, that existed in the early 16th century when the Spanish arrived on the scene.

The Maya

The Maya are another indigenous people that are part of Mexico's history and its contemporary reality. Like the Aztecs, the Maya are considered one of the Western Hemisphere's great pre-Columbian civilizations, with impressive achievements in the realms of social organization, architecture, and astronomy. The Maya are concentrated throughout the Mesoamerican region, which today encompasses the national territories of a number of Central American countries as well as southeastern Mexico. Although Mayan peoples are dispersed throughout the southern regions of the country, the traditional centers of ancient Mayan civilizations in modern Mexico are clustered predominantly throughout the jungle regions of the Yucatan Peninsula.

Many historians divide the pre-Columbian history of the Maya into two major periods, which also parallel in many ways the historical evolution of the civilizations of central Mexico. The first period is what many refer to as the classic period, which stretches from about AD 300 until about 900, when a still inadequately explained decline set in and the city centers of the classic Maya civilization were abandoned and their people dispersed. Nevertheless, during the classic period, Maya culture and civilization flourished and the Maya recorded many impressive achievements in science, arts, and architecture. One of the more important characteristics of the classic Maya was the decentralized nature of their political and social organization. Many thriving, but relatively small, population centers arose that had their own social and political dynamics distinct from other population centers in the region. Thus, no great imperial centers of power existed during the classic Maya period, and no one group emerged over others to dominate the region.

During the classic period, the Maya recorded impressive achievements in architecture, ceramic and visual arts, and science and mathematics, particularly in astronomy. In the realm of architecture, the classic Maya constructed pyramids noted for their geometric precision and their structural soundness. Maya sculpture was intricate and refined, with a precision in detail and proportion, as well as a complexity of design, that could compare with any of the great sculptors in other civilizations throughout the world at the time. The classic Maya also produced elaborate and beautiful pictorial manuscripts that charted the evolution of their history and their cultural practices. Most of these manuscripts are lost to us, but a select few remain, which have given us an invaluable window into the fascinating world of the classic Maya.

Perhaps in no other realm were the achievements of the classic Maya as impressive as in the realm of science and astronomy. For instance, the precision of the Maya calendar is unrivaled in its accuracy of charting the passage of the seasons and time by any other calendar produced in the world at the time. And the unique positioning and precise construction of Maya pyramids and other edifices in relation to the natural environment has demonstrated the mathematical complexity of the efforts executed by Maya scientists and architects, not to mention their engineering skills.

Archaeologists and historians are still debating the specific causes and the timing of the decline of the classic Maya civilization, but the fact of this decline is undisputed and is generally placed historically ca. AD 900. From that time, and for about the next 200 years, the region experienced its aforementioned dark age. During this time, the jungle reclaimed and hid many of the classic Maya centers, some of which would not be rediscovered until some thousand years later. During this time, the collapse of the great centers of classic Maya civilization and the dispersal of its citizens allowed the peoples of other regions of Mexico to penetrate the zones of the Maya and to reshape the life and culture of the region, establishing in the process new centers of authority and power. After some 200 years following the decline of the classic civilizations, a reemergence of social and political organization in the region began to take shape. This marks the second major period of Maya civilization, often called the postclassic period. During this period, strong influences from the peoples of central Mexico are evident in the renaissance of Maya civilization. Such influences included a militarization of society and politics characterized by the emergence of a centralized theocratic ruling elite. A social structure dependent on warfare and the expansion of empire also defined postclassic Maya civilization, and this structure included the incorporation of ritual human sacrifice as part of the new order, with clear parallels in religious and cultural practices to the peoples and civilizations of central Mexico.

Perhaps the most famous center of power during the early years of this Maya renaissance was Chichén Itzá. Among the Maya of Chichén Itzá, religious practices and rituals were characterized by their own versions of the deities of the peoples of central Mexico. For instance, Kukulcán was the Maya equivalent of Quetzalcoatl, both in appearance and in popular mythology. In Chichén Itzá, the architecture and sculptures of the postclassic Maya show clearly the influence of the great civilizations of central Mexico.

By the time the Spaniards arrived at the Yucatan Peninsula in the early 16th century, the Maya, through internecine warfare and other factors, had been dispersed and had become relatively disorganized, presenting only a hint of the magnificence and greatness of both the classic civilizations and the early postclassic empires. The Spaniards, who encountered the native Maya inhabitants of Mexico first on the shores of the Yucatan Peninsula, did not consider the Maya to be either a serious threat to their ambitions of conquest or an opportunity to fulfill their desires for the accumulation of power and wealth. They gave a passing glance to the Maya and left their conquest to another time. Instead,

The Temple of the Warriors at Chichén Itzá. The temple complex consists of a large stepped pyramid fronted and flanked by rows of carved columns depicting warriors. (Kristine Kikisky)

they set their sights first on the preeminent civilization and empire of the Aztecs in central Mexico.

The Spanish Conquest of Mexico

The story of the Spanish Conquest of Mexico is the stuff of legend. First, the arrival of the Spaniards in the early 1500s to Mexico came at an inauspicious time in the calendrical cycle of the Aztecs. There was evidence that the Aztec empire at the time of the arrival of the Spaniards was stretched beyond its economic and administrative capacity and was facing a major political and social reorganization, if not an entire imperial collapse. The landing of Hernán Cortés on the Mexican mainland precipitated what some argue was the inevitable fall of the Aztec empire. On top of this, Aztec religious mythology had predicted the return of the God of Wisdom, Quetzalcoatl, to reclaim his kingdom from the Aztecs at the very moment of the arrival of the Spaniards, who were intent on accumulating as much wealth and land as possible.

Soon after the famous voyages of Christopher Columbus to the Americas in the final decade of the 15th century, Spanish adventurers arrived in droves to explore and colonize the "newly discovered" lands. Cortés, a young and headstrong soldier from the Extremadura region of Spain, was one of these very early adventurers. Cortés first came to the island of Cuba in the Caribbean, where he initially settled and nurtured his growing ambition to explore and seek greater conquests in other parts of this strange, new world. Through a series of astute political maneuverings, Cortés managed to launch an expeditionary force to explore the lands to the west of Cuba, which were rumored to possess great wealth and be home to a magnificent civilization. Defying the authority of the Cuban governor, Diego Velázquez, Cortés set sail for these lands with a force of some 500 men and about a dozen horses.

In early 1519, Cortés landed on the southeastern Caribbean coast of what is today the state of Tabasco, Mexico. Over the next few months, Cortés found himself faced with a unique set of fortuitous connections and circumstances that would be decisive in his future endeavors to defeat and conquer the mighty Aztec empire. However, his adventures on the lands of Mexico did not begin with conflict. In fact, his first contact with the indigenous peoples of the area was relatively cordial. These hospitable natives informed Cortés of other "white" men who had arrived previously and had become integrated with the local peoples. One of these men was a Spaniard named Jerónimo de Aguilar, who was part of an earlier expedition that had shipwrecked some seven years prior to Cortés's arrival. Aguilar happily reunited with his Spanish countrymen and, given his facility with the Maya language, provided Cortés with an invaluable service as translator. Not long after this initial encounter, the Cortés expedition continued along the coast and eventually encountered more hostile Maya peoples, whom he proceeded to subdue with relative ease. As compensatory tribute, the defeated Maya provided Cortés with a gift of a cadre of young women as slaves. Among these was a woman by the name of Malinche, who came from the Nahua peoples of the central valley. As such, Malinche spoke both Nahuatl, the language of the Aztecs and Montezuma, and Maya. With Malinche and Aguilar now part of his expedition, Cortés found himself with a decided communications advantage at the most opportune moment in his conquest expedition. It would not be the last of the lucky breaks that befell Cortés along his charmed path.

Cortés and his crew continued their march westward along the Caribbean coast of the mainland toward the heart of the great Aztec empire and its many riches. However, fearful that an angry and vindictive Spanish Crown might nullify whatever gains he might obtain because of his mutinous behavior against Velázquez, Cortés founded the city of Vera Cruz in the name of the Spanish king according to established legal procedure, and he promptly appointed city officials, who then exercised their traditional authority to elect Cortés as their captain and chief military official. Fearful of a mutiny among his own men, Cortés promised them a more than fair share of the spoils while he scuttled their ships to prevent the possibility of retreat back to Cuba. With his authority thus legitimized and the loyalty of his men secured, Cortés began his march on Tenochtitlán, forging allies with natives itching to escape the yoke of the Aztecs or winning their allegiance through victory on the battlefields. By the time Cortés reached the outskirts of Tenochtitlán, he had, by virtue of cunning diplomacy or outright military victory, won the allegiance of such native groups as the Cempoalans, Tlaxcalans, and Cholulans, among others. On a number of occasions, Malinche was instrumental in warning

Cortés of planned attacks and of duplicitous intentions on the part of the Aztecs, who always publicly behaved deferentially and cordially in their exchanges with the Spaniards but schemed in private for their undoing. Because of Cortés's skillful machinations and Malinche's effective espionage activities, on November 8, 1519, Cortés and his troops entered the Aztec capital of Tenochtitlán without incident, as the invited guests of Montezuma, the Aztec emperor.

Tenochtitlán, a city constructed in the middle of Lake Texcoco and connected by a maze of waterway canals, completely awed the Spaniards. Its bustling urban activity and its impressive temples and palaces impressed the Spaniards in its organization and efficiency. Bernal Díaz del Castillo, one of Cortés's Spanish comrades who chronicled the events of the conquest, declared that the Spaniards had never seen a city so elaborately designed and filled with so many people, remarking that even those Spaniards among them who were acquainted with the important cities of Europe and the Middle East claimed that Tenochtitlán by far exceeded the magnificence even of Constantinople, then the most illustrious city of the Old World. Montezuma, whose feet never touched the actual soil on the grounds outside of his palaces and whose subjects neither touched him nor looked him directly in the eyes, made a great show of treating the Spanish newcomers with courtesy and sumptuous hospitality, even offering them residence in the well-fortified royal palace of Axayácatl. However, taking note of the hundreds of thousands of people swarming throughout the city conducting their daily routines and business, many Aztec warriors among them, Cortés recognized the precarious nature of his situation and kept a watchful and cautious eye, as well as an ever-alert ear, on the words, behavior, and signals, however slight, projected by Montezuma and his advisers. As the Spaniards received royal treatment and bided their time in Tenochtitlán as special guests of the emperor, Montezuma and his advisers met regularly and privately to plot their next steps in dealing with this new threat. Not trusting the intentions of the Aztecs and sensitive to the strategic weakness of his position in the Aztec capital with few escape routes by land across the lake, Cortés took preemptive action. Using the news that a few of his soldiers in Vera Cruz had been killed by some natives, the wily Spanish conquistador accused Montezuma of being responsible for these deaths. Furthermore, Cortés accused Montezuma of plotting the massacre of the Spaniards currently residing in Tenochtitlán. Under this pretext, Cortés placed the emperor under house arrest and kept an around-the-clock surveillance over him. Throughout his captivity, Montezuma continued to exercise his authority as emperor, kept to his royal routines, and was even free to move about the city under guard by the Spaniards. For his part, Montezuma was expected to keep his citizens pacified. Cortés counted on the public's conditioned and absolute deference to the emperor to keep the Aztecs at bay. Although he initially protested his house arrest and surveillance, Montezuma eventually acquiesced to this arrangement, perhaps because his fatalistic attitude resigned him to this inevitable fate. Montezuma's willingness to be used in such a way by the Spaniards deeply wounded the citizenry's faith in his role as their emperor and leader, though it did serve for some time the intended purpose of preventing a military uprising against the caged-up and closely watched Spaniards. This situation prevailed for about half a year, with Cortés biding time while he built up his alliances and developed a comprehensive strategy to emerge victorious in the eventual, inevitable conflict with the Aztecs for control over the land and its riches. Naturally, the citizens of Tenochtitlán became ever more restless with the continuing presence of the Spaniards and the arrogant affronts they levied against their emperor and their ways of life. Furthermore, their patience with Montezuma as a compromised leader was wearing thin. Montezuma, for his part, used this time thinking of ways to convince the Spaniards simply to leave.

Such was the status quo when word reached Cortés that the aggrieved governor of Cuba, Velázquez, had sent another expedition led by Pánfilo de Narváez to capture Cortés and bring him back to Cuba for trial as a traitor to the Crown, and that this expedition had arrived in Vera Cruz and had taken over the town. Cortés decided to return at once to Vera Cruz to defuse this threat before it had time to grow. So, he said his farewells to Montezuma, left a contingent of his expedition under the direction of Pedro de Alvarado in Tenochtitlán to guard Montezuma, and departed for Vera Cruz. Cortés defeated this punitive expedition, arrested Narváez, and even managed to win over a significant segment of the newly arriving forces to his cause with incredible stories of Tenochtitlán and great opportunities for personal enrichment. Once this threat had been neutralized, Cortés headed back to the Aztec capital to rejoin his men and to continue his negotiations with Montezuma. However, Cortés arrived back in Tenochtitlán to find the citizenry in a great state of agitation and anger and his men confined for security reasons to one of Montezuma's heavily fortified palaces. During Cortés's absence, Alvarado had ordered a massacre of Aztec priests and nobility, who had supposedly gathered for a ritualistic celebration, under the pretext that the gathering was really a plot to attack the Spaniards, capture them, and offer them up as human sacrifices to their bloodthirsty gods. Regardless of the truth of the instigation, the result was that the nervous and anxious Spaniards killed hundreds of Aztecs, and the citizens of Tenochtitlán were outraged and clamoring for justice, if not for vengeance, because of this unforgivable affront to their hospitality. The Spaniards, besieged by the angry mob of Aztecs, holed up in the palace of Axayácatl with Montezuma as their prisoner. Montezuma dutifully played his part as the

Spaniards' hostage and managed to keep the Aztecs from storming the palace.

It was in this environment, a prelude to wholesale war, that Cortés reentered Tenochtitlán and rejoined his weary companions. The fact that Cortés was able to enter the city without opposition leads one to believe that the Aztecs permitted this as part of a larger war strategy, for once in the heart of the city, the routes and possibilities of escape were few. Furthermore, the Spaniards could be shut off from any external supply routes of food, weapons, and even reinforcement troops.

Once Cortés and his new contingent had ensconced themselves with the others, the Aztecs attacked. War had begun. At one point, Cortés, reaching in any direction for a way out of this terrible situation, persuaded Montezuma to present himself to his people and order them to stand down and allow the Spaniards to leave. However, by this time, Montezuma's authority was completely ruined and his feeble effort to pacify his people resulted in nothing more than his ignominious death in the crossfires of war. The specific details of Montezuma's death are in dispute, but the one with perhaps the most currency is that Montezuma took a boulder thrown by an Aztec fighter to the head and died shortly thereafter. Regardless, whatever advantage the Spaniards possessed by keeping Montezuma as hostage was now gone with his death. Cortés, understanding the futility of continuing to fight as caged animals against a much more numerous and formidable foe, planned a desperate and daring midnight escape across the lake, using makeshift portable bridges to span the sections of the causeways that the Aztecs had destroyed to prevent precisely such an escape possibility. Silently, in the early morning hours of July 1, 1520, the Spaniards and their native allies ventured forth, burdened by as much of Montezuma's treasures as they could carry. But the Aztecs were not fooled, and not long after the Spaniards had begun this futile effort, a bloody and chaotic melee ensued. Although Cortés, Alvarado, and a number of other Spaniards were able to cross the lake, hundreds of Spaniards and a great number of their native allies died in the fighting. This event, known as *Noche Triste* and sometimes called the Sad Night or the Night of Sorrows, was the lowest point for Cortés and the Spaniards in their conquest expedition. In the context of this defeat, in the sorrow of so many friends and companions dead, and in the ignominy of retreat, Cortés grieved terribly, but he also resolved with an inflamed passion that he would return to exact vengeance and redeem his honor, even if it meant razing every building, temple, and palace of the magnificent Tenochtitlán.

But the Spaniards did not retreat without leaving a most lethal, stealthy, and gruesomely efficient weapon behind. While the Aztecs celebrated their victory and elevated Montezuma's nephew, Cuitláhuac as their new emperor, the disease of smallpox, apparently brought over by a member of the Narvaez expedition, began to cut down the Aztecs, who had no natural immunity to the disease, much more effectively than any Spanish sword or cannon. Cuitláhuac himself was an early casualty of smallpox, and he was replaced as emperor by his young but valiant cousin, Cuauhtémoc.

While smallpox was taking its toll on the Aztecs, Cortés was regrouping and developing his battle plan for the next encounter with the Aztecs in Tenochtitlán. Six months after the tragic events of the *Noche Triste,* Cortés once again made his way into the central valley. This time, his strategy was not to play the game of deceptive diplomacy and backroom intrigue but to attack, fight, and defeat. Purely and simply, he came to wage war. As a military tactician and planner, Cortés had unsurpassing skill. His strategy was multifaceted and strategically brilliant. He forged alliances with the peoples surrounding Tenochtitlán, thus choking off Tenochtitlán from its outside supply routes and weakening a population already suffering under the debilitations brought on by smallpox. In essence, Cortés was doing to the entire

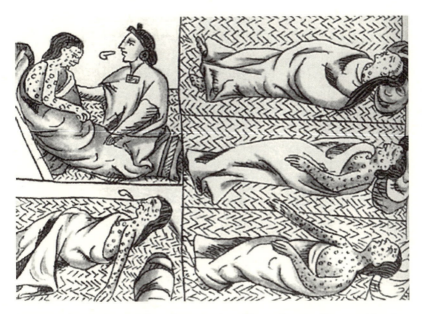

Drawing by native scribes showing the effects of a smallpox epidemic in Mexico, from the Codex Mendoza, *ca. 1542. (Courtesy David Marley)*

lake city of Tenochtitlán what the Aztecs had done on a smaller scale to the palace of Axayácatl when the Spaniards were holed up there previously. Cortés also noted that any offensive attack against a lake city such as Tenochtitlán must include both an infantry assault and a naval assault. So, Cortés had his engineers and boatbuilders design a small fleet of naval vessels outfitted for war that could be transported across land in pieces and reconstructed on the shores of the lake for launching. As soon as everything was in place to Cortés's satisfaction, he ordered the assault on the city. Instead of a quick victory, though, the Aztecs, weakened and isolated as they were, defended their city ferociously, and Cortés was only able to prevail after utterly destroying the city and its infrastructure piece by piece. The final major battle of the war took place in the famous market center of Tlatelolco, and shortly thereafter, Cuauhtémoc was captured. The Spaniards eventually would torture and execute Cuauhtémoc, both as a means to try to extract information regarding hidden Aztec treasures and as a strategy of removing any authority around which future indigenous rebellions might rally. The razing of Tenochtitlán coupled with the capture and execution of Cuauhtémoc ended the reign of the Aztecs and ushered in the period of Spanish colonial rule over Mexico, or New Spain, as the victorious Spanish conquerors would come to call the land of the defeated Aztecs.

The Conquest of the Maya.   Although carried out by similar patterns of violence and conflict, the Spanish conquest of the Maya in the Yucatan region, relative to the conquest of the Aztecs in central Mexico, was perhaps less of a dramatic military and political enterprise and more of a spiritual and cultural one. While the Maya did put up pockets of resistance to the incursions of Spanish adventurers, the Maya could not be conquered by a single assault on any imperial central authority. In part, this was due to the reality that, by the time the Spaniards had arrived to the region, the Maya were not subject to the rule of a centralized authority. Instead, the great imperial experiments of the postclassic Maya, which unified the various Maya peoples and their distinct communities under a predominant political authority, had decomposed and fragmented into a decentralized network of essentially autonomous city-states spread throughout the region. When the Spanish conquistadors ventured into the dense jungles of the Yucatan in the mid-15th century to pacify, subjugate, and convert the indigenous peoples of the region, what they found was a loosely tied network of many independent and relatively sparsely populated Maya city-states consumed with parochial interests.

The dispersal of Maya communities throughout the Yucatan Peninsula coupled with the difficulties of navigating the dense jungle terrain stretched out the conquest of the region some 150 years. This made for a very different conquest enterprise. Spanish incursion into Maya territory began by accident in 1511 as the result of an unexpected shipwreck that marooned a group of Spaniards on the mainland of the Yucatan Peninsula. A couple of other brief expeditions from the Cuba mainland skirted the coastline of the Yucatan Peninsula over the period of 1517–1519, but nothing much came of them. It was not until the Cortés expedition of 1519 that the next serious encounter between the Spanish and the Maya occurred. When Cortés landed on the shores of the Yucatan, only two of the original shipwrecked crew from the ill-fated 1511 expedition were still alive. By sheer coincidence, Cortés was able to make contact with these remaining two men. Although both of these men had been fully integrated and assimilated into the local Maya culture and society by the time of Cortés's arrival, one of these men, Jerónimo de Aguilar, eventually left his place among the Maya and rejoined the Spanish. As noted previously, Aguilar would play a critical role in the successful conquest of the Aztec empire a few short years later.

Once the Aztecs had been defeated and the indigenous peoples of the central Mexican valley pacified, attention returned to the Yucatan and the Maya. The man who, in 1526, won the legal right to conquer the Maya and claim the Yucatan on behalf of the Spanish Crown was Francisco de Montejo, who had proved his worthiness as a loyal and competent soldier in the Cortés expedition. Montejo, along with his son by the same name, spent the next 20 years pacifying the most significant of the various Maya indigenous tribes and laying the foundations for Spanish administrative and social control over the entire region. By 1546, major territorial conquest efforts had tapered off significantly, and Spanish control over the Maya of the Yucatan was firmly entrenched. Along the way, in 1542, the younger Montejo founded the city of Merida, which he used as his base of operations. To this day, Merida continues to be the most important city in the Yucatan Peninsula. Neverthe-less, in some of the more remote reaches of the jungles, pockets of Maya resistance to the Spaniards persisted, and village life completely independent of Spanish authority survived and thrived. The last of these Maya, known as the Itza Maya and located in the Petén region of Mesoamerica, were pacified and incorporated formally into the Spanish legal and colonial administrative system in 1697.

This conquest enterprise of the Maya region of Mexico was only loosely connected to the centralizing process being undertaken in central Mexico, which witnessed the decapitation of one empire and the rapid reinstitution of another. Because attempts to pacify the Maya of the Yucatan Peninsula were tedious, difficult, and remote from the centers of power in the central valley, the effort there proceeded on its own timetable and within its own context. This had the residual effect of placing the Maya and the Yucatan region on the periphery of the Spanish colonial experiment in Mexico. Consequently, Maya culture and language survived much more functionally intact over the years than did the culture and language of the central valley indigenous communities. And even within the context of nominal Spanish rule over the region, the Yucatecan Maya maintained and practiced their social, political, and religious traditions much more openly and unreservedly in spite of the spiritual conquest being undertaken with such determination and, sometimes, even ferocity, by the friars and the secular clergy. In fact, during the earlier phases of the colonization of the Yucatan and the conquest of the Maya there, the relatively slow pace of Christian conversion among the Maya and the continued practice of Maya religious rituals and ceremonies, not to mention the existence of rebellious or independent Maya peoples, were so troublesome to the Spanish religious and secular authorities that it elicited perhaps the most aggressive and thorough eradication and conversion campaign undertaken throughout the Spanish conquest of the entire region. This was partly due to the unique nature of the social and political organization of the Maya, but it was probably more largely due to the single-minded and determined efforts of one particular Spanish Franciscan friar, Diego de Landa, whom the Spanish Crown named the first archbishop of Yucatan.

The work and writings of Landa, who was originally assigned as bishop to the Maya lands of the Yucatan Peninsula during the early phases of conquest and colonialism in Mexico, gives witness not only to the brutality of the nature of the spiritual and physical conquest of the Maya but also to the persistence and richness of Mayan religious, cultural, and linguistic traditions in the face of persistent oppression and forced assimilation into mainstream Mexican life and culture as defined by the political elites in central Mexico.

Colonial Mexico

As is the case with the rapid collapse of any imperial authority, the first few years immediately following the fall of Tenochtitlán were times of turmoil and uncertainty as Cortés and his fellow adventurers attempted both to expand their reach in more remote areas of the region and to put the pieces of empire, albeit a European one, back together again. The head of Aztec imperial authority had been decapitated, and the process of building and consolidating a new social and political order out of the scattered fragments of the crushed empire was anything but settled. Cortés, even prior to the final assault on Tenochtitlán, had sent out subordinates to conquer for Spain other tributary indigenous communities that had been brought into the Aztec empire. This expansion of Spanish control simply magnified once the Aztecs were defeated. Some tributary indigenous communities had been so thoroughly integrated into the Aztec imperial framework that the Spaniards had little trouble asserting their control and authority over them. Other communities that had only reluctantly submitted to Aztec authority and thus had retained some semblance of autonomy in the face of their subordination took the defeat of the Aztecs as an opportunity for reclaiming their independence and refused to accept Spanish claims to authority over them without a fight.

This transitional period lacked a coherent administrative apparatus and a centralized authority necessary to guide the reconstruction of the social and political order in New Spain, and the Spanish monarchy stepped in to provide both. While rewarding Cortés handsomely for his handiwork in bringing such a wealthy and vast territory under its dominion, the Spanish Crown wasted no time in asserting its authority and privileges to manage this new addition to the Spanish kingdom. The next 280 years were dedicated to a great colonial experiment for Spain in the land of the Aztecs, the Maya, the Mixteca, and the Chichimeca. The Spanish colonizers and the Spanish Crown built on the ruins of the Aztec empire a colonial economy, society, and political structure oriented to serve Spain and its Spanish colonists.

Spanish Colonial Administration in New Spain.   The Spanish Crown, having observed the mutinous behavior of Cortés and the corruption of other Spanish colonial administrators and adventurers, knew quite well the risks of centralizing power in the hands of a few individuals. It also knew quite well the limits of its abilities to control and contain individuals who might behave in ways boldly defiant of its authority. It often had to walk a fine line between being forgiving and accommodating of the rebellious tendencies of powerful conquistadors and of behaving decisively and sternly in brooking no serious challenge to its ultimate authority. Thus, traditional patterns of royalism and absolutism, while certainly present in the Spanish colony of New Spain as an extension of the royalism and absolutism of Spain itself, fail to capture the uniqueness of the decentralized aspects of the public administrative system of New Spain. It is precisely this decentralizing aspect of the colonial administrative system that allowed Spain to manage and retain its control over the region for more than 300 years with minimal threats to its authority, even after its own status as a dominant world power declined and the economic dynamism of its colonies eclipsed that of the mother country itself. What was this colonial system of administration? How and why did it come about and evolve in the way that it did? And how did it function specifically in New Spain?

It behooves us to recall that with the defeat of the Aztecs, Cortés brought into the fledgling Spanish empire a territory by many degrees much more vast and wealthy in human and natural resources than anything anyone had seen previously. How Spain managed this vast and populous territory would serve as the guide for its entire system of colonial administration. Thus, one of the first and most important endeavors of the Spanish Crown following Cortés's successful conquest was the establishment of an administrative and political apparatus to assert and consolidate royal authority over the newly acquired territory and all of its resources and riches. From the Crown's vantage point, this administrative and political apparatus had to be structured in order to ensure three things: (1) that the Spanish Crown would receive its own proper share of the wealth contained in the territories conquered in its name; (2) that intimates of the Spanish Crown would protect its interests and would check the ambitions of the less-trusted conquistadors, most of whom also came from humble class origins; and (3) that the ambitions of colonial public administrators themselves, even those trusted by the Crown, could be kept in check and guarded from the temptations to assume the airs of an independent royalty.

While Cortés, by most accounts, was a faithful servant of the Spanish Crown, an able and competent administrator, and an astute financial manager whose economic policies for the colony served the financial interests of the Crown quite well, his disobedient and insubordinate behavior with regard to Velázquez in Cuba, coupled with his impressive and growing power and wealth, made him suspect to the Crown. Furthermore, Cortés was not without his enemies in New Spain, who envied his wealth and power, and these rivals did not hesitate to send reports back to Spain that painted Cortés and his loyalty to the Crown in less-than-flattering terms. Cortés, in spite of making a special trip to Spain to plead his case and demonstrate in person his unflagging loyalty to the Spanish King Charles V, could never beat down these lingering doubts, and the Spanish Crown, though it honored Cortés for his accomplishments, felt much more comfortable entrusting the administration and management of its new territories to individuals of proven loyalty and possessing proper aristocratic credentials.

Thus, the Spanish monarchy moved quickly to appoint an administrative apparatus of its own design to oversee colonial affairs in New Spain and to keep a watchful eye on Cortés and the many other adventurers pouring into the region eager to seek fortunes through their own conquest expeditions. Colonial administrative designations, known as viceroyalties, ordered the limits of the colonial administrative apparatus and were confined to loosely demarcated geographical boundaries, which often shifted as the empire expanded. Following this structure, colonial Mexico was managed as the Viceroyalty of New Spain, and a personal representative of the Crown, known as the viceroy, or vice king, exercised executive authority over the viceregal territory. The viceroy's authority was virtually absolute in day-to-day administrative matters. The viceroy was also the chief military officer of the viceroyalty and assumed direct responsibility for the maintenance of law and order in his jurisdiction, and for the defense and even expansion of the Spanish empire in the region. However, the viceroy's power

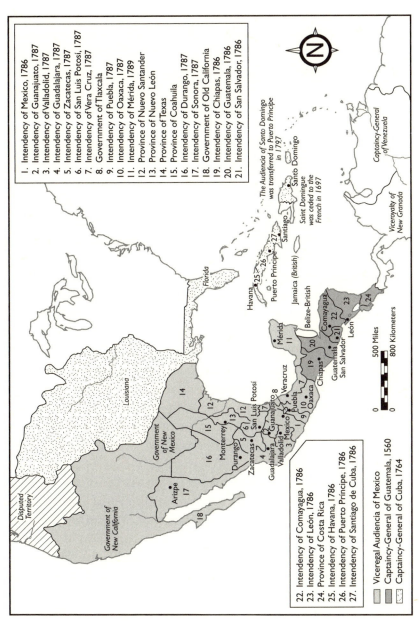

1. Intendency of Mexico, 1786
2. Intendency of Guanajuato, 1787
3. Intendency of Valladolid, 1787
4. Intendency of Guadalajara, 1787
5. Intendency of Zacatecas, 1787
6. Intendency of San Luis Potosí, 1787
7. Intendency of Vera Cruz, 1787
8. Government of Tlaxcala
9. Intendency of Puebla, 1787
10. Intendency of Oaxaca, 1787
11. Intendency of Mérida, 1789
12. Province of Nuevo Santander
13. Province of Nuevo León
14. Province of Texas
15. Province of Coahuila
16. Intendency of Durango, 1787
17. Intendency of Sonora, 1787
18. Government of Old California
19. Intendency of Chiapas, 1786
20. Intendency of Guatemala, 1786
21. Intendency of San Salvador, 1786

22. Intendency of Comayagua, 1786
23. Intendency of León, 1786
24. Province of Costa Rica
25. Intendency of Havana, 1786
26. Intendency of Puerto Príncipe, 1786
27. Intendency of Santiago de Cuba, 1786

Viceregal Audiencia of Mexico
Captaincy-General of Guatemala, 1560
Captaincy-General of Cuba, 1764

The Audiencia of Santo Domingo was transferred to Puerto Príncipe in 1797

Saint Domingue was ceded to the French in 1697

Viceroyalty of New Spain

was not unchecked. The Spanish colonial administrative system also established an institution, known as an *audiencia,* to handle judicial affairs. The *audiencia,* constituted of a panel of judges known as *oidores,* not only oversaw judicial affairs but also acted in an advisory capacity to the viceroy on executive and legislative matters. Both the viceroy and the *audiencia* had direct access to the Crown and to its colonial administrative body in Spain, the Council of Indies. The *audiencia* could report confidentially on any malfeasance on the part of the viceroy, and the viceroy could do likewise for any *oidor* on the *audiencia.*

In 1527, some six years after the fall of Tenochtitlán, the Spanish Crown constituted the first *audiencia* for the territory. This *audiencia* actively assumed its duties in early 1529. The Crown took a little longer to secure the appointment of its first viceroy, who accepted his commission in 1530 but who, for personal reasons, was unable to assume his duties until 1535.

The first *audiencia* comprised three *oidores,* one of whom was the unscrupulous and ambitious Nuño de Guzmán, who also presided over the body. This first *audiencia,* unaccountable to any competing authorities in the absence of a viceroy, fell prey to the temptations of power and wealth and was characterized by rampant corruption, unabashed greed, and coercive exploitation of native and Spaniard alike. In less than a year, this *audiencia* disbanded in the midst of a demoralized environment of its own creation, with its presiding official, Guzmán, fleeing to the west to escape the reach of an angry and disappointed Crown as well as to engage in his own conquest expeditions. By the beginning of 1530, a newly appointed *audiencia* had assumed the reins of the colonial administration of New Spain. This new *audiencia* distinguished itself for its just and competent administration of colonial affairs on behalf of the Crown, but the fiasco of the first *audiencia* drove the point home that a competing authority in the person of the viceroy was all the

Antonio de Mendoza, first viceroy of New Spain (1535–1550). (Museum of History, Chapultepec Castle, Mexico City)

more important as an effective check and balance against the power both of the *audiencia* and of the conquistadors. Any potential disputes or disagreements between the viceroy and the *audiencia,* or between individual Spanish colonists and any of the colonial administrative units, could only be resolved by royal decision. The effect was to decentralize power in the colony and to locate ultimate authority in Spain, even though daily administration was left to the colonial administrators.

The first viceroy of New Spain was a respected Spanish nobleman and aristocrat, Antonio de Mendoza, who brought with him extensive administrative and diplomatic experience. Mendoza arrived in New Spain in 1535 to carry out his duties. He was the first of a long line of viceroys, and on balance one of the most competent and able. Working in concert with the well-respected and equally competent second *audiencia,* Mendoza, during his more than 15-year tenure in the viceregal seat, established a firm foundation for a stable and functional colonial administrative structure. His successor, Luis de Velasco, who also served an unusually lengthy term of 14 years, was equally competent and successful. Under the nearly 30-year leadership of these first two viceroys, the roots of Spanish royal authority and control over New Spain had grown strong and deep.

But the unique system of checks and balances did not end with the institutions of the viceroy and the *audiencia.* In fact, it extended even further into the colonial administrative structure, reaching all the way down to the municipal level, which made nearly all colonial public officials subject to peer accountability and thus solidified an individual public official's dependence on the authority of the Crown in Spain. Other administrative innovations contributed to the dynamic. For instance, the Crown at times would send a special representative, a kind of administrative inspector general known as a *visitador,* to make periodic assessments of the state of affairs in the colony. Usually, the *visitador* was a well-respected member of the Spanish aristocracy with close personal ties to the monarchy, and almost always with legal training. During his inspections, the *visitador* took effective charge over the colony for the duration of his "visit." An interesting aspect of this institution is that such visits could be unannounced, potentially catching a viceroy and other public officials by surprise. *Visitadors* were given as much time and as much leeway as necessary to carry out a thorough inspection. The element of surprise built into the *visita,* and the extensive power accorded to the *visitador,* intended to keep public officials, especially high-ranking ones, honest and upright, lest they be caught unawares in the midst of unscrupulous or questionable dealings.

Furthermore, all public officeholders, including the viceroy and the *audiencia* judges, at the end of their terms of office, were subject to an external review of their job performance through the *residencia,* a kind of public accounting of one's job performance. The *residencia* was essentially a legal proceeding, and the individual appointed to conduct the *residencia* trial, a special *residencia* judge, presided over public hearings, gathered testimony, and issued judgment. In the case of high-ranking officers such as the viceroy or *audiencia* judges, the *residencia* was usually conducted by a *visitador,* who made a special trip from Spain for the purpose. For lower-ranking public officials, the viceroy would appoint the *residencia* judge. Once the *residencia* was announced and a *residencia* judge selected, notice of the dates of the *residencia* was made public and anyone could provide testimony over these days either for or against the public official. The person subject to the *residencia* was required to remain present, or "in residence," during the course of the *residencia* hearings.

Though the *visita* and the *residencia* often did not function as intended, since *residencia* judges and witnesses could be bribed and since *visitas* could be compromised or *visitadors* stonewalled, the institutions still had an important function in providing multiple information flows to the Crown and in decentralizing authority within the colony by adding other layers of checks and balances to the process.

And yet the labyrinthine nature of the administrative apparatus, with its multiple checks and balances, still did not end with the *residencia* or the *visita*. The Crown also constantly issued and reissued rules and regulations that governed not only how public officials administered their official duties but even particular aspects of their personal, private lives. For instance, certain individuals holding appointed office were not allowed to marry among the local citizenry, to own property, to engage in commercial activity, and so forth, without the explicit permission to do so from the Crown. Such regulations represented another way to discourage corruption and malfeasance.

As the colony of New Spain expanded, the Crown subdivided it into smaller administrative units. Additional *audiencias* presided over more settled lands that were some distance from the capital city of the colony but that had a burgeoning citizenry and a relatively established and stable environment. For the frontier regions that were still unsettled and subject to the vagaries of frontier warfare between resistant native populations and Spanish military forces attempting to pacify the region, the Crown appointed a captain general to oversee administrative affairs of the region. Such captains general, who were usually military officers, were nominally subject to the authority of the viceroy, but given the unstable nature of the environment, they had wide latitude in how they managed affairs in their captaincies general.

Throughout the early colonial period, from the establishment of the first *audiencia* in 1529 until the Bourbon reforms of 1700 (see "Reform and Rebellion in Late Colonial Mexico: Prelude to Independence" below), the Viceroyalty of New Spain contained up to five *audiencias* (Nueva España, Nueva Galicia, Nuevo Santander, Nueva Extremadura, Nueva Vizcaya) and four captaincies general (Guatemala, Yucatan, Cuba and Santo Domingo, and the Philippines). In each *audiencia* district, the presiding *audiencia* judge also served as the district governor and still reported to the viceroy. In the viceregal capital, the viceroy himself served as an *oidor* as well as the presiding officer of the *audiencia*. *Audiencia* districts were also broken down into even smaller administrative units at the municipal level. In municipal government, the local citizenry exercised a limited type of self-government. For instance, local residents of a municipality elected their own local representatives to the city council. This city council, also known as the cabildo, was composed of members of the local elite who were elected as city council members, or *regidores,* among whom two individuals were selected to function as co-mayors (*alcaldes mayores*). The cabildo was essentially the only place where criollos, or native-born descendants of Spanish settlers, could participate in public administration, for the Crown restricted occupation of almost all other public offices to *peninsulares,* or individuals born and raised in Spain. Given that criollos, always a bit suspect to the Crown in terms of their loyalty to the mother country above the colony, generally dominated the institution of the cabildo, the Crown also appointed a separate official of peninsular stock to oversee municipal administration and to monitor the activity of the cabildo. Known as a *corregidor,* this individual was often seen as a carpetbagging outsider to the local community and its leaders. Because of this, relations between *corregidores,* who could be very corrupt and abusive of their authority, and the cabildo could be tense and frosty. Throughout the colonial period, municipal cabildos and the *corregidores* assigned to oversee them managed to keep the peace out of mutual convenience if not exactly out of mutual respect. However, the cabildo would function as the local rallying point for independence when the Spanish monarch, Carlos IV, abdicated his throne following the French invasion and occupation of Spain in 1808.

The Spanish Crown also created a separate administrative apparatus that guided the affairs of the local indigenous populations. The reason for segregating indigenous peoples in this way was that the Crown had instituted a separate body of laws that applied exclusively to the protection of the indigenous peoples of the colony. Influenced by the arguments of the Franciscan Friar Bartolomé de las Casas, who tirelessly defended the humanity and the rights of the indigenous peoples, the Crown believed that, as Christian neophytes not fully capable of possessing the rights or fulfilling the obligations of full citizenship, the indigenous peoples required special protections and laws regulating their affairs and guiding their social and spiritual formation. Through this separate body of laws and administrative structure, the Spanish monarchy hoped to protect the indigenous peoples from the excesses and abuses of unscrupulous colonists and adventurers. Thus, though indigenous communities still fell under the jurisdiction and authority of the viceroyalty and its appropriate *audiencia,* an official known as a *corregidor de indios* was appointed by the Crown to oversee and administer the Crown's unique paternalistic relationship with its indigenous subjects. In practice, however, the Crown's good intentions had quite the opposite effect. Segregating the indigenous peoples in this way only encouraged Spanish colonists and public officials to continue to see and to treat the native peoples as subordinate and lesser beings. This policy invited all kinds of abuses and exploitation, even though the intent was precisely to prevent such abuses and exploitation.

The structure of the colonial administrative system encouraged a type of competitive rivalry among those who would seek to hold public office in colonial New Spain. Individuals desirous of the perquisites, privileges, and prestige that came with public office made every effort to ingratiate themselves with the Spanish Crown, which made appointments to such offices. Furthermore, aspirants to public office would also seek to tarnish the reputations of current officeholders, in the hopes of eventually making that office available for the taking. This competitive system of checks and balances had the Crown at the center as the dispassionate mediator and ultimate arbiter. In this way, problems or dissatisfactions with the ways things worked in the colonies rarely translated into a critical commentary on the authority or the legitimacy of the Crown itself, but rather with corrupt, incompetent, or abusive local public officials.

Spanish Colonial Society in New Spain. In order for the Spanish Crown, and those who engaged in conquest expeditions in its name, to recover the costs of its enterprises as well as to profit from them, sources of labor and tribute had to be preserved. The institution in colonial Mexico that served this end was principally the encomienda. The encomienda was essentially a contract between the conquistador or the Spanish settler and the Crown in which native populations were placed in the care of the conquistador/settler. The contract allowed for the encomendero (the individual awarded an encomienda) to exact tribute and demand labor from his native charges. In exchange, the encomendero promised to deliver a percentage of the tribute and the profits from the productive use of native labor to the Spanish Crown. But the encomendero also assumed responsibility for tending to the physical and spiritual well-being of his native charges.

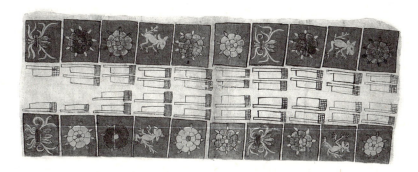

Paper leaf from the Huejotzingo Codex *depicts the variety and quantity of woven cloth given in tribute by the people of the Puebla region of Mexico to the Spanish administration, 1531. (Library of Congress)*

This arrangement suited the interests of the Crown and the individual encomendero quite well. On the one hand, the Crown had to do very little in order to receive its share of the profits. Its actions were limited to issuing a legal title to the encomienda and then having its official representatives in the region monitor the activities of the encomendero and collect its due. On the other hand, the encomendero had his claims to sources of wealth legitimized by royal sanction. This was of utmost importance to the encomendero because it provided a secure means by which he could repay whatever debts he might have incurred in financing his adventures. The encomienda added some measure of financial security to his life in the colony, and it also functioned as a means of upward social mobility in a very rigid, hierarchical social structure that offered few avenues for such advancement. In essence, holding title to an encomienda was a public manifestation of the encomendero's improved social status, both in the colony and back in Spain, that being an encomendero guaranteed.

In principle, the encomienda claimed to serve the interests of the natives subject to it. For example, as noted previously, the encomendero was obligated as part of his contractual agreement with the Crown to provide for the material and spiritual well-being of the indigenous peoples under his charge. Furthermore, the idea was also that the encomendero would have a vested personal interest in keeping his charges healthy and happy in order to maintain the source of his income. In practice, however, the institution was mostly a vehicle of abuse and exploitation of the natives.

The Church and the Inquisition: Spiritual Conquest

The Catholic Church also had an important role in the political, social, and economic life of colonial Mexico. In fact, at every stage of the conquest and colonization, Catholic priests and missionaries were present. Perhaps more importantly, though, the fusion of the Catholic Church with the Spanish monarchy made the Conquest of Mexico not only a political and economic conquest but a spiritual one as well.

For the Catholic Church, the "discovery" of new lands inhabited by peoples previously unknown to it represented an opportunity of historic proportions for evangelization and conversion. The opportunity to win literally hundreds of thousands of new converts to the faith presented a challenge to the Catholic Church in the context of the discovery, conquest, and colonization of the region. On the one hand, the Catholic Church, tied as it was to the Spanish monarchy, recognized the Crown's worldly rights and obligations to manage its empire and deferred to its authority in temporal matters, that is, in matters particular to the conduct of business, politics, and social engineering. In fact, not only did the Church accept the Crown's authority to establish policies with regard to the treatment of the Indians but its representatives in the Americas often themselves defended the necessity and justice of such policies and even directly benefited from them. After all, it was native labor that built the great churches and cathedrals of colonial Mexico, and it was native tribute and tithing to the Catholic Church in colonial Mexico that helped to enrich the Church and thus supported its evangelizing missions. On the other hand, the Catholic Church considered its authority in providing for the spiritual care and well-being of the native populations to be paramount. The fact that colonial Mexico was home to literally hundreds of thousands of indigenous people made it almost inevitable that tensions over the treatment of the natives would surface between the Catholic Church and the Spanish Crown when such treatment hindered the effective conversion or evangelization of the natives. So, in essence, the role of the Catholic Church in the conquest and colonial history of Mexico was complex. It served as an institution that would protect and defend the rights of the native peoples against unscrupulous conquistadors and colonists, yet it also buffeted and augmented the Spanish Crown in its efforts to sustain and expand its empire. Even within the Catholic Church itself, divisions between the secular clergy and the regular clergy added dimensions of complexity to the behavior and function of the Catholic Church in colonial Mexico.

The first representatives of the Catholic Church in Mexico were from the religious orders. Secular clergy came to the colony only later, after the conquest had been secured and the institutionalization of colonial life had begun to take root. The difference is important to note because clergy from religious orders tended to be more concerned with spiritual conversion and defending the humanity of the indigenous peoples than with subjecting the indigenous peoples to civil authority. Secular clergy, by contrast, tended to see the spiritual conquest as a means to bring the native peoples of Mexico under the tutelage of the Spanish monarchy and its colonial administrative apparatus in the service of temporal and more secular goals of social and economic development.

The Inquisition in Colonial Mexico.   A significant institution in colonial Mexico that bridged the divide between secular and religious authorities was the Inquisition. The Inquisition, essentially, was an agency of the state, answerable principally to the Crown and its duly appointed representatives in the colony. Hence, its purpose was not only to enforce religious orthodoxy among colonial residents but also to secure and defend the religious underpinnings of the Spanish Crown's authority in the colonies. Unlike its role on the European continent, the Inquisition assumed a much more lax tone in the colonies and exhibited much more flexibility in enforcing Catholic orthodoxy and in meting out punishments for violation of orthodox religious values and prescriptions. Nevertheless, the Inquisition in Mexico was a significant actor in promoting conformity to official Church doctrine. Because of the unique and special authority the state maintained over Church affairs in the colony through the *patronato real* (royal patronage), the Inquisition served as an important means for the state to utilize religion for secular ends.

Colonial Letters: Sor Juana

Like most other colonial experiments, the cultural and artistic life of colonial Mexico was never well developed. With a few rare exceptions, colonial Mexico did not produce any cultural or artistic innovations. In fact, the nature of the colonial mentality was such that all things noble and good and creative could not truly be generated out of the colony. Indigenous artistic achievement was perceived as exotic and interesting but was never embraced as evidence of advanced culture and was always considered inferior. As in many other areas of colonial life, the idea was that the colony existed to provide only the rough and the raw to the mother country and relied on the superior abilities of the mother country to produce the refined and the cultured, which then would work its way back to the colony for its consumption. This attitude applied to the arts and culture as well, which had a dampening effect on creative artistic and cultural production in colonial Mexico.

However, the few exceptions to this rule that did surface in colonial Mexico during the nearly 300-year history of Spanish rule over the region were extraordinary. Perhaps the best known of colonial Mexico's lettered class was a nun by the name of Sor Juana Inéz de la Cruz, who lived in the mid-1600s. Life for women in colonial New Spain was very restricted. There were few opportunities for "decent" women other than marriage or life as a religious. Marriage carried with it a very structured life within the confines of the home, and the role of the woman in marriage was strictly to care for the family. Educational opportunities were generally not available to women in colonial Mexican society, and women were actively discouraged from participating in the intellectual and administrative life of the colony.

Given these limitations, and desiring not to confine herself to the anti-intellectualism of married life, Sor Juana chose to embrace a religious vocation, which provided her the only opportunity, albeit a very limited one, to develop her passion for learning and her skills as both a scientist and a writer. Sor Juana, from the cloistered life of the convent, entertained her curiosities in scientific inquiry in natural phenomena and also wrote some of the most beautiful poetry and plays of the day. She was a brilliant essayist who did not shy away from challenging both the orthodoxy of the Catholic Church as it related to the arts and sciences and the most controversial aspects of governing and statecraft then being practiced.

Her ruminations and publications made her famous back in Spain, but they also incurred the displeasure of colonial Church authorities, who believed that a nun should refrain from such activities and should concentrate on the contemplative life of monastic prayer and on the charitable social works normally ascribed to female religious. When attacked

Sor Juana Inéz de la Cruz was one of the greatest poets and writers in the Spanish-speaking world. She was also a feminist at a time when such things were almost inconceivable. (Art Resource)

by such authorities, Sor Juana wrote a famous and oft-referenced letter in which she defended her life and activities as an intellectual. Yet, Sor Juana was a product of her times and ultimately accepted the authority of the Church and gave up her books, experiments, and writings as a sign of her conformity to the conscribed and limited role expected of her as a woman and a nun.

Spanish Colonial Economy in New Spain

The economy of colonial Mexico was oriented exclusively to the service of the mother country based on the economic philosophy of mercantilism. One of the tenets of mercantilism is that states should seek colonial possessions to expand the range of wealth and resources at the disposal of the colonizing power. In essence, mercantilism demands the creation and expansion of territorial empires. In order for the mother country to benefit from the resources offered by territories incorporated into the empire, such resources had to be extracted and then shipped over to the mother country. Territorial acquisitions were jealously guarded, and any commercial activity that involved the territory was managed through the mother country. In the Spanish empire, its colonial possessions in the New World, divided into clear administrative units, were prohibited from engaging in commerce not only directly with any other sovereign state but also among themselves. All traded commodities had to pass through the ports of Spain before they could then make it to other ports throughout the world. In this way, Spain could regulate the commodity markets and impose fees and taxes on the reexported commodities. Another tenet of mercantilism is that the colonial economy sent raw materials to the mother country, whose merchants then converted them into processed and finished goods, ready for export back to the colonies for their consumption with significant value added, as well as to the broader world market.

One of the principal motivations for conquest, which served the immediate financial interests of the Crown, was the discovery and extraction of precious metals. Mining was perhaps the most important activity of the colonial economy of New Spain. The extraction of precious metals was always a primary objective of the Spanish Crown in its approach to colonial economic management, and colonial Mexico, while not as rich in precious metals as the Andean colonies of the

Spanish empire, still produced a significant cache of precious metals to finance the Spanish Crown's enterprise. Mexico possessed a relative abundance of silver, which was found in regions just to the north and just to the south of Mexico City in the areas today known as Cuernavaca, Taxco, and San Luís Potosí. The extraction of silver from these mines constituted a significant part of the economic activity of colonial Mexico.

However, people need to eat. Thus, agriculture and livestock ranching were another important economic activity of colonial New Spain, if not primarily for purposes of trading with Spain, at least for ensuring that the labor force could be sustained for work in economic activity that did enrich the mother country.

General trade in commercial goods was another important economic activity of the colony. Spanish merchants would process primary materials imported from the colonies into finished goods, or they would contract out the production of finished goods to other producers throughout Europe and then export the finished goods back to the colonies.

Reform and Rebellion in Late Colonial Mexico: Prelude to Independence

By the late 17th century, Spain's grip on its empire was loosening, and this loosening propelled the Spanish monarchy, which passed from the Habsburgs to the Bourbons, to implement a series of administrative reforms affecting both the governance of its colonies and the economic model that defined the commercial relationship between Spain and the colonies. Ironically, these "Bourbon" reforms, which really were an attempt by the Spanish monarchy to tighten its control over its American colonies, actually planted the seeds that would later propel its American colonies toward independence. The stricter administrative regulations that tried to keep economic and political power in the hands of Spaniards alienated the criollo classes, who had come to expect a certain amount of autonomy and privilege over the lands that they called home. Furthermore, the more liberal economic policies that the Bourbons instituted to bring about greater efficiencies in an effort to improve the fortunes of the Spanish royal treasury merely whetted the appetites of colonial business elites and merchants for even greater freedoms in the realm of trade and finance.

Economic Reforms. Although the Bourbon monarchy implemented a number of economic reforms that affected Mexico, perhaps the most important of these were (1) the reduction of taxes and other levies on trade and commerce between Mexico and the mother country; (2) the expansion of officially sanctioned ports of commerce within Mexico that weakened the monopoly of a privileged merchant class throughout the region and decentralized economic power; (3) the weakening and eventual elimination of the Casa de Contratación in Spain, which reduced the bureaucratic transaction costs of doing business while simultaneously loosening the stranglehold that a centralized Spanish administrative apparatus and business class had exercised over Mexico; and (4) the development and utilization of advanced technologies in mining, which augmented the importance and power of Mexico, since Mexico was Spain's precious metals mining mecca.

Political Reforms. With regard to the restructuring of the political and administrative apparatus, the Bourbons implemented what was essentially a multifaceted process of political reform. First, the Bourbons sought to make colonial administration more manageable and efficient by decentralizing power away from the two main viceroyalties of Peru and New Spain (Mexico) by creating the additional separate viceroyalties of La Plata and New Granada as well as subdividing their entire American colonial empire into

new bureaucratic and administrative units called inten-
dencies (*intendencias*). Second, the Bourbons attempted
to reassert peninsular authority over colonial public administration by ending the Habsburg practice of selling local offices to American-born criollos and reestablishing the
practice of permitting only individuals born in Spain to
hold colonial office. Third, the Bourbons made much more
regular use of the practice of having visitors general conduct independent and comprehensive reviews and assessments of colonial public administration. Fourth, the
Bourbons attempted to reclaim in the American colonies
its privileges of authority over the Catholic Church, which
had gradually become increasingly powerful and functionally independent from the secular political representatives
of the Spanish monarchy. These political and administrative reforms, among a number of others, did create a much
more efficient management of the colonial empire in the
Americas. However, they also contained the seeds of discontent that would also come to characterize the colonies'
relationship with the Spanish monarchy over the 18th century. The criollos' loss of access to local power and privileges that accompanied these reforms left them embittered
and feeling more and more alienated from the Spanish
monarchy. Furthermore, the enlightenment ideas of efficiency in public administration, the primacy of the secular
state over religious authority, and the deregulation of certain aspects of the mercantilist economic model, when
coupled with the growing notions of popular sovereignty
that challenged the divine right of kings to rule indiscriminately over their subjects, encouraged American-born
colonists and native populations alike to claim more boldly
their rights to participate in local affairs governing their
lives and livelihoods. It was within this environment that
Mexico positioned itself for a break with Spain as the 18th
century came to a close.

Mexican Independence

The independence of Mexico, like that of most of the rest of Spanish America, emerged out of the leadership crisis in Spain precipitated by the French invasion and occupation of Spain in 1808 and the abdication of the Spanish throne by King Carlos IV. In the case of Mexico, this crisis in Spain gave rise to competing debates over who was to assume the role of governing authority in Mexico. As Mexican criollo elites were negotiating this matter with the Spanish viceroy assigned to the region, a Mexican mestizo priest by the name of Miguel Hidalgo took matters into his own hands and called for a grassroots independence movement that advocated not only the end of Spanish royal authority over the former colony but also a radical plan for social and economic reform.

In 1808, Hidalgo issued his famous *grito de Dolores* declaring open rebellion against the Spanish monarchy and on behalf of Mexican independence. The mestizo and lower-middle popular classes rallied behind Hidalgo and constituted a formidable army that attempted to use military force to dislodge the entrenched Spanish colonial authorities from power and to inaugurate an independent and social reform–minded national government. However, the more radical social reform agenda that was attached to the Hidalgo rebellion alienated the criollo elites whose vision for independence did not encompass such a radical restructuring of Mexican society. These criollos primarily desired political independence from Spain. To the extent that representatives of the criollo elite did embrace any type of social reform as part of their own calls for independence, it was certainly gradualist and to be instituted from the top down.

After a short and somewhat misguided campaign, partly characterized by mob attacks, Hidalgo was captured by the reigning authorities, tried by the Inquisition, and executed. However, this setback in the movement was only temporary,

*Mural by Mexican artist Juan O'Gorman depicting scenes from the
Mexican Revolt of 1810. Father Miguel Hidalgo's impassioned speech,
the "Grito de Dolores," is illustrated at the bottom left of the painting.
(Charles & Josette Lenars/Corbis)*

as the cause was enjoined by another reform-minded cleric,
José María Morelos, who replaced Hidalgo as the movement's de facto leader. Although he ultimately did not meet
with any more success than did Hidalgo, Morelos did manage to convene a congress at Chilpancingo in order to clar-
ify the goals of the independence movement and to craft a
constitution that would guide the new country upon Spain's
ultimate defeat. Morelos, who at least managed to keep the
movement organized and cohesive, led Hidalgo's grassroots,
popular movement until his own capture and execution in
1815. After Morelos's death, the movement fragmented and
began to operate as a rather uncoordinated collection of regional insurgencies that were never able to mount any significant threats to the Spanish authorities. Instead, these
groups engaged in the practice of guerrilla warfare, capable
of making only minor sorties here and there, just enough to

remain bothersome to the colonial Spanish authorities, but not enough to end Spanish control altogether. The most important of the insurgency leaders were Vicente Guerrero, Nicolás Bravo, and Guadalupe Victoria.

The persistence of the independence movement inspired by Hidalgo and Morelos, along with its radical ideological underpinnings, had the effect of leading many of the criollo elite into an alliance of convenience with the peninsular royalists. Reluctant to declare openly and decisively against Spanish authority while the popular revolt that threatened their own social position and privileges festered, the criollo elite of Mexico, even though sympathetic to the potential benefits of independence from Spain, tolerated continued Spanish rule over the territory. However, this alliance of convenience was only tenable as long as Spain itself remained committed to continue running colonial affairs in a manner that preserved traditional social values and conserved a traditional social order. Thus, when reform-minded elements within the mother country, those that shared some of the same troublesome ideological convictions of the rebels in Mexico, successfully declared against the Spanish monarch, Ferdinand VII, forcing him to accept liberal reforms in exchange for retaining his crown, the reactionary elements of the elite in Mexico, fearing what this turn of events in Spain would mean for Mexico, saw fit to turn the tables and to themselves declare Mexico's independence for a second time. However, the person who would assume the leadership of Mexico's second serious push for independence was not a reform-minded liberal cleric or a firebrand ideological radical, but a reactionary criollo soldier, General Agustín de Iturbide. Iturbide's independence movement, in fact, was decidedly absolutist, conservative, and traditionalist in nature. However, Iturbide also shrewdly recognized that his vision of an independent Mexico would never fully succeed without some kind of accommodation with the remnants of the Hidalgo rebellion and a show of national unity.

Thus, betraying the Crown for which he fought, Iturbide forged common cause with the rebels against Spain and crafted a plan with rebel leaders Vicente Guerrero and Guadalupe Victoria that would secure Mexico's independence, appease the weary rebels, and yet preserve the traditional social and political order. The declaration of independence articulated in this Plan de Iguala sought not to usher in a new era of republican government in Mexico, but the reestablishment of absolutist monarchy, this time of the Mexican variation.

The Plan de Iguala had a number of provisions, but the most important of these are the "Three Guarantees," which declared (1) the Roman Catholic faith to be the official state religion for an independent Mexico, whereby the Catholic Church would continue to enjoy all its corporate rights and privileges; (2) that the new Mexican government would be a constitutional monarchy, headed by a member of a European royal family; and (3) that the state would not discriminate between criollos or *peninsulares,* treating both as equal participants in the new national order. Furthermore, the Plan de Iguala called for the creation of a new army that would protect and defend these three guarantees. When the last Spanish viceroy of New Spain, Juan O'Donojú, recognized the inevitability of Mexico's independence and the futility (not to mention Spain's inability) of fighting against the Army of the Three Guarantees, he capitulated to Iturbide and signed off on a treaty that recognized the independent nation of Mexico. Known as the Treaty of Córdoba, this document not only reiterated the fundamental principles and guarantees of the Plan de Iguala but also contained another interesting provision that declared that, should Mexico be unable to secure a monarch from among the European royalty, the country would be free to choose its new emperor from among its own people. In this way, Iturbide had not only craftily co-opted the legacy of the independence struggle that originated with

Hidalgo's *grito* in 1810, but he also laid the groundwork for his own elevation as the first emperor and formal leader of a brand new country.

The Plan de Iguala also set a precedent for the use of the "military pronouncement" as the most common means by which political contestation and power transfer would take place in Mexico over the remainder of the 19th century and into the early 20th century. Elections were certainly a feature of Mexican political life following the country's independence from Spain, but they were hollow events in the face of disgruntled military officers and their civilian political allies who refused to accept the results of elections as legitimate. Even Iturbide would fall prey to this tactic, one that he himself so effectively used with the Plan de Iguala.

The liberal undercurrents that had characterized Mexico's push toward independence from Spain, once unleashed, could not be contained just because Mexico happened to be in control of its own destiny. What Iturbide failed to appreciate was that the push for independence, initiated by Hidalgo in 1810, was much more than simply separation from Spain. At the very least, it represented a new way of thinking about governing, if not about social transformation. Even the criollo elites of Mexico, who had always chafed under the restrictions and the exclusivity of Spanish imperial policies regarding public administration and government, understood this to be the case. And it was not long before these criollo elites wearied of the absolutism, not to mention the haughty pretentiousness and absurd extravagance, of Emperor Iturbide.

Following the signing of the Treaty of Córdoba in August 1821, and after a brief period of political posturing and maneuvering, Iturbide was declared by a compliant and browbeaten Mexican Congress to be the newly independent country's first emperor, Emperor Agustín I. His coronation took place on July 1, 1822, with all the symbolic and ritualistic trappings typical of European coronations. But almost as soon as the crown was placed on Iturbide's head, the glamour of monarchy began to fade. With the Iturbide government unable to make any serious headway in improving the social and economic conditions facing the country, and with such conditions beating back the initial heady excitement of the reality of independence, a critical restiveness began to surface among a fairly significant cadre of criollo civilians, who were never fully comfortable with the absolutism of monarchy to begin with, and certain criollo military officers. On December 1, 1822, one of these officers, a military commander by the name of Antonio López de Santa Anna, declared against the monarchy in favor of a republic. Immediately, Iturbide called upon one of his own trusted captains general, José Antonio Echáverri, to suppress the Santa Anna rebellion. However, in an ironic and fitting coup de grâce for Iturbide, Echáverri made common cause with Santa Anna, and together these military officers, along with others, put forward in early February 1823 their own plan, the Plan de Casa Mata, which called for an end to the empire and for the creation of a constitutional republic. When word of this pronouncement spread throughout the country, both civilian and military supporters lined up behind it in rapid succession. Recognizing the inevitable end to his rule, Iturbide did not even try to fight. By the end of the month, Iturbide had abdicated his throne and left with his family for exile in Europe.

The rise and fall of the first Mexican empire revealed the divisions between conservative and liberal factions that would dominate Mexican politics until the early 1870s, when Porfirio Díaz came to power and, through a mixture of coercion and co-optation, would unify the country under what has come to be called the Pax Porfiriano. Conservatives had backed at least the traditional policy prescriptions of the Iturbide empire and the principles expressed in the Plan de Iguala, if not the imperial form of government.

Liberals, on the other hand, not only disavowed monarchical government but also embraced policies that would move Mexico away from other traditional expressions of social and political organization. Nowhere was this division more evident than in discussions concerning (1) the role of religion and the place of the Catholic Church and (2) whether Mexico should embrace a centralized unitary republic or a decentralized federal form of government.

With regard to the issue of the Catholic Church, the more conservative faction embraced a close and intimate relationship between the Church and the state, and it also sought to protect and defend the Catholic Church's special rights and privileges. The more liberal faction, on the other hand, embraced a secular approach to government and sought to distance the Church from the state. On the subject of a unitary versus a federal republic, conservatives emphasized the need for a strong central authority that could unify the country and maintain the order necessary for national security and for economic growth. Liberals, though, tended to view centralized authority as an invitation to absolutism and autocracy, and they believed that a federal republic with power decentralized among the various states would act as a deterrent to this temptation, so recently manifested in the example of Iturbide.

The Plan de Casa Mata called for a triumvirate caretaker government while a constitutional congress was convened to produce a guiding document that would decide the contours of the Mexican republic. Conservative and liberal factions debated the provisions of such a constitution passionately and convincingly. In the end, the Constitution promulgated by the Congress in 1824 clearly favored the liberal faction and established the basis for a decentralized federal republic. Perhaps the most radical example of the liberal faction's victory in this instance was the constitutional provision that the president and vice-president of the country be elected neither by direct popular vote nor by a national electoral college, but rather by the state legislatures. However, the conservative faction did not leave empty-handed, as the Constitution also contained provisions that would grant the federal executive, with the approval of the federal Congress, extraordinary emergency powers in moments of national crisis. Ironically, over the next 40 years, both conservatives and liberals would make selective use of these countervailing principles contained in the 1824 Constitution to legitimize the implementation of their own different governing philosophies. Instead of unifying the country under the banner of constitutional republicanism, the 1824 Constitution would become the justification for continued civil discord and factional squabbling, evident in the fact that over a period of more than 30 years (from 1824 to 1855) the country would see the presidency switch hands more than 35 times; it would be invaded by foreign powers numerous times; and it would suffer the loss of more than half of its national territory to the United States.

The individual who surfaced as Mexico's most powerful leader during this volatile period in Mexico's history was the enigmatic Santa Anna. One might argue that his crass opportunism essentially created the discordant environment from which he personally benefited, but from which Mexico as a country suffered tremendously. Whether from behind the scenes or from the seat of presidential authority, Santa Anna ruled over the country. Initially, Santa Anna threw his support behind the liberal factions. He came to the defense of Guadalupe Victoria, the country's first elected president under the 1824 Constitution, and suppressed an uprising in 1827 led by conservative Vice-President Nicolás Bravo. In the subsequent presidential election to replace Victoria, Santa Anna also threw his weight (and his military forces) in support of the liberal candidate Vicente Guerrero against his conservative rival Manuel Gómez Pedraza. In spite of the fact that the conservative Gómez Pedraza had won a majority of state

Antonio López de Santa Anna depicted at the time of the Mexican-American War. Santa Anna was Mexico's president and military leader when Mexico City was seized by General Winfield Scott. (Stephenson, Nathaniel W. Texas and the Mexican War, *1921)*

legislatures, and thus the national presidency, the liberal faction refused to accept this result. In fact, when the very system of federalism championed by the liberals and written into the Constitution produced a result not to their liking, they simply ignored the Constitution and rose up in rebellion against Gómez Pedraza. Santa Anna used his power and his influence over the military to rally support behind Guerrero in an armed rebellion against the Gómez Pedraza government. His efforts succeeded and Gómez Pedraza resigned; Guerrero assumed the presidency. In an effort to appease the slighted conservatives, General Anastasio Bustamanate was installed as vice-president. However, sensing that winds of change were blowing in the direction of the conservative faction, Santa Anna moved toward an affiliation with this camp. Also, as Santa Anna's power and prestige grew, so did his autocratic pretensions and his desires for unchecked centralized authority. Mexico's conservatives were much more ideologically disposed to support this vision of government and to embrace dictatorship trending toward monarchical absolutism.

Up until the mid-1850s, Santa Anna would effectively control Mexican politics, becoming ever more autocratic and enigmatic in the process. During his fabled tenure, Santa Anna would drag his country through some of its most humiliating and lowest points, but he would always, like the phoenix, find a way to rise out of the ashes of Mexico's ruin to reassert himself as the national hero and the only leader capable of saving Mexico from utter destruction. Perhaps the story that best exemplifies the Santa Anna legacy in Mexico's history, and one that bears closer scrutiny because of its long-term impact on the nature of U.S.-Mexican relations, is the story of the secession and independence of Texas, its eventual annexation by the United States, and the resulting U.S.-Mexican War of 1846–1848, an ignominious war for Mexico that resulted both in the fall of Mexico City to U.S. marines and in the subsequent loss of nearly half of its national territory to its northern neighbor.

The U.S.-Mexican War

The westward expansion of the United States under the mantra of Manifest Destiny collided with the chaos and instability of early independent Mexico. This collision took place in the territory of Texas. Prior to Mexico's independence from Spain, the lands to the west of the Sabine River on the North American continent belonged to Spain and were administratively managed as part of the Viceroyalty of New Spain. Mexico, in declaring its independence from Spain, also claimed sovereignty over all of the territory of the Viceroyalty of New Spain previously under Spanish administration. However, the territory constituting Texas was sparsely populated, and the Mexican authorities concocted a plan to accept colonization from Anglo-Americans as a means of populating the region, developing it, and collecting income from the colonists in the process.

In an effort to maintain its claims to authority over the region in a practical way, the Mexican government granted concessions for colonization on certain conditions: that the colonists would convert to Catholicism, that they would conduct all transactions and the business of daily life in Spanish, and that the colonists would integrate themselves into the Mexican cultural milieu. The rapid increase in the numbers of Anglo colonists in the Texas territory, coupled with the territory's status as an often-ignored outlier region in the Mexican national political dynamic, led to resentments among the Anglo colonists toward the central Mexican government and a growing sympathy toward retaining and expanding closer connections with the culturally and linguistically similar territories and peoples of the United States.

The factor that propelled Texas onto the path first of declaring independence from Mexico and later of annexation to the United States, however, was Santa Anna's abrogation in early 1935 of the 1824 Federalist Constitution in Mexico, which had, to some extent, preserved local autonomies from the central government in Mexico City. The loss of this autonomy not only increased resentments among Texas's Anglo colonists for being even more marginalized and excluded from influencing national policies that affected their parochial interests, but also inflamed the passions of Mexico's own federalist sympathizers, who saw ex-federalist Santa Anna's abrogation of the Constitution as a violation of the prerogatives of all regional authorities throughout the Mexican Republic to have a greater say in managing their own local affairs. Spurred on by the increasingly centralizing tendencies of Santa Anna, both Mexican nationals and Anglo colonists in the Texas region found common cause against the assault on federalism and local rights to self-governance. The consequence was an alliance between these Mexican nationals and Anglo colonists living in the region that advocated the autonomy of Texas and ultimately declared, in 1835, secession from the Mexican union and the establishment of the independent Republic of Texas.

Unable to tolerate this threat to the territorial and political integrity of the Mexican nation, Santa Anna embarked upon a military mission of forced reintegration of this renegade territory to the Mexican national fold. Of course, Santa Anna's campaign is best remembered for the famous Battle at the Alamo, in which the Mexicans, after facing fierce and brave resistance, defeated a vastly outnumbered contingent of Texas soldiers. However, it was Santa Anna's ordering of the execution of 365 Texan prisoners of war after the Battle of Goliad that turned the tide of military engagement as well as public opinion irrevocably against the Mexicans and in favor of the Texans. A short while afterward, Texas troops under the direction of General Sam Houston defeated the Mexicans in a battle at the San Jacinto River and captured Santa Anna, who, in order to ransom his own life, capitulated to the victorious Texans by agreeing to sign two

Santa Anna's surrender to General Sam Houston after the battle of San Jacinto in 1836. (Library of Congress)

treaties that would formally end hostilities and pave the way for the recognition in Mexico of Texas's independence. Even though the Mexican legislature refused to recognize the legitimacy of these treaties, Texas was able to maintain its independence from the moment of Santa Anna's defeat and capture in 1836 until 1845, during which time the U.S. government began in earnest to move inexorably toward the annexation of Texas.

The first step for the United States toward this end was to recognize formally in 1837 the Republic of Texas as an independent nation against the protests of the Mexican government. It was not until some eight years later that the U.S. government formally declared the annexation of Texas into the union. For its part, Mexico had never accepted Texas's declaration of independence as legitimate and still considered its frontier territory as part of the nation. Thus, Mexico viewed the annexation of Texas by the United States in 1845 as a direct and illegitimate appropriation of its national territory and as constituting a clear violation of Mexico's sovereignty. Mexico considered such a blatant attack on what it considered its national territory as an act of aggression against the country and its sovereign rights. In order to defend its interests, Mexico began to make preparations for war.

However, the chaos and divisions within Mexico's internal politics at the time precluded any serious ability to conduct a war in the defense of its claims, and the defeat of Mexico at the hands of a much better organized and militarily superior U.S. army was a foregone conclusion. Under the direction of General Winfield Scott, the U.S. army methodically whittled away at the Mexican defenses as it worked its way slowly, but definitively and confidently, toward Mexico City. After a series of bloody battles from the port city of Vera Cruz to the walls of Chapultepec Castle in Mexico City, the U.S. army emerged victorious and Mexico was forced to negotiate what it considered to be a humiliating treaty of surrender in early February 1848. This treaty, known as the Treaty of Guadalupe Hidalgo for the city in which it was negotiated, added the vast Mexican territories of California and New Mexico to the dominion of the United States of America for the bargain price of $18,250,000. Mexico lost nearly one-half of its richest northern frontier lands for an amount that was less than the Mexican federal government's yearly budget.

The psychological and ideological wounds inflicted on Mexico as a consequence of this humiliating defeat contributed to a subsequent crisis of identity and serious financial difficulties that would turn inward and would fuel a vicious and equally bloody civil war between Mexico's liberal reformers and conservatives. The result of this internal conflict was another foreign intervention and occupation some 15 years later.

The War of the Reform

The violent struggles between Mexico's liberal and conservative factions erupted into outright civil war in the mid-1950s. The major issues that divided Mexico at the time were centered around church rights, land reform, and indigenous rights. The liberal factions were led by a group of reformers bent on institutionalizing a secular vision of government and society. These reformers embraced notions such as the separation of church and state, economic liberalization, universal and free public education, and a resistance to absolutist forms of government. The leading figures in this group included Benito Juárez, Melchor Ocampo, and the Lerdo de Tejada brothers, among others. However, among this group, none would embrace and represent the ideals and spirit of the reform movement as completely as did Juárez, a full-blood Zapotec Indian who rose through the political establishment to serve first as governor of the state of Oaxaca, then as a justice on the Supreme Court of Mexico, and finally as president of Mexico.

This liberal group assumed control over the Mexican central government in 1854, after leading a movement to depose the corrupt and authoritarian conservative administration of Santa Anna. The movement was based in the principles contained in the Plan de Ayutla, which would serve as the guiding document for Mexico's Constitution of 1857. Following the fiscal and intellectual bankruptcy of the conservative faction, which had been intimately associated with the extremely unpopular Santa Anna government, Mexico's liberal reformers had virtually unchecked authority to implement their alternative vision and governing philosophy in the country. Emboldened by their weakened and demoralized opposition, the liberal governments that assumed power during this period initiated a series of radical reforms that polarized Mexican politics further and eventually regalvanized the conservative opposition.

This reform project began first with the presidency of Ignacio Comonfort in 1854, who brought Juárez, Ocampo, and other reformers into the central administration from their state outposts. Some of the controversial initiatives and laws implemented by these reformers are known primarily by the names of their authors and sought to institutionalize the cornerstones of the liberal platform. The primary source of controversy was the combination of clericalism and militarism that had imbued the entire political and social order, and the reform movement faced these elements head on and unapologetically. One of the first controversial and important reform measures was a piece of legislation known as the Ley Juárez, named after Benito Juárez, minister of Justice at the time. The Ley Juárez sought to curb the special legal privileges and immunities (*fueros*) granted to military and ecclesiastical authorities. Up to that point, military and ecclesiastical authorities who committed crimes or violated the civil law were not subject to trial and prosecution in civil courts. Instead, they had the right to have their cases heard in special courts composed of and regulated by fellow military or ecclesiastical authorities. The Ley Juárez did not eliminate such privileges, as is commonly misunderstood, but rather restricted them. Clerics and soldiers still maintained their own courts, but such courts could only hear cases that pertained specifically to church or military affairs. The Ley Juárez merely mandated that all other legal proceedings or cases that involved military or religious authorities be held in their appropriate civilian courts. This law was followed by another legislative initiative known as the "Ley Lerdo," named after Sebastián Lerdo de Tejada, minister of the Interior at the time, which commanded the forced sale to the state or to private interests of dormant property owned by various social institutions. In essence, the "Ley Lerdo," the second of three important legislative reforms, was the 19th-century

Despite the limited effectiveness of Benito Juárez' reforms, he remained the hero of Mexican nationalism, a leader who weakened colonial practices and created a new Mexico in the mid-19th century. (Library of Congress)

equivalent of "eminent domain," and this law affected not
only the Catholic Church but also the indigenous system of
community landownership known as the ejido. And what is
often considered the third pillar of the liberal reform was the
Ley Iglesias, which required that church-based services to
the poor be provided indiscriminately and at no cost and
that fees for services provided to people of means had to be
modest. Each of these legislative mandates either dismantled or severely compromised the long-standing and vigorously defended rights and traditions valued and preserved
by Mexican conservatives and their ecclesiastical and military allies. When these laws were incorporated into the Mexican Constitution of 1857, the stage was set again for civil
war, since refusal to accept the Constitution or to declare allegiance to it was tantamount to treason.

Throughout this time, dissension also crept into the ranks
of the liberals, separating those who advocated swift, radical
reform from those who embraced deliberate, moderate reform. The former, known as the "puros" (or the "purist" liberals), pushed their agenda from the margins of the scene
and embraced an antagonistic relationship with the conservatives. The moderates, led by President Ignacio Comonfort,
attempted to hold the country together and to chart an accommodationist path of reform without completely alienat-
ing or antagonizing the conservatives in the country. With
the promulgation of the 1857 Constitution and the incorporation of the famous reform laws listed previously (the Ley
Juárez, the Ley Lerdo, and the Ley Iglesias) into the Constitution, it was clear that the radical puros were ascendant.
The inability of the moderates to rein in the radicals created
a crisis of confidence in the leadership of Comonfort. And
when the conservatives launched their own armed uprising
against the Comonfort government in protest of the excesses
and attacks they perceived to be levied against them in the
1857 Constitution, Comonfort was forced to resign his office. The 1857 Constitution mandated that the next in line

to the presidency was the chief justice of the Supreme Court, who, at the time of Comonfort's resignation, was none other than Benito Juárez. Thus Juárez assumed the presidency in the context of a factionalized and divided liberalism and faced a significant armed uprising by the conservatives.

After a series of disputes and military engagements that temporarily altered the balance of control over the seats of power in Mexico City, the conservatives were finally able to dislodge Juárez and his liberal consorts from Mexico City and forced them to establish a rival government in the coastal city of Vera Cruz. From there, the liberal faction laid claim to its legitimacy as the true government of Mexico, and the conservatives, now entrenched in Mexico City, refused to accept this claim, arguing that their faction represented the legitimate national authority. Each faction organized an armed movement both to defend its claims and to wage war against its rivals. So, from the period of 1858–1860, Mexico witnessed a very bloody and violent civil war, know as the War of the Reform, in which no one faction could deliver the final knockout blow to the other.

However, in 1860, after this protracted struggle, the liberal factions came out on top, and Juárez and his chastened liberal entourage once again marched into Mexico City as the uncontested national authority. However, the War of the Reform, in addition to being a very violent and costly war in terms of the loss of human life, was financially a very costly war, with both sides having accrued debts with their international sponsors that they were unable to repay. Faced with the prospect of imminent insolvency, the liberal Juárez government repudiated the debt incurred by the conservatives and refused to entertain a repayment of such debt to the foreign powers that held claim to it, including Britain, Spain, and France. In an effort to enforce recognition of their claims on the liberal government of Juárez, they organized an alliance that sought to realize their claims to debt repayment through military intervention and occupation of the country.

However, Napoleon III of France had larger ambitions of imperial conquest beyond the restitution of its pecuniary claims. When Britain and Spain realized the extent of France's intentions, each country backed out of the alliance at the final moment. Disaffected conservatives, seeing a natural ally in the imperial monarchy of Napoleon III, collaborated with France in order to oust the liberals from Mexico and to go one step further in promoting a return to conservative notions of political, economic, and social relations by inviting a European monarch to claim Mexico as part of his kingdom.

The Maximilian Empire

Emboldened by the occupation of Napoleon III's troops in Mexico, and persuaded by Mexico's conservative community in exile at the courts of Europe that he would be welcomed as a force of order and stability in the country, Maximilian von Habsburg accepted the invitation to become Mexico's second royal authority in the country's independent history. Maximilian arrived in Mexico with his wife, Carlota, under heavy French escort in 1862. During his reign, Maximilian disappointed his conservative supporters with his refusal to undo completely the more controversial reforms that his liberal predecessors had promulgated. However, Maximilian was equally unable to win the critical support he needed from other countries in the hemisphere, particularly the United States, because his regime was seen as illegitimate and incompatible with the constitutional republicanism and notions of popular sovereignty that defined the political culture of the Western Hemisphere. Maximilian's unfamiliarity with Mexico and its unique social and cultural realities, coupled with his more progressive outlook, only contributed to the hastening of his demise. His regime, faced constantly with local rebellions against his authority, not to mention the existence of a liberal government in exile, depended completely on French troops for its political survival and for keeping the exiled liberal government of Benito Juárez and his considerable military forces at bay.

As long as Napoleon III remained committed to the military defense of the Maximilian empire against the various movements and international pressures facing it, the monarchy was able to survive. However, Napoleon III, in the face of his own troubles in Europe, ultimately decided to abandon his ambitious experiment in Mexico and brought French troops back home in 1864. From that point forward, in spite of Empress Carlota's futile efforts to secure support from the various courts in Europe, the Maximilian monarchy was doomed. It was only a matter of time, absent the continuation of French military support, before the liberal forces under the command of Juárez succeeded in defeating what remained of Maximilian's local army. Maximilian refused to abandon Mexico and return to Europe, still convinced that he would prevail. In the end, Maximilian was captured and executed, and Juárez returned triumphantly to Mexico City to reestablish and continue the liberal project that he had started during the years of the reform period. The defeat of Maximilian also represented the end of Mexico's conservative movement as it had existed up to that time. From that point forward, Mexico would embrace fully the notions of a secular society and a liberal market economy, even if its commitment to political democracy would still require a social revolution and take the entire 20th century to realize.

The Porfiriato

From 1864 until 1872, Mexico occupied itself with the restoration of republican government, the rebuilding of its national economy, and the recovery of its compromised sovereignty.

The humiliation of occupation by a foreign army and the failed experiment of installing a European monarch to govern the country led to a period of national healing and relative civil calm. Benito Juárez ruled with the strong support of most Mexicans and without any serious threat to his authority, ratified through an electoral process. However, the relative tranquility of Mexico's post-Maximilian recovery depended a great deal on the tested abilities and the immense popularity of Juárez. When Juárez died unexpectedly in 1872 of a massive heart attack, having just been narrowly reelected to a controversial fourth term of office, divisions within the liberal political establishment began to surface, threatening the stability of the political system.

Juárez's successor, Sebastian Lerdo de Tejada, accelerated the pace of the liberal reform program, but Lerdo was more impulsive and did not possess the political acumen of Juárez, who was able to manage the various factional interests within the liberal political establishment. Eventually, tensions among the liberal factions erupted into open hostility, and a young general who fought for the republic against the Maximilian monarchy, Porfirio Díaz, pronounced against the Lerdo government in an effort to reestablish authority and to hold the liberal coalition together. His military movement succeeded in removing Lerdo from office, and the dictatorship that ensued maintained political order through autocratic practices while simultaneously ushering in a period of unprecedented economic growth and development.

During the reign of Porfirio Díaz, commonly known as the Porfiriato, which lasted from 1872 until 1910, Mexico transitioned from an agrarian and traditional society into an export-oriented, outward-looking, modern society. And in many ways the transformation was quite remarkable. The cadre of elites that carried out this transformation did so by embracing the philosophy of positivism as the intellectual foundation for inserting Mexico into the modern world. The scientific determinism and social Darwinism that shaped the

Mexican dictator Porfirio Díaz, a towering figure in Mexican history who ruled from 1876 until being deposed in the Mexican Revolution of 1910. (Library of Congress)

mentality of these elites, known also as the *cientificos* for their training in and reliance on science as the rationale for social, political, and economic life, perpetuated a political system and an economic system that embraced the necessity and legitimacy for exclusion and discrimination on the basis of natural selection. In other words, Mexican social, political, and economic life throughout the Porfiriato was imbued with the idea that each individual had a particular set of abilities, a predetermined function, and a fixed social station in the Mexican polity and society.

The order that was associated with the positivist ideology was considered a necessary requirement for progress. Indeed, during the reign of Porfirio Díaz, the chaos of what had characterized Mexico's social and political environment for most of the 19th century gave way to an unprecedented and lengthy period of relative peace and social stability. The Pax Porfiriana, as this period of peace is sometimes called, brought with it massive amounts of direct foreign investment that improved Mexico's physical infrastructure by impressive measures. Encouraged by accommodating and preferential state policies, foreign interests and capital helped to construct thousands of miles of railroads and thoroughfares throughout the country. Previously isolated rural communities and the country's major urban centers became more accessible and connected to one another. And Mexico's major urban cities as well as its rural communities became better connected to the country's ports, which were also enjoying huge infusions of capital investment. Increased investment in commercial agriculture, coupled with the rapid and extensive development of transportation and shipping infrastructure, led to a significant growth in Mexico's national wealth through expanded international trade. While the Mexican economy boomed during the Porfiriato, the political system contracted and became ossified. The very conditions of order and stability brought about by the paternalistic authoritarianism of Porfirio Díaz's closed and exclusive dictatorship also contained the seeds of its own destruction.

The Mexican Revolution

The exclusivity of the Porfirian system did not allow for the creation and nurturing of a future political and economic leadership. As the elites of the Porfirian system aged and the energy behind the Porfirian experiment waned, the foundations that kept the dictatorship afloat weakened. Furthermore, the impressive economic and social changes wrought by the *científicos* engendered new social structures and class divisions for which Mexico was unprepared. In essence, the changes that elevated Mexico into the modern, urban, industrializing world also produced a social dynamic that the rigid political system, which created the conditions and environments conducive to such changes, was ironically not capable of absorbing and containing.

The burgeoning merchant class, as well as the growing urban working class, that the Porfiriato produced, began clamoring for access to and influence in a political system closed to them. Faced with a growing restlessness among such groups, Porfirio Díaz, perhaps in a moment of carelessness, capitulated and announced in 1908 that he would permit an open electoral campaign for the upcoming presidential elections, scheduled for 1910. Seizing upon this opportunity, a young professional, Francisco Madero, announced his candidacy on a reform platform and campaigned in earnest. His candidacy was met with unprecedented popularity, which caused Díaz to back off of his previous claims to support an open and free election. Díaz, faced with Madero's open defiance of his plans to restrict the elections, resorted to terminating Madero's campaign by force. He had Madero arrested and imprisoned and then fixed the election so that he and his handpicked successor and vice-presidential running mate, Ramón Corral, emerged victorious.

However, while in prison, Madero fashioned a treatise that openly attacked the nondemocratic nature of the Porfirian regime and called for armed rebellion by Mexicans against dictatorship and for democracy. With his Plan de San Luís Potosí, Madero ignited the spark that would usher in a decade of revolutionary violence, which would cost Mexico dearly in terms of human life. Yet the Mexican Revolution would produce a profoundly radical transformation of the political system that would institutionalize single-party rule for more than 70 years and would incorporate previously excluded social groups into the governing coalition.

The Mexican Revolution was a watershed not only in the history of Mexico but also in the history of the world. It reverberated most poignantly throughout the Western Hemisphere, inaugurating a period of intense social, economic, and political transformation in the region. In fact, the Mexican Revolution can be considered the first successful modern social revolution, predating the Bolshevik Revolution in Russia. It encompassed much more than a protest against an autocratic dictatorship by advocates for democracy.

It began slowly, first as a manifestation of frustration with the political exclusivity of the Porfirian regime. Later, it mushroomed into a full-blown rejection of the Porfirian political, social, and economic model by a multiplicity of very different actors from all social groups and classes. Peasants and rural workers in southern Mexico found expression through the movement for land reform and peasant rights led by Emiliano Zapata. Disaffected northern elites, chafing primarily at Porfirian cronyism and the dictator's evergrowing efforts to dismantle long-established patterns of semiautonomous regional power structures, found their voice first in the person of Francisco Madero and later in the great northern landowner *caudillos,* or political strongmen, Venustiano Carranza, Alvaro Obregón, and Plutarco Elías

Calles. The independent-minded popular classes of northern and central Mexico threw their lot in with the charismatic populist caudillos Pascual Orozco and Francisco "Pancho" Villa. These different factions, along with many other local and regional movements, coalesced to produce 10 years of brutal and chaotic conflict and at least 10 more years of difficult efforts at reestablishing national order and peace.

The extended history of the Mexican Revolution plays out like a soap opera melodrama, with alliances forming and breaking seemingly at whim. Allies fought side by side one day only to be plotting and carrying out one another's assassinations the next; the tides of war turned from one moment to the next between revolutionary and counterrevolutionary forces. Some estimates maintain that 1 out of every 10 Mexican citizens perished as a consequence of the Revolution, either as a victim of the fighting itself or of the poverty and desperation caused by the war's devastating impact on the Mexican economy and social infrastructure. When the dust settled, Mexicans found themselves with a radically different country and society. It would take Mexico 30 years to recover, regain some sense of normalcy, and place itself once more on the path to economic growth and political stability. Such a prolonged and psychologically traumatic experience influenced every aspect of Mexican life and culture, and these influences persist to the present. The specific story of the Revolution arguably begins, ironically, with the dictator Porfirio Díaz.

While pockets of dissent or opposition had surfaced here and there in the early years of the first decade of the 20th century, Díaz had been able to neutralize and contain such movements fairly effectively. These movements were launched by former Porfiristas such as Bernardo Reyes and Jose Yves Limantour, who had become mild and generally unthreatening voices of change within the Porfirian framework. Others, such as Francisco Madero, expressed a desire for an end to the political authoritarianism of the Porfirian system, working outside of the system to effect democratic change. But these actors were not advocates of wholesale transformation of the economic and social framework of the Porfirian system. Still others critiqued the entire Porfirian model and considered it untenable to brook any accommodation with Porfirismo. Such people, like the famous Flores Magón brothers, rejected the regime's legitimacy and did not shy away from advocating armed rebellion against the regime if necessary to force change. However, Porfirio Díaz was able to resist and control these critics as long as he could keep a tight rein on a system dependent exclusively on his personalistic authority. Thus, when Díaz indicated in an interview with North American journalist James Creelman in 1908 that he was effectively retiring from politics at the end of his current term of office, that he would not seek reelection, and that he would respect an open electoral competition to replace him as Mexico's next president, he whetted the appetites of his opponents for power and he encouraged the enthusiasms for reform that were bubbling in the imaginations of the broader Mexican population.

Díaz's announcement had the dual effect of opening some divisions within his own supporters over who would succeed him and of allowing his opponents to overcome some of their own divisions to rally under the common cause of defeating the Porfiristas in the election. The internal divisions within the Porfiristas led to calls for Díaz to reconsider his decision and to run again for reelection in the interests of keeping the ruling coalition together under his leadership. Díaz acquiesced and, following his past patterns of intolerance for any challenges to his authority, immediately initiated efforts to quash the campaigns of his opponents through his usual tactics of intimidation and repression.

Francisco Madero, who, following Díaz's surprise announcement, had published a tract on the importance of the 1910 election for carrying out essential political reform in the post-Díaz era, positioned himself as the anti-

Porfirista candidate for the presidency on the Anti-Reelectionist ticket. He campaigned throughout the country on the basis of the ideas in his book. Soon after Díaz entered the race, he arrested and incarcerated Madero in the state of San Luís Potosí. During the course of Madero's imprisonment, the election was held and Porfirio Díaz was, unsurprisingly, easily reelected. After the election, when political tensions had subsided, Madero escaped and fled north across the border into the Southwest of the United States. From there, recognizing the futility of peaceful electoral challenge to the Porfirian system, Madero published his famous Plan de San Luís Potosí, which declared the recent electoral victory of Díaz illegitimate and called on his countrymen to rise up in arms against the illegitimate Díaz government on November 20, 1910.

After a rather inauspicious start to the uprising, the rebels began to experience a few victories in remote municipalities. Under the bold military leadership of Pascual Orozco and Pancho Villa, the Maderistas eventually succeeded in defeating federal troops in such important cities as Ciudad Juárez and Torreón in the north. From this point, Porfirio Díaz was prescient enough to see that his presidency was untenable and capitulated to the rebels. In the subsequent Treaty of Ciudad Juárez, among a few other minor concessions, Díaz and his vice-president agreed to resign and to go into exile. Pending the results of a new election, the government of Mexico was placed in the hands of Francisco León de la Barra, Díaz's minister of Foreign Relations. After a six-month transitional period, the people of Mexico elected Madero as president. Madero, believing that the intended goal of the uprising was achieved, began the process of dismantling the rebel movement. However, his naivete and his patrician tendencies prevented him either from seeing or from embracing more profound social and economic reforms that those who fought for his cause desired and expected. Madero's vision embraced mild democratic political reform while keeping

*After garnering a heroic reputation in the Mexican
Revolution of 1910, Francisco Madero served as
president of the turbulent nation from 1911 to 1913.
(Library of Congress)*

most of the Porfirian system intact, including the federal militia. His short-sightedness angered and alienated some of his important initial allies, such as Pascual Orozco, and his patronizing dismissiveness of the demands for substantive land reform made enemies of Emiliano Zapata and the peasants he represented. This fragmentation among the insurgent forces also toughened the resolve of pro-Porfirian elements, which still constituted the bulk of the federal and state bureaucracies and the federal militia, to plan a counterrevolutionary challenge to Madero. In the interests of appeasing the defeated opponent and achieving reconciliation, Madero made the mistake of keeping the pre-Porfirian federal armed forces and their command structures intact. In fact, Madero relied on such forces to contain whatever pockets of rebellion remained or whatever new pockets of revolutionary activity bubbled up in opposition to his regime. In this way, Madero hoped to placate those against whom he and his allies fought, all the while keeping many of his former allies who fought for him at arm's distance in constructing the new post-Porfirian political order.

As Madero relied more and more on the Porfirista federal military to contain and suppress his disaffected and rebellious former allies, his standing with both groups became ever more precarious. The federal armed forces not only were suspicious of even his modest reformist agenda but also were not exactly enthusiastic about defending an upstart who represented a threat to their institutional interests and who had also actually overthrown a system and a leader to whom they owed much of their loyalty. And the more Madero embraced the ancien régime in such ways, even perpetuating the Porfirian patterns of personalistic cronyism, the more his previous allies thought of him as compromising the principles of the Revolution that he himself had proclaimed. For instance, Madero's unwillingness to entertain more sweeping land reform proposals led very quickly to his rejection as a legitimate authority by Emiliano Zapata and his followers, who openly declared their opposition to Madero in early 1912 in the famous Plan de Ayala.

Madero's timidity as well as his insensitivity to the animosities underlying both the revolutionary and counterrevolutionary forces in Mexico resulted ultimately in an orchestrated movement to forcefully remove Madero from office. While the growing hostility toward Madero among the likes of Orozco and Zapata simmered in the provinces, counterrevolutionary elements in the federal military, unimpressed with Madero, took action. On February 9, 1913, federalist General Felix Díaz, the ex-dictator's nephew, along with imprisoned Porfirian General Bernardo Reyes, implemented their coup plot against Madero. Madero, for his part, turned to the Porfirian General Victoriano Huerta to defend his besieged government. And for the first time since the Pax Porfiriano, revolutionary violence engulfed the capital city. After 10 days of gruesome and debilitating urban warfare, and encouraged by the meddling U.S. Ambassador Henry Lane Wilson, General Huerta abandoned Madero and forged common cause with General Díaz to end the bloodshed and to reestablish the peaceful calm and civility with which the residents of Mexico City, foreign and national alike, had come to take for granted. After hammering out a power-sharing deal with Díaz in the halls of the U.S. Embassy under the watchful eye of Ambassador Wilson, General Huerta had Madero and his vice-president, José María Pino Suárez, arrested and incarcerated. Within a few short hours of the arrests of Madero and Pino Suárez, and after manipulating constitutional succession provisions to avoid the need for conducting a new presidential election, Huerta was named president of the republic and order was restored to Mexico City. Thus, the reactionary forces led by Huerta and Díaz prevailed.

The story may have ended there but for a tragic blunder on the part of Mexico's new rulers. The victorious counterrevolutionary factions, in an inexplicable move, without a trial and lacking even common decency, unceremoniously murdered Madero and his vice-president, Pino Suárez, in a late-night execution. In spite of Madero's disappointment to so many of his previous allies, the manner of his and Pino Suárez's deaths made revolutionary martyrs and heroes of them, and it served to galvanize once again the various antireactionary insurgent forces under common cause. Even the United States, under the presidency of Woodrow Wilson, which was embarrassed by the interventions of Henry Lane Wilson in such shocking events as well as the farcical method by which Huerta laid claim to the presidency, protested this unconstitutional seizure of power and the gruesome execution of Madero and Pino Suárez not only by cutting off all military and economic support to the reactionary Huerta government but also by sending U.S. marines to occupy the Mexican port city of Vera Cruz.

With opposition coming from all sides, the reactionary regime of Victoriano Huerta did not last long. Immediately following news of the assassination of Madero and Pino Suárez and the assumption of power by Victoriano Huerta, Madero's supporters in the north rose up in armed rebellion against Huerta. In late March 1913, Venustiano Carranza, Pancho Villa, and Álvaro Obregón affixed their signatures to the Plan de Guadalupe, which rejected the authority of Huerta; declared a "constitutionalist" rebellion against Huerta; and selected Carranza as "first chief" of the Constitutionalist Army, who would assume provisional presidency upon the fall of Huerta. In the south, Emiliano Zapata and his followers also rejected the authority of Huerta, but did not accept the authority of the Constitutionalists. Over the months of March and April 1913, the Constitutionalists and the Zapatistas engaged the federal army in fierce battles and scored some important victories, but the psychological tide turned decisively in favor of the antireactionary forces in May 1913 when Venustiano Carranza declared "no quarter" for captured federalist soldiers, although it would be another year before Carranza and the other antireactionary forces could convert this advantage to the defeat of Huerta. Nevertheless, after Carranza issued this famous no quarter decree, Huerta was forced to engage in an aggressive campaign of militarization, invoking the *leva* (forced conscription of Indians and vagrants) and confiscating resources in support of the war effort.

The conflict raged unabated for one year from May 1913 through July 1914, but by spring of 1914, Huerta's position was growing more untenable and he was slowly but surely losing ground to the rebels. His fate was sealed, though, not by the rebels but by actions carried out by the United States. First, the U.S. administration of Woodrow Wilson, appalled by Huerta's violent seizure of power and the subsequent assassinations of Madero and Pino Suárez, refused to accord the Huerta government official recognition. This status made it impossible for Huerta to obtain the financial and military assistance necessary to defend his government from the rebels. In addition, Wilson went one step further in defiance of Huerta's pretensions by beefing up the American fleet stationed off Mexican waters. In April 1914, two U.S. sailors were arrested by federal troops under the command of Huerta after disembarking their ship in Tampico, Mexico, which further exacerbated the tensions between the two countries, causing a diplomatic standoff between Mexico and the United States. In this environment, word came to the Wilson administration that a German ship was scheduled to arrive on April 21 in Vera Cruz with the intent to sell munitions to the Huerta government. Wilson, tying this information to the unstable situation in Europe, ordered an occupation of Vera Cruz to prevent this transaction between Germany and the Huerta government from occurring. Huerta had no choice but to call in his troops off the front lines against the forces of Carranza and Zapata in order to face the Americans and to defend the dignity and territorial sovereignty of the country in the face of a foreign invasion. This retreat from the civil war allowed the Zapatistas and

Constitutionalists a reprieve, and made it possible for Pancho Villa to capture the state of Zacatecas for the Constitutionalists, which sealed Huerta's fate. On July 8, 1914, recognizing the inevitable forces conspiring against him, Huerta resigned his office and voluntarily went into exile.

Soon thereafter, Carranza entered the capital city and set up a provisional government while the anti-Huerta forces consolidated their gains. In October 1914, Carranza called for the Convention of Revolutionaries in Aguascalientes to decide on the interim successor to Huerta as well as other matters. However, the Convention revealed a split in the revolutionary forces that pitted Carranza and Obregón (the Constitutionalists) against the forces of Zapata and Villa (the Conventionists). The Convention adopted a more radical platform and selected Eulalio Gutiérrez, against the wishes of Carranza, to serve as provisional president. Carranza, offended at the affront to his authority as first chief, ordered his delegates to withdraw from the Convention. Villa and Zapata's forces then marched on Mexico City to install Gutiérrez as president. Carranza retreated to Vera Cruz with Obregón, where they established their own functional government in opposition to that of the Conventionists and Gutiérrez.

Thus, from October 1914 through January 1915, two revolutionary factions, the Constitutionalists and the Conventionists, laid claim to power. Over this period, the Conventionists had the upper hand temporarily. But the vastly different types of movements and specific ideologies and regional sympathies represented by Villa and Zapata made the Conventionist alliance short lived.

The period of January 1915 to April 1915 was possibly the most chaotic and unstable period of the Mexican Revolution. Outright civil war raged between the Constitutionalists and the Conventionists, with two separate governments claiming legitimacy and neither able to take charge of the situation. The tide changed in favor of the Constitutionalists in April 1915 at the famous Battle of Celaya. This battle pitted the strategically and tactically superior military skills of Álvaro Obregón against the forces led by Pancho Villa. Obregón emerged victorious in a rout, and it was the turning point for Villa, presaging his eventual elimination from the revolutionary equation.

In October 1915, the Constitutionalists clearly had the upper hand, so much so that the United States afforded official diplomatic recognition to the Carranza government as the country's legitimate administrative authority. Disgruntled by the fact that the United States afforded to Carranza all the advantages that came with formal diplomatic recognition, Pancho Villa turned his attention and ire away from Carranza and toward the United States. In January 1916, Villa ordered an attack on U.S. citizens, and two months later, in March 1916, Villa made a military incursion into Columbus, New Mexico. From March 1916 to January 1917, the U.S. government responded to these acts of aggression by Villa by commissioning General John J. Pershing to outfit an expedition to cross into Mexico and to hunt down Villa. The Pershing expedition was unsuccessful, however, and merely served to strengthen Villa's image as a national hero to his fellow citizens for his defiance of the United States.

While Pancho Villa was on the run from General Pershing in northern Mexico, Venustiano Carranza called for a constitutional convention to meet in the state of Querétaro. Carranza had learned his lesson with the Aguascalientes Convention of 1914 and permitted only Constitutionalist sympathizers as delegates. But even here, sharp divisions were seen between the old, patrician reformers and the younger, more radical secularist reformers. In the end, the secularist firebrands held sway, and the Constitution that was produced was imbued with many radical articles and a heavily secular and anticlerical bias. It was only reluctantly accepted by Carranza, and the first chief's unwillingness (or

Carranza's soldiers and U.S. troops use trains during the search for Pancho Villa during General Pershing's expedition in 1916. (Library of Congress)

inability) to recognize this wing's importance to the Revolution would cost him dearly in the future. Nevertheless, in early 1917, and with only lukewarm support from Carranza, the Constitution was ratified by the Convention.

Following the establishment and ratification of the Constitution, presidential elections were called and, in March 1917, Carranza was formally elected as Mexico's first president under the auspices of the 1917 Constitution. On May 1, 1917, Carranza assumed his office with the full legitimacy conferred on him by the electoral and constitutional process. Carranza's presidency lasted from May 1, 1917, until May 1920.

Carranza's presidency was marked by his acute lack of enthusiasm for implementing the more radical elements of the Constitution, which became a source of contention among different Constitutionalist factions. Some major developments that took place during his presidency included the founding of Mexico's first nationwide labor union, the Confederación Regional Obrera Mexicana (CROM), which was headed up by Luis Morones. The establishment of the CROM marked an important step in labor politics for postrevolutionary Mexico, conferring on organized labor a privileged seat at the governing bargaining table.

But opposition to Carranza did not die with the promulgation of the 1917 Constitution and with his formal election to the presidency. Emiliano Zapata in the south had never recognized the authority of the Constitutionalists since the rupture that emerged between the Zapatistas and the Carrancistas at the 1914 Aguascalientes Convention. Carranza understood that his administration would never be conferred full legitimacy in the minds of the Mexican people until such revolutionary icons could be removed from the dynamic. Thus, in an effort to eliminate his powerful southern rival from the scene, Carranza moved forcefully against Zapata in a "scorched earth" campaign, directed by General Pablo González, with the goal of pacifying Zapata's agrarian and peasant supporters, who were still disillusioned by the federal government's continued unwillingness to enact serious land reform as the Constitution demanded. After a series of insidious deceptions, on April 10, 1919, Carranza and his subordinates tricked Zapata into walking into a trap, at which time he was assassinated.

In early 1920, as the constitutionally mandated term for a new presidential election approached, Carranza attempted to mute the power of some of his generals and to maintain control over the country by selecting a more docile subordinate as his successor. Álvaro Obregón, one of Carranza's formidable generals and a loyal supporter from the north, took offense at Carranza's efforts to deny him his perceived reward as Carranza's successor to the presidency and declared against Carranza, in alliance with other northern Constitutionalist military caudillos, Adolfo de la Huerta and Plutarco Elías Calles, under the Plan de

Agua Prieta. This new rebel movement began a march to Mexico City in May.

Still in May 1920, Carranza was forced to flee Mexico City and go into exile. In the process of doing so, he was assassinated by one of his own guards, who happened to be a loyal Obregonista. However, evidence linking Obregón to the assassination is scanty and suspect. Adolfo de la Huerta, an Obregón ally, assumed the provisional presidency until elections could be carried out, at which time Obregón was elected president.

With the death of Carranza and the ascension of Obregón to power, the so-called Decade of Violence was winding down. The nation, weary of the many years of violence, desperate for some semblance of order and stability, and with many of its great revolutionary leaders either marginalized or dead, could finally begin the tedious process of institutionalizing the Revolution and rebuilding the shattered country. Carranza, like his ideological predecessor Madero, was a man of the patrician class and ultimately could not escape this ideological formation. His experience within the struggles of the Revolution for so many years had alerted him to the social underpinnings of the forces unleashed by Madero, and consequently he at least minimally acquiesced to certain shows of social reform. However, his commitment to fundamental and profound social change was nonexistent, and his ascension to the pinnacle of power led him to think, as Madero did upon assuming the presidency, that the Revolution had succeeded and had accomplished its goals. Not only did Carranza become complacent following the defeat of both Zapata and Villa, his two most threatening internal rivals, but his efforts to rein in the Revolution by marginalizing his more powerful and less compliant partisans, such as Álvaro Obregón, ultimately cost him his life.

Obregón represented a new type of revolutionary leader. He was a hybrid of sorts between the social reform radicals and the political reform patricians. He understood that the forces behind the Zapatista and Villista movements were more than just convenient allies on the path to the presidential palace, and he understood intuitively and by experience in the trenches that the new Mexico would have to encompass, in more than just a rhetorical way, a sincere effort at reform programs that would address the desires and aspirations of the peasant and working classes. However, Obregón was also a pragmatist, and he followed a path of moderation and gradualism in his policies. Obregón was also very much the beneficiary of war fatigue. After 10 years of more or less constant violence and uncertainty, the Mexican people were ready to embrace a leader who could bring some peace and stability to the country in the context of the social, economic, and political principles that had come to shape the revolution. In many respects, Obregón was perfectly suited for this leadership role. He had proved his military agility on the battlefield; he had demonstrated at least an appreciation for a meaningful agrarian and labor reform program championed by the Zapatista and Villista factions of the revolution; and he fully embraced the secular revolutionary nationalism that replaced the patristic, detached, elitist, and foreign-oriented ideology of previous national administrations.

As president, Obregón began institutionalizing the ideology of the Revolution and putting together a formal machinery of governing that brought a semblance of order to the country. Obregón's governing strategy included the practices of co-optation, accommodation, and subtle coercion that would become the cornerstones of Mexico's single-party political model, which would endure for the entire 20th century. Obregón brought labor into the governing coalition by encouraging the formation of labor unions and by ensuring that labor had a seat at the bargaining table with the business class. He addressed the needs of the rural peasantry by engaging in some significant agrarian reform and land redistribution programs. Even though these agrarian

Mexican president Álvaro Obregón (in white) addresses a crowd in Mexico City, 1920. (Library of Congress)

reform initiatives were relatively modest in scope, they did represent at least an important symbolic break with the past in the sense that a sincere effort was being made to match the rhetoric and promises of reform with real practice. Obregón also embarked on a massive effort first to harness and then to propagate a unifying ideology of revolutionary nationalism through educational and cultural policy. He wisely appointed José Vasconcelos, one of Mexico's most respected and talented intellectuals of the time, as his secretary of Education. He gave Vasconcelos wide latitude and a significant budget to develop a revolutionary and nationalist credo, to bring this credo to the far reaches of the country in elementary and secondary school curricula, and to display this credo in magnificent pictorial artistic expression on the walls and ceilings of public buildings for all Mexicans to see and appreciate. Vasconcelos wrapped his sweeping cultural and educational reform program in the mantra of the *raza cósmica,* the "cosmic race." According to Vasconcelos, the Mexican people, a mestizo or "mixed" people, unlike any other world civilization, represented the best and most noble elements of an indigenous heritage, a Spanish European heritage, and a Latin American heritage. And it was the revolution that fully encapsulated and gave prominent voice to this cosmic race, both on the national and the global scene. In these ways, among many others, Obregón began to consolidate and institutionalize the social and political aspects of the Revolution.

In the area of economic development and foreign economic relations, however, Obregón was less aggressive and more cautious. He realized that the Mexican economy, absolutely devastated by 10 years of brutal civil war, needed direct foreign investment to spur the engines of economic recovery. The ability to secure this needed foreign investment in turn depended upon friendly relations with investor countries, with its northern neighbor, the United States, being the first among them. And foreign investors were extremely worried about the security and status of their investments given what they considered to be the troublesome and antagonistic approach to foreign investment outlined in various articles of the Mexican Constitution. Obregón had to find a way to convince foreign investors and their representative governments that there could be an accommodation suitable both to the interests of foreign investors and to the principles of the Revolution.

However, the violence of the previous 10 years did not completely abate. Pockets of disaffection would burst to the surface in violent rebellion periodically during Obregón's tenure in office, with some more serious than others. As one might expect, the most serious rebellion occurred in the context of the presidential succession. Obregón had thrown his support behind his fellow Sonoran, Plutarco Elías Calles. This decision prompted another aspirant and erstwhile

Obregón ally, Adolfo de la Huerta, to throw in his lot with those who found fault with Obregón's administration and mounted their own uprising against the president with de la Huerta as their leader. However, unlike his predecessors, Obregón was able not only to contain and put down this and other rebellions but also to complete his term of office and to transfer power to a successor government without being forced to do so at the point of a rifle.

With the support of outgoing president Álvaro Obregón, the military, and organized labor, Plutarco Elías Calles assumed the presidency in 1924. He would dominate Mexican politics for the next 10 years, the first 4 as president and the remaining 6 as the power behind three successive compliant administrations, each lasting 2 years. This latter period is known as the "Maximato" because, during this period, Calles effectively ruled behind the scenes as the *jefe máximo,* or supreme leader. The three puppet presidents during the Maximato were Emilio Portes Gil (1928–1930), Pascual Ortiz Rubio (1930–1932), and General Abelardo Rodríguez (1932–1934). During Calles's tenure, both as president and as *jefe máximo,* the lingering violence of the Mexican Revolution would effectively come to an end, but not without a last spasm of bloody warfare in what is known as the Cristero Rebellion (discussed below).

Most interpreted Obregón's selection of Calles as his successor to mean that the government would begin to pay more attention to the radical wing of the social revolutionaries and begin to implement much more fully some of the more socially progressive provisions of the Mexican Constitution, which had languished up to that point. Calles had developed a reputation as an outspoken anticleric, a dedicated nationalist, and a vocal proponent of more aggressive labor and land reform programs. For instance, the Catholic Church was justifiably fearful that its accommodation with Obregón over the role of the Church in education would be abandoned by Calles. When Church leaders took the

A cristero *praying before his execution, ca. 1928. (Hemeroteca Nacional, Mexico)*

offensive to head off such an eventuality by means of a pro-Church public relations campaign, Calles responded with unexpected severity and cracked down on the Church's public role. The tensions escalated into the Cristero Rebellion, in which dedicated partisans of the Catholic Church took up arms against what they viewed to be an oppressive and godless state. The Cristero war was perhaps the lowest point in the revolutionary struggles because of the ugly and personal viciousness attached to it; however, one might argue that it was the necessary and inevitable consequence of the long-standing and always tense church-state relationship that had plagued Mexican politics since the Hidalgo uprising of 1810. The Cristero Rebellion was nasty and brutal, and it lasted for three years, in fact the duration of the Calles presidency, before a peace was negotiated in which the Catholic Church essentially capitulated to the secularism of the Mexican state and basically abandoned any claims to a role in the public or civic life of the country. At about the same time the Cristero war was ending, the question of Calles's successor also was being debated. Álvaro Obregón, who had patiently sat on the sidelines as Calles governed Mexico, had his sights on a second term of office, in spite of the importance of the no-reelection principle that had been such a central feature of the revolutionary movement since Madero had run on the Anti-Reelectionist platform against Porfirio Díaz in 1910. The Calles government, surely in consultation with Obregón, had amended the 1917 Constitution to provide for a six-year presidential term and to allow the possibility of reelection as long as the terms were not served consecutively. Once this change was made, Calles supported the candidacy of his mentor and patron Obregón, who easily won the election. However, a short time after the election and before Obregón assumed office, a Cristero partisan who had apparently been counseled by a mystic nun assassinated Obregón at a celebratory banquet. The assassination threw Mexico into a political quandary, and Calles, still the sitting president, stepped into the breach.

Álvaro Obregón's death was significant because it produced consequences for the Mexican political system that endured and shaped Mexican politics throughout the remainder of the 20th century. One of these was the apparent need to establish a formal organization to manage electoral politics and processes of political succession. The end result of this need was the establishment of a national political party that could appropriate the values and ideals of the Revolution but that could also strengthen the governing coalition and establish mechanisms for co-opting dissent peacefully instead of undergoing a series of armed uprisings at every presidential succession and transition cycle. This political party, established in 1929 by Calles as the National Revolutionary Party, would evolve into the Institutional Revolutionary Party, or the PRI, which would control Mexican politics from 1929 until 2000. Another consequence was the reaffirmation of the principle of no reelection. From the time of Obregón's death, no elected public official would be permitted to serve more than one term in any one particular office. The hope was to establish a system that would consolidate peace, co-opt dissent, minimize violence as a path to power, ensure security, and provide for a stable transfer of power from one generation to the next. Economic development, as much as social and political stability, demanded it. For the most part, the strategy was successful, even in the short term, and the single-party, semiauthoritarian Mexican political model was born.

In spite of his tendencies toward personalist authoritarianism and the viciousness with which he attacked the Catholic Church, Calles perhaps did more to stabilize the country than any preceding president since the Revolution. And although the Maximato represented a turn toward a more conservative politics compared with the more radical tilt of Calles's politics during his presidential term of

1924–1928, the pace of social and economic reforms in critical areas such as labor and agrarian rights did accelerate. Furthermore, Calles built on the foundations laid by Obregón for a stable and peaceful country. What remained for the Revolution as it was originally conceived was to address the lingering tendency toward personalist autocracy and to deepen the progressive reforms demanded by the Revolution but still inadequately fulfilled. Each of these issues would be dealt with decisively by Calles's handpicked successor in the 1934 elections, Lázaro Cárdenas.

Lázaro Cárdenas came to the presidency from the governor's seat in his home state of Michoacan. An unassuming man with unassailable revolutionary battlefield credentials who had loyally supported both Obregón and Calles, Cárdenas brought with him a governing philosophy that matched his humble personality. He lived modestly; had a reputation for honesty and integrity; listened intently to even the most humble of his fellow citizens in formulating policies; and was sympathetic to the popular, grassroots origins of the Revolution. Perhaps it was because of his perceived lack of ambition, his modest style of living, and his patient demeanor that Calles selected him, thinking Cárdenas would be pliant and easily controllable. If such was the case, then Calles misjudged Cárdenas.

The Cárdenas presidency has gone down in Mexico's modern, postrevolutionary history as one of the country's most progressive, dynamic, and nationalist administrations. During his term of office, Cárdenas put an end to the autocratic pretensions of Calles without assuming similar pretensions for himself. He accelerated the pace of agrarian reform and land redistribution to unprecedented levels. He strengthened the hand of organized labor in its relationship both with the state and with business. And he stood up for Mexico's independence and sovereignty in the country's foreign relations by confronting the excesses and pretensions of foreign governments and foreign investors in dictating

certain aspects of Mexico's foreign and domestic policies.
Perhaps Cárdenas's most referenced and celebrated behavior in this regard was his administration's nationalization of
the petroleum industry in 1938, which is a powerful symbol
of Mexico's revolutionary nationalism and sovereignty today.

In many ways, the Cárdenas presidency was a watershed
moment for Mexico. Although uprisings and calls for continued militancy in the spirit of the Revolution continued
during the Cárdenas *sexenio,* such events were sporadic
and small scale. The period of serious warfare and aggressive factionalism wound down to a close. Mexican society
began to take on airs of normalcy again. With the threat of
major upheaval greatly diminished, Mexicans were able to
take stock of what the Revolution meant and even venture
forth to begin to celebrate its dynamism. In many ways, the
atmosphere of the Cárdenas presidency could be characterized as the excitement of the birth and infancy of a palpable nationalism and a vibrant new social order following
the painful, chaotic, and unsettling labor of the previous 25
years. Mexican revolutionary pride bubbled over in many
ways during the Cárdenas regime. It appeared in the dynamism of a land reform program that established the ejido
system of communal land grants and placed millions of
acres of land in the hands of peasant workers and cooperatives. It appeared on the walls of many of Mexico's government buildings and public universities through the vibrant
colors and themes of Mexico's rich history and revolutionary consciousness in the paintings of Mexico's famous muralists, in the fiction and poetry of a blossoming nationalist
revolutionary literature, and in the nurturing of a film industry that would usher in a "golden age" of Mexican cinema. It showed up in the long-forgotten and isolated villages
of the countryside with the construction of thousands of
new rural schools and the impressive wave of energetic and
well-trained teachers, funded by the state, who came to
teach in them. It revealed itself in the expansion of a

dynamic welfare state that inaugurated an ambitious job creation program, that advanced the rights of labor and strengthened union organizing efforts, and that gave some stability to a growing professional workforce. And it became manifest outside of Mexico to the rest of the world in an uncompromising, nationalist, and vigorous foreign policy that witnessed Mexico standing up to the stronger powers of the world and, on matters of greatest significance to Mexico, prevailing in its global confrontations. The Cárdenas period was the heyday of everything positive and exciting about what the Revolution stood for without any major internal bloodletting.

Success also had its price, and while the Cárdenas *sexenio* was undoubtedly an exciting and creative period in Mexico's postrevolutionary history, its success in many ways also laid the foundations for the subsequent institutionalization and even ossification of the Mexican Revolution and its corresponding political institutions and economic models. The fact that Cárdenas voluntarily relinquished the presidency to his handpicked successor, Manuel Ávila Camacho, in a process that, for the first time since the Revolution, did not experience a corresponding convulsion of at least some contestation or violence, symbolized in a very concrete way this process of institutionalization. And the new era that began to take shape and build upon the stability engendered by Cárdenas was one of settling down, if not of slowing down, that revolutionary impulse. For some observers and students of postrevolutionary Mexican history, the post-Cárdenas period represents the "death" of the Mexican Revolution. For others, it represented the true beginning of the Mexican Revolution. But nearly all scholars accept that Mexico entered a new phase in its history after the Cárdenas period that was characterized by a distinctly new and clearly identifiable vision of social, political, and economic order, one that did indeed represent a significant break from the past.

Mexico, 1940–1968: Institutionalization, Stability, and Growth

The expression of dissent through violence was never completely eliminated following the institutionalization of the Revolution over the periods subsequent to the Cárdenas regime, and they probably never will disappear entirely, but they never again posed a serious and sustained challenge to the government and the new order. This calm allowed Mexico to embark upon a sustained and coherent period of growth, consolidation, and stability for the three decades following the Cárdenas period.

Mexico's history over the balance of the 20th century is best characterized as a quest to realize the social, political, and economic goals of the Revolution in the context of reestablishing stability and order. Mexico's postrevolutionary 20th-century history is also one that seeks to balance the ideologies of socialism and capitalism, as well as the principles of liberal democracy, with the residual tendencies of a stabilizing authoritarianism. The transfer of the Mexican presidency from Lázaro Cárdenas to his handpicked successor, Manuel Ávila Camacho, represented a shift away from the more radical tendencies of the Cárdenas period. Some observers saw the selection of the nondescript and uncontroversial Ávila Camacho as a means for the ruling clique to move toward a moderation in social policy. And the establishment of an all-encompassing party structure to manage the process of presidential transition represented perhaps the last phases of the heavy personalist legacy that had characterized the revolutionary experiment up to that point and that set the stage for an institutionalizing phase that would make possible what has come to be known as the "Mexican Miracle."

The Mexican Miracle. The period of 1940–1968 in Mexican history spans five presidential administrations. The immediate successor to Lázaro Cárdenas was Manuel Ávila

Camacho (1940–1946). Following Ávila Camacho were Miguél Alemán Valdés (1946–1952), Adolfo Ruiz Cortines (1952–1958), Adolfo López Mateos (1958–1964), and Gustavo Díaz Ordáz (1964–1970).

Over the span of these administrations, Mexico experienced an unprecedented political and social stability, which permitted dramatically high levels of sustained economic growth. For instance, Mexico's economy as measured by gross domestic product grew at a remarkable and sustained average annual rate of 6 percent over this extended period, while the population growth rate averaged about 2 percent annually. The "Mexican Miracle," as this period is sometimes called, was the product of an economic policy that blended an unabashed embrace of free market capitalism, coupled with the tempering effects of targeted state intervention and management of strategic sectors of the economy. A term frequently used to describe this economic strategy is "import substituting industrialization," whereby internal industrialization was perceived as the key to long-term economic success and for which the state protected nascent domestic industry from foreign competition. There is no doubt that this policy produced significant economic gains for Mexico and its citizens during this period. The commitment to industrialization as an economic development strategy was evident in the economic policy of the Ávila Camacho administration, which moved away from the economic populism and perceived radicalism of the Cárdenas presidency. And the subsequent administration of Miguél Alemán consolidated and deepened the capitalist model of industrialization and market-based development. From that point onward and continuing through the present day, Mexico's economic development strategy would remain firmly in the procapitalist camp, with only token concessions to the forces calling for progressive wealth redistribution and centrally planned economic policy.

In order for Mexico to move toward the consolidation of this development model over the period of the Mexican Miracle, however, one of the primary challenges for Mexican leaders was to find a way to balance this managed free market approach to economic development with the demands for wealth redistribution that constituted part of the revolutionary legacy. The answer to this challenge was the establishment of an overarching hegemonic political party structure that could co-opt dissent, incorporate differing perspectives on governing, and involve the various disparate sectors of Mexican society formally into the decision-making process while establishing a mechanism of control that would minimize political competition and social conflict. The effectiveness of the Mexican political model in achieving this goal of single-party hegemony was such that Peruvian author Mario Vargas Llosa saw fit, in a 1990 debate with Mexican intellectual Octavio Paz, to term the Mexican model a "perfect dictatorship."

The genius of this political model and its success in achieving social and political stability following such a violent and extended social revolution was its flexibility and its inclusiveness within the context of an authoritarianism that still permitted space for relatively open and critical debate within Mexican society. The process of presidential transition, often the flashpoint for social upheaval and conflict, was consolidated in the practice of the *dedazo,* or the hand-picked selection of the incoming president by the outgoing one, and was afforded legitimacy during the transition between Lázaro Cárdenas and Manuel Ávila Camacho by Cárdenas's willingness not to attempt to disrupt or micromanage the Ávila Camacho administration from behind the scenes.

Another important element of the formation of the hegemonic party system that created the stability necessary for the successes of the five administrations during the middle period of the 20th century was the demilitarization of the political environment by gradually weaning the military from the halls of power and by subordinating the military to the civilian authority of the ruling party elites. From the beginning of the Mexican Revolution through the administration of Manuel Ávila Camacho, every Mexican president claimed both high military rank and significant battlefield experience in the armed phases of the Revolution. And the military, as an institution, had been formally incorporated as a separate sector of the early manifestations of the ruling party. However, the military was finally removed as a formal sector of the ruling party in 1946. And Ávila Camacho, in picking Miguél Alemán as his successor, chose a civilian with no direct military experience or involvement in the military campaigns of the Revolution to lead the country.

Also impressive during the period of regime consolidation was the successful balancing act that the ruling party managed to maintain within the ruling coalition between the more radical, prosocialist elements who embraced the revolutionary legacy of the Cárdenas period and those who embraced the procapitalist policies of the Ávila Camacho and Alemán administrations.

One of the more important social consequences of the Mexican model was the transformation of Mexico over this period from a principally agrarian society to a predominantly urban one. The focus on industrialization was centered in the country's major cities, and the development of supporting infrastructure was concentrated in the cities as well.

Cracks in the Model: Tlatelolco 1968. The Mexican model began to weaken throughout the 1960s as the state-managed process of import-substituting industrialization exhausted itself. The rapid urbanization, and even the economic successes of the model itself, created a burgeoning working and middle class that congregated in the major cities of the country with such rapidity that the ability of the state to keep up with the social demands of this population lagged. Eventually, bending under the weight of this pressure, the formidable hegemonic construct of power and social control that characterized the perfect dictatorship began to crack. In the meantime, the state, under the guidance of the ruling party, had become complacent after a long period of calm and stability. Thus, the PRI and the ruling elites were not prepared to seal these fissures and address the concerns bubbling up among the citizenry. Instead, their reaction was, first, to ignore the signs of growing discontent and, second, when it could no longer avoid them, to do something it had astutely refrained from doing previously: publicly and dramatically repress them with brutal force.

While social repression was not unheard of during the consolidation phase of the Mexican ruling apparatus, its appearance was generally isolated, limited, and often hidden. And as long as the economic model could manage sustained growth, Mexicans overall were less disposed to complain about such repressive moments when they did occur. All this changed in the fall of 1968 when the government engaged in a violent and massive repression of administration critics at a student protest in Tlatelolco plaza.

The specific events leading up to the military crackdown were primarily political in nature. But also providing grist for the protestors were an underlying general dissatisfaction with an economy showing signs of weakness and a political elite seemingly unconcerned about the growing social and economic disparities that were beginning to affect negatively the pocketbooks of working-class citizens. The particular context of the moment also contributed to the conditions that led to the tragedy of the Tlatelolco incident.

As in most of the Western democracies, the 1960s were turbulent times. Mexico, especially, being physically near to and culturally influenced by the United States, was experiencing many of the same generational and cultural clashes

A soldier prods a protester with the butt of his rifle in Mexico City's Tlatelolco plaza on October 3, 1968, after a night of violence between protesting university students and soldiers. Exactly how many died is still hotly contested (with claims between 38 and 300), but the incident brought the repressive tactics of Mexico's government into sharp focus. (AP/Wide World Photos)

that were characterizing European and North American societies. In Mexico, young and idealistic students, alienated by an authoritarian and exclusivist political system that seemed not to respect voices even mildly dissenting from official state policy, embarked upon a path of public protest that sought to challenge the entrenched machinery of the hegemonic, single-party dominant state. The ruling party only half-heartedly embraced mild and insignificant reform of the electoral system in an effort to paint at least the picture, if not the reality, of involving meaningful opposition participation in the governing process. On top of this social context, Mexico had been selected by the International Olympic Committee to be the first country of the developing world to host the Olympic Games. The awarding of the 1968 Olympics to Mexico, to be hosted in the capital, Mexico City, created enormous pressures, both psychological and financial, on the Mexican government. The 1968 Olympics brought international attention to Mexico at a level arguably unprecedented in the country's modern history, and the country and its political elites wanted to put its best foot forward. Because of this, the Mexican government was especially sensitive to any kind of internal manifestation of trouble or instability that might damage the country's reputation in front of the world. On the line were not only the country's prospects for garnering potentially massive windfalls of international investment but also Mexico's pretenses to claim entry into the ranks of first world nations. So, even the slightest perception of internal instability elicited a swift and immediate response by a state accustomed to the use of authoritarian methods of social control. All of these factors—a weakening economic model, a climate of intergenerational cultural conflict, a large and alienated youth population, and an authoritarian single-party state under the microscope of intense international attention—came together and found a tragic expression in the violent military repression of students gathered in protest in Tlatelolco Plaza in Mexico City on October 2, 1968, just one month before the scheduled start of the 1968 Olympics.

On this day, students had gathered for a peaceful rally to protest the government's recent takeover and occupation of the national university and to address other concerns relative to the government's unwillingness to accede to popular demands for greater transparency and more liberal reforms of the political system. In the early evening of October 2, after a series of emotional and passionate speeches against the government had been delivered by protest organizations and student activists, police and military units arrived to disband the meeting and to disperse the crowds. When the protestors failed to heed the orders to disband and disperse, riot police moved in to force the end of the protest. At this point, a few isolated shots were fired. Whether they came from the armed forces or from within the ranks of the civilian protestors is contested. The official government report blamed radicalized protestors, while sources sympathetic to the protestors blamed trigger-happy armed forces. Regardless, in short order, chaos ensued after the initial shots were fired, and the armed forces responded by what can only be described as an indiscriminate and random firing of weapons into the crowds. No one knows the exact death toll from this event, but reliable sources claim that the most accurate numbers are in the range of 300–400 dead, including innocent women and children. More than 2,000 civilians were arrested and taken prisoner in the melee.

The events at Tlatelolco stunned the Mexican population and neutralized what had been, until then, a growing show of public dissent. The government had succeeded in tamping down social unrest and preventing the situation from expanding and developing into a more destabilizing, nationwide, regime-threatening social movement. And the 1968 Mexico City Olympics were free of any major protests or violence. But the massacre at Tlatelolco had its costs and represented the beginning of the end of the hegemonic single-party political system and the import-substituting model of capitalist development. The following years witnessed a brief lurch to a more populist and nationalist rhetoric in order to heal the wounds of the fractured national psyche caused by the repression of 1968, but the country and its leaders would ultimately find themselves forced to accept a political and economic reform project that would, in many ways, bid farewell to the revolutionary nationalism and the semiauthoritarianism of the perfect dictatorship. Even along this path, Mexico's options would continue to be conditioned and limited by the world around it.

Oil Boom and Debt Crisis

Mexico's long march of political and economic reform began in the early 1970s under the regime of Luís Echeverría. Echeverría was secretary of the Interior during the Díaz Ordáz administration, and the tragedy of the 1968 Tlatelolco massacre happened under his watch. Therefore, Echeverría had a personal as well as political need to reverse the damage done to the PRI and to the Mexican state, to reestablish the legitimacy of the PRI government, and to win back popular trust in the regime. His shift to a more populist, left-leaning rhetoric was meant to project an image of greater openness and inclusiveness toward those disaffected elements of Mexican society. In order to project this image, Echeverría acceded to a process of political and economic reform that addressed some of the fundamental underlying problems that had precipitated the crises of the late 1960s. Some of these reforms included an economic policy of "shared development," which promised more equitable redistribution of the gains from economic growth, a commitment to greater political dialogue under the mantra of what he called a "democratic opening," and a highly nationalist and populist foreign policy. But the unwillingness to go beyond mere cosmetic reforms would just prolong the conditions that would later unravel the political and economic model completely. The discovery of vast amounts of oil off the Gulf Coast of southern Mexico created a windfall of revenues that, at least for a while, sustained the economy and breathed new legitimacy into the decaying political model. Echeverría's successor, José López Portillo, leveraged Mexico's petroleum reserves to secure large loans from international creditors. López Portillo then used these loans to finance Mexico's economic development and to redistribute these resources to the Mexican population through generous social welfare programs. However, the precipitous collapse in global oil prices, coupled with rising interest rates, created a financial crisis of unprecedented proportions for the

López Portillo administration such that, by 1982, Mexico was no longer able to service its international debt and announced that it would have to suspend debt payments. Panic ensued in the Mexican economy, and a rapid process of capital flight took place. Faced with this growing crisis in the financial sector, López Portillo nationalized the Mexican banking system in the hopes of stemming the financial hemorrhaging of the economy. This ill-advised bank nationalization turned out to be even more damaging to the Mexican economy and the political system that permitted such an outcome. In an effort to preserve the old order, López Portillo unwittingly created the conditions that led to its permanent dismantling.

Miguel de la Madrid succeeded López Portillo as president of Mexico, and his only course of action was to begin the process of substantive reform of the political system while radically reorienting Mexican economic policy. De la Madrid and his team of technocrats, led principally by his secretary of Programming and Budget, Carlos Salinas de Gortari, dismantled the statist economic model and abandoned the import-substituting industrialization strategy in exchange for an export-oriented, market-driven reform program. Under de la Madrid, Mexico opened up its economy and began to look outward for solutions to its economic problems. In order to reignite investor confidence in the Mexican economy, the de la Madrid government adopted the strict neoliberal prescriptions of stabilization and structural adjustment policies advocated by the World Bank and the International Monetary Fund (IMF) as preconditions for debt refinancing. De la Madrid gradually weaned the Mexican economy off of its dependence on the government by selling off state enterprises to private entities. The administration further tightened the economic reform belt by dramatically curbing state expenditures on social welfare programs. While the economic policies of the de la Madrid government did impose needed order on a Mexican economy that appeared to be spiraling out of control, and while it did reestablish Mexico's

financial credibility to the world, these successes came at a
significant social cost. The average Mexican citizen saw
his standard of living decline during the de la Madrid administration, and indices of economic inequality grew at
alarming rates. While many Mexicans were suffering from
the shock of de la Madrid's reforms, a small percentage of
well-connected Mexicans were entering the ranks of the
world's richest people.

As is usually the case in Mexico, popular discontent with
the harsher aspects of de la Madrid's economic reform program bubbled up in the process of presidential succession
toward the end of his term of office.

The 1988 Presidential Elections, Neoliberal Reform, and Institutional Breakdown

The 1988 presidential elections marked a watershed in many
ways for Mexico. The context leading up to the elections revealed a serious breach within the governing party and shook
the hegemonic single-party system to its core. In the years
leading up to the 1988 elections, neoliberal technocrats
within the PRI, led by Carlos Salinas de Gortari and with the
backing of the international financial community and the
Mexican business sector, had muscled their way into positions of near absolute control over both the government and
the party apparatus. This was, in part, driven by the imperative need to address the fallout from the 1982 debt crisis and
the nationalization of the banking sector, which privileged
the skills and neoliberal policy orientation of the technocratic wing of the ruling party. Additionally, de la Madrid's decision to adhere to the General Agreement on Tariffs and
Trade further strengthened the hand of the technocrats
because it committed the country to a process of economic
reform whose implementation required their sophisticated
technical knowledge, training, and skills. In the process
of consolidating their control over the party and state

apparatuses, the technocrats marginalized the revolutionary old guard of the PRI, sometimes called the *dinosaurios* (dinosaurs). In fact, partly because they had made their careers without ever having to engage in the rough-and-tumble business of electoral politics and backroom horsetrading, these technocratic elites resisted even a symbolic inclusion of the old guard in the long-established process of give and take among competing factions within the governing coalition. The politically unseasoned technocrats did not respect the long-standing rules of the game, which generally followed an alternating pattern of presidential succession between the two competing factions. So, when de la Madrid broke tradition by selecting a like-minded technocrat for his successor instead of someone from the more traditionally political wing of the party, many of those from the traditional political wing of the party broke from the PRI and established a populist and leftist alliance around the person of Cuauhtémoc Cárdenas, the son of Lázaro Cárdenas and heir to his reformist political legacy.

Salinas, a Harvard-trained economist and public finance specialist, had served as Miguel de la Madrid's secretary of Programming and Budget. He assumed the presidency under the dual clouds of electoral fraud and a persistent economic stagnation. While he acted quickly to consolidate his authority and to shore up the reputation of the ruling party, both of which had been seriously damaged by the official handling of the very election that brought him to power, Salinas would leave office six years later with the political system in a severe state of crisis, with social discord and political violence at alarming levels, with a culture of corruption among governing elites in full display, and with the overheated economy on the verge of collapse.

The dissatisfaction with the hegemonic party structure that characterized the student movements of the 1960s and that contributed to a process of electoral reform that sought to involve opposition voices more fully in the governing process emboldened what came to be called the "democratic current" of Mexican opposition outside of the formal rules of electoral politics. This breakaway faction was also alienated by the economic reform program undertaken by de la Madrid. This program required Mexico's acquiescence to IMF and World Bank neoliberal orthodoxies, which threatened the social welfare and wealth redistribution policies that had become synonymous with revolutionary principles since the days of Lázaro Cárdenas.

On the other hand, the outcome of the election put Mexico on an economic path of neoliberal reform that represented in many ways a decisive break from the economic legacy of the Revolution. With the ascension of Carlos Salinas de Gortari to the presidency, the institutionalized Revolution that originated in the idealism of Madero's movement in 1910 effectively began its closing chapters after a very long run.

Salinas began an ambitious process of consolidating the neoliberal reform program initiated by his predecessor. In practice, this reform program involved a profound process of privatization of state-owned enterprises, a liberalization of foreign investment policy, a contraction of government spending, and a dismantling of government welfare and entitlement programs. On the political front, Salinas halted serious democratic reform and instead opted for a strategy of reconstituting the official party's hegemony by aggressively asserting the prerogatives and traditions of unchecked presidential authority. In the social arena, Salinas attempted to address the concerns that Mexicans continued to express regarding the neoliberal economic model and the authoritarian political system through a program of targeted welfare and decentralized development in his ambitious and fairly successful National Solidarity Program (PRONASOL or *Solidaridad*).

The year 1994 was a watershed for Mexico, and it started ominously. On January 1, 1994, the North American Free

Carlos Salinas de Gortari, president of Mexico (1988–1994). (Sergio Dorantes/Sygma/Corbis)

Trade Agreement, which had been ratified by all three of the signatory countries (Canada, Mexico, and the United States) just a few months previously, formally went into effect. On the same day, a group of armed and masked indigenous rebels from the Zapatista National Liberation Army took over five municipalities in the southern Mexican state of Chiapas and engaged in sporadic violent confrontation with state and federal militias for almost two weeks, until a cease-fire agreement was brokered between the government and the insurgents by the Catholic archbishop of the Diocese of San Cristobal de las Casas, Samuel Ruiz.

Even though the armed skirmishes ended a few short weeks after the initial uprising, the Zapatistas continued to exercise de facto jurisdiction over a significant part of the Chiapas countryside. To this day, the Zapatistas have continued their political campaign for greater autonomy and have kept the issues that precipitated their actions present in the nation's political dialogue.

The year 1994 was also a presidential election year, and
Luis Donaldo Colosio, Salinas's former social development
secretary, was campaigning for the presidency as the PRI's
candidate handpicked by Salinas in accordance with traditional practice. On March 23, 1994, while campaigning in
the northern border city of Tijuana, Colosio was assassinated at point-blank range. The shooter, Mario Aburto, was
immediately arrested and interrogated, and has consistently
maintained that he acted alone. However, rumors of a coor-
dinated conspiracy surrounding this assassination abounded
then and continue to circulate among the Mexican people.
We may never know the full details of this tragic event, but
the incident threw Mexico into political chaos and turmoil.
Not since the assassination of Alvaro Obregón in 1928 had
such a high-profile, politically charged murder taken place
in the context of a presidential succession electoral cycle.
And the Colosio assassination had occurred less than three
months after the Zapatista uprising, which was still very
much an ongoing conflict, a source of instability, and an em-
barrassment to the Salinas administration. From the standpoint of the presidential succession process, the Colosio
murder also created additional problems for the government. With the presidential election less than six months
away, none of Salinas's cabinet members nor any other
member of the PRI still holding elective office was constitutionally eligible to run for the presidency. The situation
elicited suggestions that President Salinas simply ignore the
constitutional provision that prohibited these officeholders
to run or that he find a creative way to bypass the Constitution within the bounds of some legal argument. It also generated debate within the governing party concerning the need
to create an internal mechanism within the PRI, such as a
primary system, that could institutionalize and depersonal-
ize the process of presidential succession. Thus, the Colosio
murder revealed in even starker terms the outmoded and

archaic nature of the single-party dominant, and overly presidentialist, political system.

In the end, Salinas wisely decided to follow constitutional
procedures and settled on Ernesto Zedillo Ponce de León as
the PRI's official replacement candidate. Zedillo was a relative unknown from among the ranks of the top-tier PRI
politicians. Before his selection as the PRI's official candidate, Zedillo had served in the Salinas cabinet as secretary
of Education. Because Zedillo had left the Salinas cabinet in
order to direct Colosio's campaign, he was constitutionally
eligible to run for the office. Even though Zedillo had more
than sufficient experience in the upper ranks of the government and in the PRI to make a competent president, very little was known about him, and he was never considered a
serious, top-ranking contender among the possible PRI candidates. Although he had only a very short window to mount
his own campaign for the presidency, Zedillo won the July
election convincingly, an election that nearly all observers
considered to be the fairest and cleanest in Mexico's recent
history, and certainly much more legitimate than the previous presidential election. However, before Zedillo could assume office in December of that year, Mexico was rocked by
another political murder, which implicated a number of
high-ranking PRI politicians, including President Salinas's
brother. Thus, Zedillo took office following one of the most
tumultuous years in modern Mexican political history, and
with public trust and confidence in the PRI and the single-
party state system badly shaken.

In contrast to the scandal-plagued and corrupt administration of his predecessor, Zedillo presided over a government that was basically honest and transparent. Zedillo,
himself a Yale University–trained economist, came out of
the same technocratic tradition and ideological mold that
shaped Salinas. He embraced and deepened Mexico's commitment to the neoliberal reform agenda in his economic

policy, and he did not allow the continuing challenges from
the Mexican left and the Zapatista movement to sidetrack
this reform agenda. In the political arena, however, Zedillo
distinguished himself considerably from Salinas. Whereas
Salinas minimized calls for greater democratic political reforms, Zedillo listened to them. Whereas Salinas chose to
act decisively and authoritatively, and sometimes autocratically, Zedillo embraced moderation and collaboration.
Whereas Salinas practiced a politics of privilege and self-
aggrandizement, using the presidency as a bully pulpit and
sinecure, Zedillo behaved deferentially and modestly, re-
fraining from abusing the power and privilege of his office for
personal or partisan gain. In fact, one might argue that
Zedillo did not have much of an option in the matter, given
the serious damage done to the hegemonic PRI government
system by the Salinas administration, which had stretched
the patience and tolerance of Mexicans with the PRI to its
limits and which had only propelled Mexicans to clamor for
greater democratic political reform.

Zedillo responded favorably to these calls for reform: he
strengthened the independence and autonomy of Mexico's
Federal Electoral Institute. He resisted pressures to use his
position to manipulate and massage the outcomes of the
1997 midterm elections. He separated administration of the
Federal District from the national government, and he recognized opposition party leader Cuauhtémoc Cárdenas's
victory in the first popular election for the governorship of
the Federal District. Also, he broke with long-standing and
well-entrenched tradition by promoting and implementing
a transparent primary system within his own party, the PRI,
for the selection of candidates to public office. And most
significantly, he gracefully and unhesitatingly accepted the
victory of the National Action Party's (PAN) Vicente Fox in
the 2000 presidential elections, thus ending the PRI's extended reign over the country's government at the federal
level. Many Mexicans, both within and outside of the PRI,

considered Zedillo to be a weak and ineffectual president because he either would not or could not exercise the power that Mexicans had for so long come to expect from their national leader. Within his own party, he suffered harsh criticism for appearing to have led the PRI into defeat. But one should not diminish the importance, the courage, and the accomplishments of Zedillo. He made the inexorable process of democratic transition in Mexico a relatively peaceful and painless one, which occurred without an accompanying paroxysm of violence and crisis. He also restored economic growth and stability in Mexico following the calamitous peso crash of December 1994, an economic crisis that brought Mexico to the brink of financial insolvency and that was precipitated by the disastrous events of that year and by the economic mismanagement and corruption of his predecessor. In many ways, the mild and uninspiring Zedillo was exactly the president that Mexico required at this moment in its history, and he lived up to the challenges and expectations of the moment. Those character traits of Zedillo that one might argue contributed to his consistently unimpressive levels of popular support, as well as to the undoing of his political party, the PRI, were traits that one might also argue ultimately served his country and his people well. Without a leader of his temperament and character, the 2000 elections may very well have produced a different and less peaceful outcome.

The presidential election of 2000 was a transformative moment in Mexico's modern history. For the first time since the 1910 Revolution, a member of the opposition to the ruling party assumed the reins of government. Vicente Fox, who ran as the nominee of the PAN, won convincingly against his two principle challengers, Francisco Labastida of the PRI and Cuauhtémoc Cárdenas of the Party of the Democratic Revolution (PRD). Fox's victory came as a result of a variety of factors. Fox had compiled a solid record as a competent executive during his tenure as governor of the state of Guanajuato. Fox was also a physically imposing and austere individual, which played well within a political culture that still likes its leaders to be confident, strong, and authoritative, even within a democracy. Additionally, Mexicans were ready and enthusiastic for change, and Zedillo had encouraged them that change was not only possible but acceptable. Fox also had developed a reputation as a kind of maverick politician, unbeholden even to the militants within his own party.

Democracy's Challenges: The Rise of Andrés Manuel López Obrador and the 2006 Presidential Elections

The failure of the Fox administration to meet the almost unrealistic expectations of the Mexican citizenry for substantive transformation of Mexico's political system and its entrenched corrupt practices and structures, coupled with the continuing disparity in the quality of lives of Mexicans of various socioeconomic classes that accompanied a neoliberal model under attack, resulted in a kind of ideological and philosophical backlash against Fox's continued commitment to the more conservative neoliberal project. As a measure of the public's disenchantment with neoliberalism and the PAN's conservative political platform, left-of-center politicians espousing a more populist agenda began to enjoy increasing success in the court of public opinion. The ideological leader of this neopopulist surge in Mexico was Andrés Manuel López Obrador, the leftist politician from the state of Tabasco, who used his charismatic personality and his popular appeal among Mexico's lower classes to win election to the powerful office of Mexico's head of government of the Federal District in the same year that Vicente Fox was elected president.

From his perch as the head of government of the Federal District, López Obrador was able to consolidate his power over the leftist PRD, prove his abilities to govern effectively, and extend his reputation for leadership at the national level. Furthermore, López Obrador was able to contrast his governing of the massive Federal District directly with that of the national government headed by Vicente Fox, and thus establish himself as an ideological counterpoint to a national administration that was struggling to meet public expectations.

Like many left-leaning politicians of his generation, López Obrador began his political career as a member of the ruling PRI. When Cuauhtémoc Cárdenas left the PRI in the mid-1980s out of frustration with the growing consolidation of power within the party of its technocratic and economically conservative contingent, and forged a coalition of disaffected leftists to challenge the PRI, López Obrador also left the PRI and joined the Cardenista movement, which found organizational expression in the creation of the PRD. From that point on, López Obrador worked tirelessly for the PRD and helped to develop its more populist social policy platforms as well as its grassroots organizational efforts.

As a candidate of the PRD, López Obrador ran for the governorship of his home state of Tabasco in 1994. Although his opponent from the PRI in this election, Roberto Madrazo, won the election in a year when the PRI's popularity and strength had recovered considerably from the contested 1988 elections, López Obrador made a name for himself nationally by forcefully contesting the outcome of this election and successfully highlighting some of the shady campaign practices of Madrazo. Capitalizing on the attention he received in the wake of his challenge to the outcome of this gubernatorial election, López Obrador carefully developed his populist agenda by staging dramatic events in which he could cultivate his populist image as a defender and a savior of the dignity of the marginalized and the oppressed from the ravages of a neoliberal and conservative agenda represented, first, by the PRI regime of Ernesto Zedillo, and, later, by the PAN administration of Vicente Fox.

During his tenure as head of government of the Federal District, López Obrador became perhaps the best-known political personality throughout the country. His policies governing the Federal District met with widespread public approval, and the image he cultivated as a regular, down-to-earth Mexican resonated with many of his fellow countrymen. His intense and strict daily regimen confirmed his reputation as an austere and dedicated public servant, far removed from the out-of-touch and corrupt political class of previous years. López Obrador eschewed the traditional perquisites of public office. He did not surround himself with a coterie of government-provided security officers, he rarely used government-assigned luxury transportation, and he chose to live in his modest, personal, neighborhood home instead of in the official residence pertaining to his office. By the time he declared his intention to run for the presidency and resigned his position as head of government of the Federal District in order to do so, his public approval ratings were above 80 percent. He entered the presidential campaign as the clear front-runner.

However, he was not above criticism and controversy, and he did have to weather some important accusations and challenges during his tenure as head of government of the Federal District. Chief among these was an attempt to remove López Obrador's constitutionally guaranteed immunity from prosecution in order to require him to face a misdemeanor charge of ignoring a court order in a land expropriation case that had its origins in the previous Federal District administration. This particular incident had implications for López Obrador's eligibility to run for the presidency, since federal law prohibits any individual facing criminal charges from competing in a presidential election. The incident also demonstrated a defiant character trait in López Obrador, whose demagoguery of the issue bordered at times on an open contempt for the rule of law. While the issue was ultimately resolved in favor of López Obrador, whose candidacy for the presidency proceeded without legal impediments, it proved to be an ominous sign of things to come.

A number of political scientists specializing in democratic theory and democratic transitions argue that the true test of the consolidation of democracy in a transitional political system is not just the singular transition of power peacefully between opposition political parties at the highest levels of political office through a fair and impartial democratic election, but the continuation of this peaceful transfer of power over multiple administrations and electoral cycles. The end of PRI hegemony in the 2000 elections and the peaceful transition of power to the PAN's Vicente Fox that represented this democratic milestone were merely the first part of this test of democratic consolidation. The 2006 presidential election in Mexico represented the second critical test of the process of Mexico's democratic transition. The prospect of a peaceful transition of power from the PAN to the PRD represented not only a continuation of the process of democratic consolidation in Mexico but also a deepening of it, as a PRD administration would represent the third political party to occupy the presidency in as many elections.

For a while, if polls are to be believed, López Obrador appeared likely to succeed Vicente Fox. However, in the late stages of the presidential campaign, López Obrador began a precipitous decline in the polls, and his PAN opponent, Felípe Calderón, gained on him. By the time the election actually took place on Sunday, July 2, 2006, the polls indicated the race to be a toss-up. In what most observers considered to be one of the cleanest and fairest elections in Mexico's recent history, the preliminary counts were so close that the Federal Electoral Institute delayed announcing a winner until four days later, at which time Calderón was declared the winner with a razor-thin 0.58 percent margin over López Obrador. López Obrador, resorting to the demagoguery and populist tendencies that had served him well in past conflicts of this sort, refused to accept the results and concede

Andrés Manuel López Obrador, presidential candidate for the Party of the Democratic Revolution (PRD), greets supporters gathered in Mexico City's central plaza on July 9, 2006. (David de la Paz/epa/Corbis)

defeat. Instead, he not only mounted an aggressive campaign to contest the election results through the formal and legal procedures designed for such a purpose, demanding an unprecedented nationwide recount as part of a "vote by vote" campaign, but he also openly rejected the authority of the Federal Electoral Institute to announce the winner, and he defiantly declared himself to be the legitimate president of Mexico, refusing to accept any other outcome.

With the support of the administration of the interim PRD head of government of the Federal District, himself a López Obrador protégé, the political supporters of the defeated candidate staged a number of massive, largely peaceful and respectful public protests in the *zocalo,* or central plaza, of Mexico City. Additionally, López Obrador supporters carried out a two-month, round-the-clock occupation of a swath of the Avenue of the Reform, the main public thoroughfare and traffic artery in the downtown district of Mexico City. The disruption of commerce and the defiant posture of the movement was a strategic blunder on the part of López Obrador, as it posed an implicit threat to Mexico's nascent democracy, betrayed an autocratic tendency in López Obrador's character that caused many of his ideological allies to distance themselves from him, and diminished López Obrador's reputation in many other parts of the country.

For its part, the Federal Electoral Tribunal, the final judicial arbiter of electoral disputes, ordered a partial recount of votes in response to López Obrador's complaints and legal challenges, but the results remained the same. And on September 5, 2006, two months after the election, the Federal Electoral Tribunal officially declared and certified Felípe Calderón as Mexico's next president. The last symbolic effort among López Obrador supporters to find a way to keep his aspirations to the presidency alive took place during the official swearing-in ceremony of Calderón before the Mexican Congress on December 1, 2006. As required by the Mexican Constitution, the president-elect must take the oath of office before Mexico's Lower House of Congress, or the Chamber of Deputies. López Obrador's supporters in the Chamber of Deputies, hoping to provoke a constitutional crisis of succession that would create a potential path for López Obrador to assume the presidency, planned to try to prevent Calderón from carrying out this task. However, Calderón managed to find his way into the Chamber of Deputies through a back door and was able to take the oath of office as required by the Constitution and put to rest any further talk of constitutional challenges to his presidency, albeit amidst a noisy chaos and even brawling on the Chamber floor.

Although the public protests, manifestations, and street occupations in support of López Obrador gradually ended soon thereafter, López Obrador himself still refused to accept the results and announced that he was organizing a parallel government, which still currently exists, although with minimal public support and no legal recognition.

Since assuming the presidency, Felípe Calderón has largely continued the policies of his predecessor, especially in the realm of economics and foreign affairs. His conservative platform advocates for a continuation of neoliberal and free market policies, as well as domestic fiscal austerity. In his foreign policy, Calderón has stressed that his administration will approach its relationship with the United States as one of cooperation, collaboration, and friendship. However, like Vicente Fox before him, Calderón has promised to address the subject of Mexican out-migration to the United States both through a domestic jobs creation program and through continued lobbying for comprehensive immigration reform in the United States. In this matter, Calderón will find himself often at odds with the United States, and this will undoubtedly constitute a strain in the bilateral relationship. But the impact and importance of migrant remittances on the Mexican economy will continue to grow, which will only tend to exacerbate the problem.

Where Calderón has distinguished himself from his predecessor, and where his efforts have been greeted enthusiastically by the United States, is in the realm of national security, specifically in terms of cracking down on illegal drug-trafficking operations in Mexico and on the U.S.-Mexican border. One of his most difficult challenges will continue to be addressing the social and economic disparities caused by his continuation of a neoliberal economic program and the sluggish performance of the Mexican national economy. Another important challenge for Mexico under the leadership of Calderón will be the continuation of democratic reform. The controversy surrounding the elections of 2006 revealed fissures and fault lines in Mexico's still nascent democracy. Electoral reform, especially with regard to campaign financing and the use of media resources, is something that the Calderón administration and the national political parties will likely continue to work on. And the balance of power between the legislative and executive branches of government at all levels will perhaps be the single most important evolution within the Mexican political system in the near future.

Mexico's history is rich with the accomplishments of magnificent indigenous civilizations; with the complexities and refinements of Western civilization and its philosophies of global economy, empire, and political and social organization; and with the idealism of reform and revolution. However, Mexico's history is also one rich in conflict, division, and painful struggles. Mexico today is a product of this history, which resonates profoundly among all Mexicans who are passionate about and proud of their historical roots and legacies, but who also continue to struggle to make sense of the opposing forces and conflicting emotions that such a history naturally engenders. All things Mexican are rooted in this history, and the remainder of this study of Mexico, which will focus much more intently on the postindependence political, economic, and cultural elements of the country, should always be understood with this historical context as an ever-present backdrop.

References

Anna, Timothy E. *Forging Mexico, 1821–1835*. Lincoln: University of Nebraska Press, 1998.

Arnold, Linda. *Bureaucracy and Bureaucrats in Mexico City, 1742–1835*. Tucson: University of Arizona Press, 1988.

Beezley, William H. *Judas at the Jockey Club and Other Episodes of Porfirian Mexico*. Lincoln: University of Nebraska Press, 1987.

Bethell, Leslie, ed. *Mexico since Independence*. New York: Cambridge University Press, 1991.

Chevalier, François. *Land and Society in Colonial Mexico: The Great Hacienda*. Berkeley: University of California Press, 1963.

Coe, Michael D. *Mexico: From the Olmecs to the Aztecs*. London: Thames and Hudson, 1994.

Cypress, Sandra. *La Malinche in Mexican Literature from History to Myth*. Austin: University of Texas Press, 1991.

Fisher, Lillian Estelle. *Viceregal Administration in the Spanish American Colonies.* Berkeley: University of California Press, 1926.

Fisher, Lillian Estelle. *The Background of the Revolution for Mexican Independence.* Gainesville: University of Florida Press, 1966.

Greenleaf, Richard E. *The Mexican Inquisition of the Sixteenth Century.* Albuquerque: University of New Mexico Press, 1969.

Hale, Charles A. *Mexican Liberalism in the Age of Mora, 1821–1853.* New Haven, CT: Yale University Press, 1968.

Haring, Clarence H. *The Spanish Empire in America.* New York: Oxford University Press, 1947.

León-Portilla, Miguel. *Aztec Thought and Culture: A Study of the Ancient Nahuatl Mind.* Translated by Jack Emory Davis. Norman: University of Oklahoma Press, 1963.

Padden, Robert C. *The Hummingbird and the Hawk: Conquest and Sovereignty in the Valley of Mexico, 1503–1541.* New York: Harper & Row, 1970.

Poniatowska, Elena. *Massacre in Mexico.* New York: Viking Press, 1975.

Prescott, William H. *History of the Conquest of Mexico.* New York: Bantam, 1967.

Ricard, Robert. *The Spiritual Conquest of Mexico.* Berkeley: University of California Press, 1966.

Richmond, Douglas, ed. *Essays on the Mexican War.* College Station: Texas A&M University Press, 1986.

Scholes, Walter V. *Mexican Politics during the Juárez Regime, 1855–1872.* Columbia: University of Missouri Press, 1957.

Simpson, Lesley B. *Many Mexicos.* Berkeley: University of California Press, 1959.

Simpson, Lesley B. *The Encomienda in New Spain.* Berkeley: University of California Press, 1960.

Thomas, Hugh. *Conquest: Montezuma, Cortés, and the Fall of Old Mexico.* New York: Simon & Schuster, 1993.

Thompson, J. Eric S. *The Rise and Fall of Maya Civilization.* Norman: University of Oklahoma Press, 1985.

CHAPTER TWO
The Mexican Economy

This chapter focuses on the Mexican economy and the current business environment. The goal of the chapter is to introduce the reader to the history of Mexican economic development as well as the interactions between the state and nongovernmental actors in shaping the pattern and path of this development. Also, this chapter explores the relationship between the realities and structures of Mexico's domestic economy and the forces at work in the global economy. The aim is that readers understand better not only the paradoxes and the complexities that have characterized these interactions within Mexico's internal, domestic environment but also the very important place Mexico occupies in the world economy. Additionally, the chapter will introduce the most important sectors of the Mexican economy and will flesh out some of the major characteristics of these sectors.

CAPITALISM, STATISM, AND SOCIAL DEVELOPMENTALISM IN THE MODERN MEXICAN ECONOMY

Since the Mexican Revolution of 1910, and up until the economic crisis of the 1980s, the Mexican economy is best described as state-managed capitalism. It is not exactly a fully free market economy, but one in which state regulation and state control over key sectors is important. Also, the Mexican business and economic environment includes the significant role that corporate interest groups, such as labor unions and business associations, play in the construction of economic policy and planning. From a structural point of view, the Mexican economic and business environment comprises private enterprises, semiprivate/semipublic parastatal entities, and state-owned companies.

Prior to 1940, the Mexican economy functioned primarily in recovery mode following the destruction and economic contraction caused by the violence and instability of the Revolution. Further, the political elites who were born out of the Revolution vacillated between two competing tendencies. The first tendency involved a conservative, hands-off approach to the economy that also embraced accommodation and compromise with private national entrepreneurs and international investors. The second current involved a more radical, interventionist approach that catered to the demands of the nationalist and redistributionist elements of the Revolution. Regardless of the way the winds were blowing at any particular time, though, Mexico never rejected the underlying importance of market-based capitalism as the engine of economic development and growth. The question for postrevolutionary leaders in Mexico with regard to economic policy and development strategies was not whether Mexico would be a capitalist country but how Mexico would guide and manage capitalist development.

Economic policy questions that concerned the Mexican leadership included how much and to what degree the state should manage and operate economic development, how much the state should supplant or complement private capital as the principle investor in economic development projects, to what extent the state should promote protectionist policies in support of developing a national entrepreneurial and industrial class in the face of foreign competition, what the state's proper role was in balancing the demands of labor and the interests of business elites, and whether the state should emphasize agrarian reform and modernization of the agricultural sector of the economy or whether it should emphasize the development of an urban industrial sector, or whether it should do both. These questions, among others, fashioned economic policy debates in Mexico in the postrevolutionary period. And how they were answered depended on the inclinations and proclivities of the various presidents. Some presidents, like Lázaro Cárdenas and Luís Echeverría, embraced a more socialist, populist, and redistributionist approach to economic policy. Others, like Miguel Alemán Valdés and Carlos Salinas de Gortari, were partial to the interests of the business class and were unabashed advocates of unfettered free market capitalism.

As a consequence of these competing tendencies, Mexico's contemporary economic history can best be understood as the product of a mixed-development model, one that embraces capitalism as the driving engine for growth and development, but one in which the state has played an active and interventionist role in managing and directing this growth. In many ways, this is a product of the traditional statism that has been the fundamental pillar of the economic philosophy that has guided Mexico's economic development since colonial times. To reiterate, in contemporary Mexico, the question is not whether the state should reject its traditional function in managing economic growth and development in favor of an unfettered free market, but rather the question has been and continues to be what is the appropriate balance between an interventionist state and the free market in managing economic affairs.

Bases of Mexico's Mixed Economic Policies

While the Mexican state has always been more or less a central and active manager of the national economy, the Mexican Revolution and its product, the 1917 Constitution, not only institutionalized the state's formal relationship to the national economy but also outlined its obligations to assume an interventionist role in shaping the contours of the economy. For example, Article 27 of the Mexican Constitution of 1917 recognized the state as the sole proprietor and guardian of the nation's natural resources, from subsoil minerals and other underground deposits to all the surface water bodies; the forests; and the wildlife, flora, and fauna resident in them. In its capacity as guardian of the national patrimony, the state reserved the exclusive right both to give concessions to private interests for the exploitation of such natural resources and to expropriate at any time and under any circumstances any concessions granted. Furthermore, Article 27 provided the state the authority to confiscate or nationalize any private property in the service of the national interest as defined by the state. In the realm of finance, Article 28 established the creation of a state-controlled national bank, which would be the only financial institution capable of issuing national currency. And Article 73 of the Constitution outlined the state's role as the regulatory authority over credit-granting institutions and in the issuance of the national currency. With regard to the relationship between capital and labor, Article 123 of the Constitution gave explicit rights to the state to mediate relations between capital and labor and to arbitrate in a definitive and binding manner any disputes between capital and labor. This meant protecting and advocating for the rights of the working class in its relationship to the business class. In this vein, Article 123 also mandated the working conditions of labor, guaranteeing labor the right to organize, to a minimum wage, and to other health care and educational benefits. With regard to the regulation of international economic relations, Article 27 of the Constitution placed strict provisions and limitations on what kinds of real estate foreigners could own and under what conditions. Pursuant to Article 27, the Mexican government also promulgated legislation regulating the amount and percentage of ownership permitted to nonnational investors in any productive national economic activity. In the agrarian sector, where the Constitution assumed an even more expansive role of the state in the rural economy, Article 27 of the Constitution recognized the rights of peasants to their own land and authorized the state to allocate productive farmlands to dispossessed peasant farmers through state-managed agricultural cooperatives known as ejidos, which were loosely modeled upon the pre-Columbian Aztec tradition of communal operation and management of agricultural farming. The state would retain title over these communal lands, granting the legal use of such lands to peasant communities for as long as such communities could keep the lands in productive use.

The net result of these constitutional provisions, among others, was to cement the state's role, as distinct from the free market, as the primary engine for economic growth and development. The logical outcome of this was the creation and expansion of a state apparatus whose hand in the national economy not only served as a guide to encourage individual initiative and private entrepreneurship but also required that the state itself become a major entrepreneurial organization in its own right.

As the application of this very hands-on, interventionist state/economy model evolved over time, the Mexican state developed and operated more than 1,200 public enterprises. Some of these state-run enterprises, such as the Bank of Mexico or the National Bank of Agricultural Credit, were direct extensions of federal government agencies, called into being by legislative action and wholly owned by the state; but others were semiautonomous enterprises with only loose connections to the institutions of state but whose management and leadership were determined by and answerable to the state. These semiautonomous institutions are known as parastatal agencies, some of the more prominent of which were Petroleos Mexicanos (PEMEX), the state petroleum monopoly, and the Comisión Federal de Electricidad, the state utility monopoly.

Although the Mexican state exercised direct control over enterprises that constituted the bulk of the national gross domestic product (GDP) for an extended period of time,

Mexico's mixed economic development model also encouraged the simultaneous development of private enterprise in other sectors. While most of the state-run enterprises did not have to face challenges to its market shares from private-sector competitors, competition for market share among private entrepreneurs was often fierce and constantly looked toward protection and privilege from the guiding and regulatory hand of the paternalistic state. The Mexican state did not disappoint its nascent entrepreneurial class. In fact, those privately owned Mexican companies today that are thriving and competitive in the global market, such as Grupo Televisa or Banamex, owe their current successes to the nurturing and protectionist policies of the Mexican state in their early days of development.

As the mixed statist/capitalist model evolved postrevolution, it went through fairly regular phases during which one side of the equation would be emphasized and would assume primacy in guiding the country's economic development over the other. Yet, always and everywhere, the managerial eye of the state was present, at least until the state voluntarily weaned itself from the business of business in the 1980s, a process that has continued and deepened until the present day. Nevertheless, Mexico's 20th-century economic history can be defined by pendulum shifts between greater and lesser state interventionism. The periods of these pendulum shifts can be described and demarcated accordingly, as follows.

The period of 1917–1928 can be characterized as one in which a strong statist and interventionist rhetoric existed but that was never substantively realized in practice. From the moment of the promulgation of the Mexican Revolutionary Constitution in 1917 until the end of the Maximato period (1934) (see "The Mexican Revolution" section in chapter 1), the application of the more radical statist, labor-friendly, agrarian reformist, and nationalist revolutionary economic principles was limited mostly to campaign rhetoric and the paper upon which the Constitution was written.

Essentially, private enterprise and a very procapitalist, pro-foreign investment economic regime, reminiscent of the Porfiriato (see chapter 1), functioned as it basically always had. While a few concessions were made to the newly organized and powerful labor and peasant constituencies within the ruling coalition, the economy for the most part relied on market forces instead of government intervention to recover from the devastation of the civil war. Certainly, the Revolution's early leaders embraced those nationalist economic principles of the Revolution that called for a radical shift away from the promarket and probusiness practices of the Porfirian system as long-term goals for the country's economic development in a just and more equitable way, but the desperate condition of the country's economy in the wake of the conflict, and its need for large infusions of capital from foreign investors as well as from the bank accounts of the privileged families of the Porfirian system, kept the early revolutionary governments at a safe distance from truly threatening the interests of the private sector.

With the violent phase of the Revolution drawing down to a close, and with the beginnings of the institutionalization of the political and social system taking shape under the budding hegemony of a national governing party, the 1928–1940 period saw a substantive shift toward actual attempts to implement some of the more radical elements of the Constitution and its promises to redistribute the country's wealth through agrarian reform and enforcement of the rights of organized labor. In terms of the global economy, this period encompasses the years of the Great Depression and the overall contraction of most national economies. In this context, Mexico was no different than other countries in seeking a more interventionist and activist role for the state in managing economic affairs. While Franklin Roosevelt, president of the United States during much of the Depression, was developing and implementing his New Deal program in the United States under a Keynesian model of state-led

Former Mexican president Lázaro Cárdenas meeting with oil labor leaders in the state of Tamaulipas in 1938. That same year, he announced that Mexico's oil industry would be nationalized. (Library of Congress)

development, the Maximato presidents (1928–1934) and the Lázaro Cárdenas administration in Mexico were doing very much the same. It is during this period that massive amounts of agricultural land were redistributed to the peasantry with great fanfare. This was also the time when organized labor was exercising considerable influence with the state in terms of extracting concessions from the business class. And the end of this period saw the Mexican state nationalize the entire petroleum industry.

Following the populist and statist economic policies that crescendoed in the latter part of the Cárdenas administration with the nationalization of the petroleum industry in 1938, the limits of the strategy revealed themselves, and even Cárdenas himself realized that Mexico needed to pull back from his brand of economic populism and give some breathing room to the market and some encouragement to private entrepreneurs. His selection of Manuel Ávila Camacho was a clear sign of an impending change in the country's economic policies and directions. Land redistribution slowed considerably and overtures were made to international investors and the private sector, which indicated that the Mexican state would be interpreting the Constitution and adopting policies that would protect their investments, properties, and economic interests, instead of threaten them. The process of repairing state-business relations within a procapitalist framework began slowly and deliberately during the Ávila Camacho administration, but it accelerated exponentially during the subsequent Miguél Alemán administration. Not only did Alemán declare Mexico to be a country whose economy was firmly in the capitalist camp but he also used his unfettered power as president to blur the lines between business and the state. The Alemán administration's unabashed collusion with the private sector and its commitment to a capitalist model of development set the stage for a sustained period of economic growth in the Mexican economy, which would later be termed the "Mexican Miracle." However, another legacy of the Alemán administration's probusiness economic policy was a pattern of corruption that saw the state, as opposed to the market, function as the vehicle for capitalist wealth accumulation. The period of 1940–1952 thus can be understood as a period in which economic policy in Mexico moved toward a probusiness, capitalist, but still state-centric economic model of growth and development.

The next three presidential administrations continued along the path of state-led capitalist economic development that the Ávila Camacho and Alemán administrations had designed. This period of sustained levels of economic growth and relative economic stability were, in many ways, the golden years of Mexico's economic development. Even though problems of inequality persisted, especially between the rural and urban economies, average wages and incomes for the majority of working-class Mexicans generally grew across the board. The Mexican peso remained stable, with its value relative to the U.S. dollar at a steady 12.5/1 ratio. Private investment, both from domestic and international sources, continued to grow, and Mexico's commitment to a vigorous industrialization strategy proceeded apace. This period of relative wealth in Mexico contrasted with the economic uncertainty that had characterized the revolutionary period and its immediate aftermath. The violence and accompanying radicalism of the Revolution, which expressed itself in economic terms through the advocacy of a wealth redistribution policy, an agrarian reform policy, and an antiforeign economic nationalism, had been satisfied to some extent and had certainly exhausted itself. Mexicans were ready to step back and give the market and the state a chance to construct a stabilizing growth model. Socially, the wealth that accompanied the economic miracle also brought with it a relative calm throughout Mexican society. Organized labor, co-opted by the ruling party, did not seriously agitate against business; and why did it need to, with real wages rising and with the state covering its back? For its part, the business sector had developed a comfortable modus vivendi with the state in which the state protected and collaborated with Mexican entrepreneurs against foreign competitors and yet gave space for businesses willing to cooperate with the government, allowing much more breathing room to operate independently from state control. State-business relations were solidified through a number of formal and information organizations that served as conduits both for the exchange of information and expectations and for "sweetheart" deals and perquisites. The state's firm control over labor, now almost fully subordinate and docile to the Institutional Revolutionary Party (PRI) government, acted as both a carrot and a stick in state-business relations and helped to keep businesses ingratiated to the state. For their part, business elites, finally convinced that capitalism would be the guiding economic ideology supported by the state, recognized that their interests would be best served by working with and through the state to maximize the benefits of capitalist development. The Mexican economic miracle was quite real and produced significant benefits for Mexicans and undoubtedly helped to modernize the Mexican economy. But it was not without its weaknesses, which were both political and economic in nature. When these weaknesses manifested themselves in the late 1960s and produced destabilizing convulsions within the political system, the Mexican state reached back into the past and revived that latent pattern of economic populism and nationalism that was always a part of the revolutionary tradition.

From 1970 to 1982, the Mexican economy floundered and Mexican economic policy drifted leftward toward old-style Cardenista populism. Even though political leaders never really abandoned a capitalist model of economic development, the state actively stepped up its interventionist rhetoric regarding the economy and followed it up with interventionist practice. The threat of expropriation and nationalization of private enterprise grew, sending chills through the business sector. The state extended its tentacles more fully and deeply into the economy through the creation of even more state-owned enterprises in strategic economic sectors, and sought to place even greater controls over business. And instead of modifying fiscal and monetary policy to address the exhaustion of the state-led import-substitution industrialization model of economic development, the state borrowed heavily to keep the economy afloat. The discovery of vast petroleum reserves in Mexican territorial waters in the Gulf of Mexico was both a blessing and a curse for Mexico. On the one hand, it provided some relief to the political stresses and the economic imbalances within the economy. Yet, on the other hand, it emboldened the state to continue pursuing its nationalist economic policies without moving toward a reform of the underlying statist model of economic development. During this period of renewed economic populism and statist expansion into the national economy, Mexico experienced its first currency devaluation in years. Inflationary pressures were chronic, and unemployment became a serious problem. In terms of the Mexican economy, the period ended disastrously in 1982 with Mexico defaulting on its international debt obligations. Capital flight from the economy followed, and the government, desperate to contain the fallout, went toward the extremes of economic nationalism by nationalizing the entire banking industry in the same year.

The subsequent period in Mexico's economic history, which covers 1982 through the present, marks the end of the state-led capitalist development model. Both the populist/socialist variant of the model, sometimes called the Cardenista model, which characterized the 1928–1940 and the 1970–1982 periods of Mexican history, as well as the probusiness/free market capitalist variant of the model, sometimes called the Alemanista model, which characterized the 1940–1970 period in Mexican economic history, gave way to a neoliberal economic model that still embraced free market capitalism but that extracted the state from its role as manager. In essence, Mexico's contemporary economy is an unregulated, nonstatist, market-driven economy. In practical terms, this has meant the privatization of state-owned enterprises, a liberalization of investment policy, austerity in fiscal policy, and an embrace of free trade and export-oriented development. While the consequence of this neoliberal strategy improved macroeconomic stability in Mexico and restored private-sector confidence in Mexico, it did so at a high social cost. Wages stagnated as prices rose, income inequality increased dramatically, and poverty and quality-of-life indices failed to improve. The wholesale abandonment of the Cardenista model also had a residual effect among those who felt the harsher edges of the neoliberal project: More Mexicans were suffering the effects of the contraction of the Mexican economy as it took the painful medicine necessary for its recovery, and many felt abandoned by the state as welfare programs and social safety nets were gradually reduced in scope or eliminated altogether. In essence, many felt that the state had abandoned the goals and principles of the Mexican Revolution for the establishment of an economic system that harkened back to the days of Porfirio Díaz. The corruption and venality that had characterized the Alemán presidency and that was revealed in his administration's unseemly collusion with the private sector returned in the administration of Carlos Salinas de Gortari, which led to its own economic crises.

Currently, the Mexican economy continues to embrace the basic contours of the neoliberal model, only now under the direction of the conservative, probusiness National Action Party (PAN). But the social costs of the neoliberal policy have grown, and the neoliberal model's failure to address the problems of growing inequality and wealth redistribution in Mexico have met with a reemergence of the populist and statist expectations of the old revolutionary left. The Cardenista model, which advocates a strong and interventionist state operating in a climate of economic nationalism, resonates with a growing percentage of the Mexican population. The institutional voice for the advocates of a return to this economic model is the Party of the Democratic Revolution; and its candidate for the presidency in 2006, Andrés Manuel López Obrador, embodied all the characteristics of old-style economic populism. López Obrador lost the 2006 election in an extremely close contest to the PAN's Felípe Calderón, but his strong showing will require that subsequent administrations address some of the harsher elements of the neoliberal economic strategy and engage the state more fully and actively once again in managing national economic policy. Calderón remains committed to a free market approach to Mexico's economic development, but the nagging problems of poverty and income inequality will continue to push the state toward a more activist and perhaps even interventionist role.

Economic Sectors

Mexico's economic history clearly shows the pull of competing capitalist development models in the context of a strong, semiauthoritarian political system. This history has conditioned the place and importance of various different sectors in the evolution of the country's economic development strategies. This section explores the main sectors of the Mexican economy, describing their principal features and their relative importance to Mexico's economic development prospects. The section will also show how the sectors have fared over time and how they are positioned for the future likely course of Mexico's economic development.

Agriculture.   For most of its existence, Mexico's society has been rural and agrarian, with landownership and farming as vitally important components to the identity of the country and its individual citizenry. Hence, control over Mexico's rural lands and the resources that such lands produce have been the source of struggle and conflict among Mexicans for generations. Modern Mexico is undoubtedly moving away from its agrarian past and is becoming increasingly urbanized, but even today the agricultural sector of Mexico's economy employs and sustains a significant number of Mexicans. It is still a principal engine for earning foreign exchange through trade, and the wealth that Mexico's farms produce for the country have played, and continue to play, an instrumental role in the development of the other sectors of Mexico's economy. Hence, agriculture remains important not only to the success of Mexico's future

Farmers on a commercial farm in Mexico use a combine to harvest wheat, 1961. (Rockefeller Foundation)

economic development prospects but also to the health and well-being of a large portion of its population.

Structurally, Mexico's rural economy bears two distinct attributes: (1) a landless peasantry engaged in small-scale subsistence farming and (2) large-scale plantations, ranches, and commercial farms engaged in market production. The former tend to be some of the poorest, most disenfranchised, and most exploited of Mexican citizens, many of them indigenous, and the latter tend to constitute the owners and beneficiaries of Mexico's rural wealth. Many of the large-scale agricultural enterprises that exist in Mexico today are oriented toward the export market, producing goods that average Mexicans either have no use for or cannot afford to consume. It was not until the middle of the 20th century, when the Mexican government adopted the import-substituting industrialization strategy of economic development, that the main engine driving the Mexican economy shifted from agricultural production to industry and manufacturing. In contemporary Mexico, industry and manufacturing compete with tourism, services, and remittances from abroad for the top contributing shares of Mexico's total gross national product. Nevertheless, prior to 1940, the agrarian question, which addressed the nature and condition of landownership as well as the economic importance of agricultural production to overall GDP compared to industrial production, dominated Mexican political, economic, and social life. And the importance of agriculture and agrarian reform in the Mexican Revolution of 1910 has meant that the rural sector continues to have at least a symbolic importance in the Mexican national consciousness. Indeed, many Mexicans still depend on both commercial and subsistence agriculture for survival.

Social relations in the countryside are still reminiscent of the encomienda system, which awarded individual landowners control over the productive capacity of rural, indigenous populations. The control over peasant labor through the encomienda system eventually evolved into ownership and title over the lands worked by the peasants. Thus, landownership in Mexico has traditionally been an important and a necessary requirement to guarantee an improved quality of life as well as an opportunity for upward social mobility. One of the major thrusts of the Mexican Revolution, in fact, and what motivated the peasant-based armies of Emiliano Zapata, was to address the problem of landownership and the concentration of land in the hands of a very few rural elites. Prior to the Revolution, the concentration of landownership had reached unprecedented levels, with 1 percent of the population owning upwards of an astounding 97 percent of the land. In order to address this gross inequality, agrarian reform and land redistribution became one of the cornerstones of the Mexican Constitution of 1917. Article 27 of the Mexican Constitution specifically declares that large landed estates will be broken up as needed and parceled out to landless communities as a matter of redistributive justice.

Although successive Mexican administrations did expropriate and redistribute agricultural lands in accordance with the Constitution, the massive restructuring of the agrarian sector did not occur as many had hoped it would. When the government did implement agricultural land redistribution programs, the scope was almost always limited to what was politically necessary. Instead, the government tended to invest in commercial agriculture and the development of a modern agribusiness sector that could generate foreign exchange through export production as part of its overall economic development strategy. Land concentration basically continued as before, with more and more people abandoning the countryside for the urban industrial centers.

One of the unique aspects of the Mexican agricultural sector is the existence of communal farms know as ejidos. Ejidos are rural collectives that date back to pre-Columbian times. Essentially, members of a particular village or local community did not own private property, but instead worked the land together for the benefit of the community. And while the community plots served to support the local economy, formal ownership of the land actually pertained to the nation. The ejido became the primary place where postrevolutionary governments carried out their land redistribution schemes. The ejido system continues to function today, but now *ejidatarios* (peasants who work and live on ejidos) have the opportunity to obtain personal title to their plots and to dispose of such titles as they desire. *Ejidatarios* still account for the majority of agricultural farmworkers, although they remain the poorest and least productive actors in the agricultural sector. With a few exceptions, ejido lands are of relatively poor quality and *ejidatarios* have minimal access to credit and modern farming equipment, seeds, and technology. Mexico's adoption of neoliberal economic policy has reversed whatever small gains may have been made in addressing the imbalances in landownership and concentration in the countryside. In fact, some have argued that the opening of Mexico's economy to foreign competition and the elimination of protectionist measures have had devastating effects on Mexico's agricultural sector and its peasant class. The 1994 Zapatista uprising by indigenous peasant corn and bean farmers on the day that the North American Free Trade Agreement (NAFTA) went into effect was, in part, a clear and visible protest of the negative effects that NAFTA was likely to impose upon subsistence farmers (see below for a discussion of NAFTA). Largely because of neglect from the government for so long, these peasant farmers feared that their inability to compete against the much more efficient and modern corn and bean agribusinesses in the United States and Canada in an open market would put them out of business, drive them off their lands, and subject them to the exploitations of contract labor on Mexico's commercial farms, if they did not drive them to labor in Mexico's urban slums. To date, there is evidence that indicates that these fears of peasant farmers have been justified. For example, Mexican internal rural-to-urban migration has steadily grown since the implementation of NAFTA, and Mexican rural outmigration to the United States has also increased. This trend would indicate that opportunities for peasant farmers to sustain themselves by agricultural production are giving way to the need for other forms of generating income that require abandoning or selling their farms. Additionally, these migratory trends parallel an equally significant increase in the amount of corn and beans imported from foreign producers, indicating a drop in Mexican farmers' share of the national corn and bean markets.

Petroleum.   Within the energy sector of the Mexican economy, no commodity is more important than petroleum. As a natural resource, petroleum has been the single most important source of income for the country. It is also the natural resource that elicits the most passionate and nationalist responses from Mexican citizens. It is not just a resource that has practical economic import, it is also a symbol of national identity and sovereign independence. As such, the history of petroleum is as much a part of Mexico's nationalist folklore as is the history of the Ford Motor Company to the United States's national mythology. It continues to occupy a special place in Mexico's economic and national identity today.

The oil industry in Mexico had a modest beginning in the late 19th century. Mexico's president at the time, Porfirio Díaz, noting the rising energy consumption that was fueling the industrial revolution in Europe and the United States, encouraged foreign capitalists to invest in oil exploration in Mexico. For Díaz, petroleum represented simply another way to entice foreign investment to Mexico. The probusiness and proforeign dictator was only too happy to provide exclusive extraction contracts and licenses to foreign investors willing to take the risk. For the investors, given the supportive and probusiness climate fostered by Díaz, it was a convenient and minimally risky proposition. These early exploration efforts proved fruitful, and foreign-owned petroleum companies were poised to begin extracting and exporting petroleum from Mexico right at the moment that the Porfirian dictatorship collapsed and the Mexican Revolution took off at full steam.

The exploration and production of petroleum did continue during the first years of the Revolution, albeit at much reduced levels, and nearly all of the oil produced was exported to the United States. However, the economic nationalism of the Mexican Revolution made the heavily invested, private, foreign-owned petroleum companies anxious. The 1917 Constitution's provisions declaring subsoil minerals part of the national patrimony increased the anxieties of petroleum and mining concessionaires. However, the foreign-owned, private petroleum companies were basically

Pemex offshore oil rigs in the Gulf of Mexico. (Bohemian Nomad Picturemakers/Corbis)

untouched until the Lázaro Cárdenas administration, under the authority of the 1917 Constitution, took advantage of a growing crisis involving petroleum workers and the private companies' foreign management over labor concessions, and made an example of the petroleum industry by ordering the wholesale expropriation and nationalization of the industry. This event took place in 1938, and the date that Cárdenas signed the nationalization order is still celebrated as a national holiday.

As one might imagine, the reaction to such a radical and controversial decision varied greatly among the parties involved. Mexican citizens celebrated the overwhelmingly popular decision as a victory for Mexican nationalism and a sign of Mexico's strength relative to the rest of the world. The Mexican government was able to use the nationalization as a means to improve its standing with a citizenry anxious to see some of the more radical promises of the Revolution finally realized. The foreign oil company owners were out-raged, but ultimately powerless on their own to prevent nationalization, so they turned to their governments to seek redress. The Franklin D. Roosevelt administration in the United States, in the process of implementing its own nationalist New Deal project and taking note of the growing tensions in Europe, refused to force Mexico's hand and encouraged the oil companies to accept the compensation deal that the Mexican government was offering them as restitution. The petroleum nationalization did bear some significant costs to Mexico, however. It sent a chill throughout the global financial community and made foreign investors much more reluctant to view Mexico as a stable place in which to conduct business. Recognizing the potential long-term economic damage that his very popular decision could cause, Cárdenas himself immediately sought to repair relations with foreign investors and international businesses. He gave clear indications that there would be no additional nationalizations during the remainder of his presidency, and he selected as his successor the more moderate and economically prudent General Maneul Ávila Camacho, in whom the international business community could be confident.

Out of this nationalization emerged two things: (1) a massive, new state-run petroleum business, Petroleos Mexicanos (PEMEX), and (2) a powerful symbol of Mexican nationalism. Having a state-owned petroleum industry in PEMEX proved critical to Mexico's import-substituting development strategy. In addition to making petroleum products affordable to the individual Mexican worker, and thus reducing the costs associated with urban living, PEMEX was also able to supply a cheap source of energy to Mexico's nascent industrial, manufacturing, and transportation sectors of the economy, a critical component to nurturing these sectors along toward competitive status in the global market in the future. PEMEX played a significant role in bringing about the Mexican economic miracle that took shape over the 1940–1970 period.

Still, in spite of its political and economic importance to Mexico over this time, petroleum production accounted for a relatively small percentage of overall GDP. Not until the 1970s, when vast amounts of new reserves of oil and natural gas were discovered in Mexico, did petroleum assume its place as Mexico's leading export commodity and PEMEX emerge as its largest industry, which was by far the single largest component of the country's wealth.

The discovery of such reserves of petroleum came at a critical juncture in Mexico's economic history. Mexico's currency was unstable and had just been devalued for the first time in decades, and inflationary pressures were great, as were downward pressures on real wages. The discovery of petroleum deposits helped resolve some of Mexico's economic challenges in two ways. First, it eased Mexico's employment woes and provided a boost in the country's revenues. Second, it attracted huge infusions of foreign capital through direct private investment and through borrowing. However, it made the Mexican economy ultimately dependent on a single commodity. When petroleum prices collapsed in the early 1980s and global interest rates soared, the overheating of the economy caused by expanding and developing the petroleum sector created even more pressures on the Mexican economy, which ultimately collapsed under its own weight. Petroleum was approached as the salvation and future of Mexico's economic prosperity, but it was also the commodity that suffocated it. Following the economic crisis of the 1980s, the Mexican state tightened up and reformed the petroleum sector in accordance with the neoliberal structural adjustment policy prescriptions. The symbolic significance of oil to Mexico's national identity kept the government from privatizing the petroleum industry and subjecting it to foreign competition, but the government did decentralize PEMEX's operations and allowed for limited private and foreign investment in certain aspects of the oil and petroleum product subsidiary industries. Today,

PEMEX is still the national petroleum provider and still generates a significant portion of the country's national income. And oil reserves are still useful as collateral to obtain loans and to leverage Mexico's influence in the international economy. But Mexican leaders have moved away from an over-reliance on petroleum as the main engine for economic growth, instead promoting greater economic diversification by encouraging investment in the financial services and export manufacturing sectors of the economy.

Industry and Manufacturing.   The industrial and manufacturing sectors of the Mexican economy also constitute a significant component of Mexico's overall national wealth. The recent commitment by Mexico to more open and unrestricted international trade has strengthened the industrial and manufacturing sectors of the economy, particularly in the U.S.-Mexican border region, where production for export to the U.S. market has boomed in what are called maquiladora factories. As a very special and particular element to the Mexican manufacturing sector, the maquiladora industry will be treated more extensively below.

In general, Mexico's industrial and manufacturing sector concentrates around export commodities in precious metals, food and beverages, clothing and textiles, and electronics. Prior to the discovery and development of Mexico's petroleum sector, its plentiful silver deposits dominated the natural resource extraction industry, and its silver mines drove industrial development and industrial policy. While the nonpetroleum mining industry has diminished in significance relative to other productive sectors of the modern Mexican economy, it nonetheless continues to occupy an important place in the country's economy. In fact, Mexico is still the world's leading silver producer, accounting for about 15 percent of total global silver production. In addition to silver, iron ore and other metallic minerals are extracted from mines throughout Mexico.

The manufacturing of food and beverage products is also important to Mexico's contemporary economy, with this sector employing more than 600,000 Mexicans. For example, multinational companies such as Grupo Bimbo (bakery products), Grupo Modelo (beer), and Jose Cuervo (tequila) are well-known food and beverage manufacturers headquartered in Mexico.

Mexico's manufacturing and industrial sector was nurtured and protected through implementation of an import-substituting industrialization policy. This policy relied heavily on state subsidies for Mexican-owned and -operated industrial and manufacturing plants. Additionally, the Mexican state sheltered its manufacturing and industrial sector from foreign competition through protective trade measures and preferential investment and tax codes. While all levels of the Mexican industrial and manufacturing sector benefited from these protections and incentives programs, none experienced as much growth and profitability as the maquiladora manufacturers located primarily in the U.S.-Mexican border region.

Maquiladoras are a very special kind of manufacturing operation in which low-wage workers, primarily young, single women, are contracted to work in factories where component parts for particular kinds of consumer durable goods are imported from abroad and assembled, and the finished products are then exported out of the country. The presidential administration of Gustavo Díaz Ordáz (1964–1970) formally set up the program on the Mexican side of the U.S.-Mexican border as part of a strategy to industrialize the border region and to ease growing unemployment in Mexico caused by the termination of the Bracero program, a guest-worker program that provided Mexican workers legal jobs in the United States. Once finished with their temporary U.S. jobs, returning Mexican workers needed jobs to come home to, and the creation of the maquiladora industry, or the Border Industrialization Program as it was formally known, was the answer.

The border zone that the Mexican government had dedicated to the establishment of the maquiladora industry was exempt from the high taxation levels and the restrictive labor and environmental regulations that governed the business sector in the rest of the country. Furthermore, the protective trade barriers and foreign investment restrictions that the Mexican government had in place to shield domestic producers from foreign competition and to promote the development of a national industry did not apply to these maquiladora factories. On the economic front, the impact was immediate and impressive. From the initial handful of manufacturing plants established on the border region in the mid-1960s, the maquiladora industry grew by leaps and bounds such that there are now around 3,000 maquiladora plants operating on the border. Employment over the same time period grew from a few thousand workers in the mid-1960s to more than 1 million employees today. And what was once a sleepy and sparsely populated region in the north of Mexico is now a bustling, thriving, and relatively wealthy part of the country. One interesting and unexpected consequence of the maquiladora program was the arrival of manufacturers from all across the world. Manufacturers from Germany, Japan, South Korea, France, and many other countries set up shop on the Mexican side of the border. The prospect of easy access to the U.S. market, the absence of strict governmental regulation, and the reality of cheap Mexican labor represented an opportunity that these global manufacturers found very difficult to pass up. And the investment resources that these companies brought with them became fundamental to the financial health and well-being of the entire country. The further loosening of trade restrictions under NAFTA merely cemented the importance of the maquiladora manufacturing sector in the Mexican national economy.

Yet, the story of the maquiladoras in Mexico is not always and everywhere a rosy one. The social and environmental costs have not been insignificant. Lax environmental regulations, coupled with the incredible growth in the number of manufacturing factories, have permitted an alarming increase in the amount of pollution and industrial waste being irresponsibly pumped into the environment. Air quality has diminished, as has the quality of the water supply, and this has had serious impacts on the health of the citizens and workers in the border regions. The fact that maquiladoras employ primarily young, single women has dramatically altered the social structure within Mexico, particularly as it relates to gender roles and the family, and has created tensions that some argue have led to increasing levels of violence in these border towns, particularly against women. Further, the apparent unwillingness of Mexican authorities to enforce even the minimum of worker protections in the maquiladoras has contributed to growing levels of distrust among the maquiladora laborers regarding the government and its system of justice.

Trade

Of course, trade is another major component of Mexico's economy, accounting for a significant part of Mexico's overall wealth. After a prolonged period of restricted trade and high protective barriers to trade, Mexico embraced a free trade regime as part of the neoliberal economic strategy pursued by its leaders in the wake of the 1982 debt crisis. The culmination of this about-face on the subject of trade was Mexico's adhesion to the North American Free Trade Agreement, which committed Mexico to the elimination of all tariff and nontariff barriers to trade in its economic relationship with both the United States and Canada.

On January 1, 1994, after a lengthy negotiating and ratification process in each of the three signatory countries, NAFTA went into effect. This agreement, negotiated between Mexico, the United States, and Canada, sought to liberalize trade between the three countries by engaging in a gradual process of eliminating tariff and nontariff barriers to trade. This agreement was quite comprehensive in that nearly all major sectors of each country's economy was affected; the one significant exception was the energy sector.

Interestingly, it was Mexican President Carlos Salinas de Gortari who first proposed the idea of a free trade agreement between Mexico and the United States in 1989. It followed on the heels of the free trade deal negotiated between the United States and Canada. Soon after Salinas pitched the idea to the United States, Canada also joined in the discussions. The idea of a free trade agreement was consistent with the neoliberal proclivities of Salinas in terms of economic reform, but it was not Salinas's first strategy for improving Mexico's economic situation.

One must remember that in 1989, when Salinas proposed NAFTA, Mexico was still reeling from the economic crisis of 1982 and trying to claw its way back into patterns of stable economic growth and back into the good graces of international lending agencies and private investors. Salinas's predecessor, Miguel de la Madrid Hurtado, began the process of economic reform, but left the more difficult and contentious phases of reform to his successor.

Salinas, worried about the increased dependence on the U.S. economy that would necessarily result from an economic integration proposal such as NAFTA, did initially attempt to diversify Mexico's economic dependence by seeking greater partnerships with European and Asian countries. However, the powerful economies of Europe and Asia had their sights focused elsewhere. The collapse of the Soviet Union and the subsequent disintegration of the Eastern bloc led to an unprecedented opening of the formerly closed Eastern bloc economies. European countries were directing their energies to managing and exploiting the new economic possibilities that came with these dramatic changes in the Soviet Union and Eastern Europe.

Furthermore, the Western European countries themselves were at a critical point in terms of their own regionwide economic integration and trade liberalization process. So, even though Salinas's early overtures in Europe met with positive affirmation in principle, his visits failed to produce concrete results in terms of securing substantial promises of investment in Mexico's economy. With regard to Asian alternatives, this region's economic powers also had their gaze directed at the Soviet Union and Eastern Europe. But even more so, the impressive record of high economic growth rates among the Asian "Tigers" (Singapore, Taiwan, South Korea, etc.) continued to make investment in these countries at the time a much more attractive and less risky venture for the capital-rich countries of the region than the risky and troubled Mexico.

It was in this context that Carlos Salinas threw Mexico's lot in with that of the North American economies of Canada and the United States by taking the initiative and proposing NAFTA. Since then, Mexico has experienced a rapid and sustained increase in the volume of trade with the United States and Canada. But NAFTA has not come without its costs. Mexico's highly protected domestic manufacturing and industrial sectors have experienced a contraction, and overall wages have stagnated. It is true that aggregate wealth has increased in Mexico along with the policy of trade liberalization that NAFTA represents, but the distribution of this wealth is more skewed now than it was prior to NAFTA and the neoliberal reform program. Nevertheless, in spite of growing public dissatisfaction with NAFTA, Mexico has continued down the path of even greater trade liberalization. The last and most difficult round of phased-in tariff reductions that NAFTA calls for will be undertaken in 2008.

Mexico continues to actively seek out additional bilateral free trade agreements with other countries throughout the world. Today, Mexico has functioning free trade treaties with several nation-states, continues to support World Trade

Organization initiatives that call for the continued reduction of global barriers to trade, and is committed in principle to the establishment of the hemisphere-wide Free Trade Association of the Americas. The liberalization of trade, however, has not produced enough new jobs to meet the supply of a young labor force, so many of Mexico's young, working-age population are becoming more reliant on migration to the United States as their principal means of income generation than on the low-paying, low-skilled jobs in Mexico that match the comparative advantage Mexico maintains in cheap labor.

In short, the North American Free Trade Agreement may be considered the culmination of Mexico's transition from a statist and protectionist economic development model to one based on the neoliberal reform model promoted by the developed, industrialized countries of the world and the most important international financial institutions such as the IMF (International Monetary Fund), the World Bank, and the IADB (Inter-American Development Bank). Under the current administration of Felípe Calderón, this transition is likely to continue and to deepen.

BUSINESS ENVIRONMENT

Business in Mexico has always had a close relationship with the state, but it has also maintained a relative degree of independence compared with other functional interest groups in the country. In modern Mexico, the business environment has been conditioned profoundly by Mexico's mixed economic development model. Since the Revolution, the Mexican state has often exercised its constitutional prerogative to regulate business and to harness national resources and businesses for the greater good of the country as defined by the governing leadership. The constant specter of greater state regulation, or even control or expropriation, of business has led business to behave cautiously in terms of how it approaches economic activity and its investment in economic development. Furthermore, the state's ability and demonstrated willingness to control investment and monetary policy that affect the fortunes of business have also conditioned the business environment and the way entrepreneurs behave in Mexico. The resultant business environment in Mexico is one that is much more conservative in terms of taking risks.

Additionally, periods of irresponsible behavior on the part of the state in terms of economic decision making has adversely affected the business and economic climate of the country. For instance, the nationalization of the petroleum industry in 1938, while politically popular and successful at the time, clearly conveyed to both Mexican and foreign investors and entrepreneurs that the Mexican state at any point could appropriate for itself any private investment or any private property in the country. The unexpected and shocking 1982 nationalization of the banking industry by the José López Portillo administration merely drove this point home and reinforced the need for caution and risk-averse behavior by national and foreign business interests in Mexico.

Nevertheless, the economic environment has encouraged capitalist behavior and has allowed for the accumulation of private wealth through entrepreneurial activity. Thus, even though business leaders and foreign investors have recognized the need to behave cautiously in their approaches to business and economic activity, there has never been any question as to the availability of opportunities for business growth and development, however uneven and unstable, in the country.

Another facet of the Mexican business environment has been its reaction to and assimilation of the state-led capitalist development model that guided the economic development of the country at least from the mid-1940s up through the early 1980s. Because this model placed the state as the principal engine for business development and economic growth strategies, private business and entrepreneurs benefited from developing an intimate relationship with the state for access to the opportunities managed by the state. Hence, most of Mexico's important businesses and industries are grounded in a concept of reliance and dependence upon a paternalist state for access to markets; for business opportunities; and, perhaps most importantly, for protection against market competition.

A closer look at Mexico's business sector, however, reveals a significant split between large corporations and entrepreneurs whose interests are global and the mainly domestically oriented small- to medium-size businesses. The former tend to be concentrated in the more industrial and modernized northern region of Mexico, and the latter tend to be concentrated around the Federal District and the other major consumer markets in the central and southern parts of the country. Known as the Monterrey Group, the large industrialists in the northern parts of the country have had more strained relations with the state simply because the state-led capitalist model of development placed constraints and limitations on their abilities to act independently and subjected them to a government oversight that they deemed onerous and counterproductive. The smaller, domestically oriented businesses and industrialists developed strong and intimate relations with the state, primarily because their ability to compete and to earn market share for their products in the face of the more developed and capital-rich industrialists from the northern part of the state and foreign multinational corporations depended heavily on the protectionist policies of the state. In order for this very nationalist entrepreneurial class to become more effective in lobbying their cause against their more formidable competitors, they allied with one another to form the National Chamber of the Industry of Transformation (CANACINTRA). This group, as its name indicates, supported state efforts to promote an import-substitution industrial capacity that would transform the Mexican economy from its dependence on agricultural exports and foreign imports into an economy grounded in industrial self-sufficiency. Through CANACINTRA, these small entrepreneurs and domestically oriented industrialists were able to articulate their demands and interests to the political elite more clearly and effectively. More importantly, the state itself was able to develop an alternative institutional conduit to an emerging small- to medium-size business and industrial class that functioned in many ways similar to the corporatist structure of interest articulation that the political elites had established with organized labor, the peasants, and the urban professional classes through the PRI. While CANACINTRA never relinquished its operational independence to the state-party apparatus, its vocal support for and practical alliance with the government and its statist and protectionist economic model were never questioned. Even the Monterrey Group recognized the value of negotiation and dialogue with the state and the ruling party. However, the members of this powerful group pointedly refused to articulate their interests through an officially sanctioned and government-regulated business association. Instead, these powerful industrialists and entrepreneurs preferred direct access to the highest levels of government, and they expected that Mexican presidents and their cabinet secretaries (who managed the financial and economic portfolios) would ultimately privilege their points of view when major economic policies were discussed. Still, this group chafed at what it perceived as state overreach into business and financial affairs and often vocally challenged and resisted such policies when it deemed necessary.

As the capitalist model of economic development became more entrenched, and as the weakness of the statist model began to show in the late 1960s and 1970s, the differences that had previously characterized the competing entrepreneurial interests in Mexico began to dissipate. And as the administrations of Luís Echeverría and José López Portillo tilted toward the left and rattled the sabers of populist economic rhetoric that seemed to stoke and agitate working- and popular-class resentments against both domestic and foreign entrepreneurs and businesses, the business classes of Mexico began to look beyond their minor differences and to concentrate on their fundamental areas of agreement: currency stability, price stability, sound monetary and fiscal policy, transparent economic policymaking, and guarantees of private property protections. Also, one of the consequences of the economic miracle was the creation of wealth, and it became increasingly concentrated. This concentration of wealth also contributed both to a strengthening of the business classes relative to the state and to the consolidation and blending of business-class interests. The successful expansion of Mexican industry, the proliferation of healthy and competitive corporations, and the robust growth of the Mexican economy naturally led to the convergence and merger of many of Mexico's powerful corporations and entrepreneurial activity. In fact, in 1964, the most powerful of Mexico's independent business class formed an association amongst themselves, which they called the Mexican Council of Businessmen (Consejo Mexicano de Hombres de Negocios, or CMHN). The stated purpose of this group was, in fact, to oppose directly the statist model of economic development, and particularly the state's active ownership of businesses that directly (and unfairly, as they saw it) competed with them. Through the CMHN, Mexico's powerful entrepreneurial class organized a number of spin-off or related organizations to promote their interests. One such group is the Business Coordinating Council (Consejo Coordinador Empresarial), which came into being in the mid-1970s in order to promote individualism and private property, as well as an end to state expansion in the business world. Other business organizations that emerged to represent the various interests of the business classes are the Employers'

Confederation of the Mexican Republica (Confederación Patronal de la República Mexicana) and the Mexican Bankers' Association (Associación Mexicano de Banqueros).

Nevertheless, the history of state-business collaboration might have permitted continued cordial relations between political elites and entrepreneurs had the state not violated its long-standing compact to respect business autonomy at the fundamental level of ownership, or at the very least to involve business elites in the decision-making process when such a radical path of action was being considered. The bank nationalization of 1982 severely damaged the state's relationship with the business class and had the effect of unifying business against what they saw as a major threat to the success of their operations. This one single event rallied the business classes out of their apathy and into the political arena, and encouraged them to put their considerable financial resources and energies into transforming the state apparatus that had outlived its usefulness to them.

In the immediate aftermath of the bank nationalization, the business community almost universally criticized the government's action. Even CANACINTRA, which did not openly oppose the nationalization scheme, did agree with other business organizations that the secretive manner in which the López Portillo administration carried out this nationalization scheme, without seeking input and consultations from the business community, was wrong. Business leaders became even more strident in demanding that the state extricate itself from the private sector. From 1982 to the present, that is precisely what the state has done. López Portillo's successor, Miguel de la Madrid, began the process of rapprochement with the business community by adopting more probusiness policies. Over the course of the de la Madrid administration, the Mexican state privatized a significant number of state-owned companies. It successfully negotiated an economic restructuring package with private

Interior view of the Mexico City Stock Exchange. (PhotoDisc)

lenders and the international financial institutions that restored Mexico's credit, prevented its debt default threats from becoming realized, and began to attract capital back into the country. De la Madrid supported his promises by having Mexico adhere formally to the General Agreement on Tariffs and Trade (GATT), which made Mexico subject to binding commitments to pursue a trade liberalization program in accordance with GATT provisions. Further, he selected his secretary of Programming and Budget, Carlos Salinas de Gortari, to succeed him in the presidency. Complications surrounding the legitimacy of Salinas's election notwithstanding, the Salinas administration made important strides in repairing state-business relations. Salinas accelerated the pace of privatizations, presided over NAFTA negotiations and NAFTA's implementation, and implemented a host of other probusiness reforms, especially in the finance and credit services sector of the economy, all of which were continued under the Zedillo administration that followed. When Vicente Fox of the conservative, probusiness National Action Party won the 2000 presidential elections and unseated the PRI, the business community could claim not only that its efforts to completely restructure the Mexican economy had been successful but also that they had played a critical role in the transformation of the Mexican political system to one that would be openly supportive of their goals and interests. The Mexican business community restored its amicable collaboration with the state, and one might also argue that it is now effectively guiding the state.

Today, Mexico is home to some of the world's largest and wealthiest multinational corporations, many of whose stocks are traded openly on the Mexican Stock Market, or the Bolsa Mexicana de Valores. And many of the chief executive officers of these corporations rank among the richest and most powerful businesspeople in the world. In fact, in the most recent *Forbes* listing of the world's wealthiest individuals, 10 Mexicans are among the world's billionaires, and Mexican telecommunications magnate Carlos Slim Helú's net worth of $49 billion makes him the third richest man in the world, trailing only Warren Buffett and Bill Gates of the United States.

Currency and Currency Stability

Mexico's national currency is the peso. Today the value of the peso relative to the U.S. dollar is about 11.5/1. That is, one dollar in the United States is worth about 11.5 pesos. In recent years, the Mexican peso has been one of Latin America's more stable currencies. In large measure this is due to the fact that the Mexican economy is so heavily tied to and dependent upon the United States. This means that the Mexican economy, including the stability of its currency, rests heavily on the strength and stability of the U.S. economy. Furthermore, given the importance to the United States of maintaining a stable economy in Mexico, the United States is not likely to let the Mexican currency experience a prolonged crisis. And this simple fact in itself has kept Mexico's currency relatively stable. However, moments of crisis in the stability of the Mexican currency have occurred and Mexican leaders have met these crises in a variety of ways. Mostly, those ways have involved adjustments in the value of the peso. Since the 1970s, the Mexican peso has been devalued six times.

The first devaluation occurred in 1976, the second in 1980; in 1982, the Mexican government devalued the peso three times; and the last devaluation of the peso occurred in 1994. In each case, the devaluation occurred as a product of fiscal mismanagement, and in each case, it created residual crises in the national economy. Sometimes, the devaluations were the product of forces outside of the Mexican government's abilities to control; at other times, the devaluations were directly caused by poor decisions on the part of Mexican economic and financial policymakers.

In addition to monetary crises affecting the value of the peso, Mexico has had serious struggles with its public debt. Perhaps the most difficult and trying moment for Mexico in its modern public finance history was the country's debt crisis of 1982. In that year, a confluence of events beyond Mexico's control coupled with financial mismanagement led to Mexico's announcement that it would be unable to make its scheduled interest payments on its substantial public debt, thus throwing the global financial market into crisis. The long-term damage done to Mexico's creditworthiness was substantial, and the situation crashed Mexico's economy, sending the country into a period of economic stagnation for most of the 1980s. Some of the contributing factors to Mexico's 1982 debt crisis included a precipitous drop in oil prices and a rise in interest rates. Mexico had borrowed heavily to finance expansion in its petroleum sector and had used future earnings based on sustained inflated prices for petroleum as its collateral for debt repayment. However, when the Organization of Petroleum Exporting Countries (OPEC) oil cartel could not sustain its price and production policies, the price of oil dropped. Mexico, which had benefited peripherally from the inflated prices for petroleum brought about by OPEC's policies, was unable to sell its petroleum at prices that would allow the country to repay its debt. The problem was compounded by the fact that rising interest rates increased Mexico's debt liabilities even further.

MEXICO'S ECONOMIC FUTURE

Mexico's economic future is likely to continue to be a mixed bag. Mexico's economy is increasingly open and integrated into the global economy along the lines envisioned by the neoliberal reformers and policy elites. The current PAN administration of Felípe Calderón is still very much committed to embracing probusiness and promarket policy as the preferred solutions to Mexico's economic challenges. And the Mexican economy is likely to continue along a path of modest economic growth and the creation of more wealth as a consequence of such policy directions. However, income inequality and poverty, especially in the countryside, are persistent and nagging problems, which will continue to persist. In fact, they are likely to grow as the economic gains from probusiness and promarket policies continue to be concentrated in the hands of fewer and fewer Mexicans. The social problems associated with the continuation of these obstacles are becoming more acute and pose challenges to the stability of the political system, as the controversy and conflicts surrounding the last presidential election demonstrated. Calderón and successive regimes must address the issues of wealth concentration, poverty alleviation, and rural underdevelopment in order to maintain social and political stability, without which even the modest growth of the Mexican economy is not possible.

References

Camp, Roderic A. *Entrepreneurs and the State in Twentieth Century Mexico.* New York: Oxford University Press, 1989.

Domínguez, Jorge I., ed. *Mexico's Political Economy: Challenges at Home and Abroad.* Beverly Hills, CA: Sage, 1982.

Grayson, George W. *The Politics of Mexican Oil.* Pittsburgh: University of Pittsburgh Press, 1980.

Grinspun, Ricardo, and Maxwell Cameron, eds. *The Political Economy of North American Free Trade.* New York: St. Martin's Press, 1993.

Hansen, Roger D. *The Politics of Mexican Development.* Baltimore: Johns Hopkins University Press, 1971.

King, Timothy. *Mexico: Industrialization and Trade Policies since 1940.* London: Oxford University Press, 1970.

Lustig, Nora. *Mexico: The Remaking of an Economy.* Washington, D.C.: Brookings Institution, 1992.

Middlebrook, Kevin J. *The Paradox of Revolution: Labor, the State and Authoritarianism in Mexico.* Baltimore: Johns Hopkins University Press, 1995.

Orme, William A., Jr. *Understanding NAFTA: Mexico, Free Trade, and the New North America.* Austin: University of Texas Press, 1996.

Otero, Gerardo, ed. *Neo-liberalism Revisited: Economic Restructuring and Mexico's Political Future.* Boulder, CO: Westview, 1996.

Roett, Riordan, ed. *Mexico's Private Sector: Recent History, Future Challenges.* Boulder, CO: Lynne Rienner, 1998.

Story, Dale. *Industry, the State, and Public Policy in Mexico.* Austin: University of Texas Press, 1986.

Teichman, Judith A. *Privatization and Political Change in Mexico.* Pittsburgh: University of Pittsburgh Press, 1995.

Vernon, Raymond. *The Dilemma of Mexico's Development: The Roles of the Private and Public Sectors.* Cambridge, MA: Harvard University Press, 1963.

Weintraub, Sidney, ed. *NAFTA's Impact on North America: The First Decade.* Washington, D.C.: Center for Strategic and International Studies, 2004.

CHAPTER THREE
Politics and Institutions

Mexico is a constitutional, federal republic. Its political affairs, as well as its governing institutions and procedures, are regulated by the 1917 Constitution, which has been discussed in chapters 1 and 2. Formally and officially, the country is divided into 31 separate states and the Federal District. Each state has its own executive and legislative bodies. Until 1994, the Federal District, home to approximately 20 percent of Mexico's people and the administrative, economic, and intellectual center of the country, was managed by an individual appointed as part of the presidential cabinet. Since 1994, governance of the Federal District has been separated from the federal government and is now determined by electoral competition through direct popular vote.

MEXICAN POLITICS AND GOVERNMENT IN HISTORICAL CONTEXT

Mexican politics and government cannot be disassociated from their historical political and governing legacies. It is not far-fetched to note that modern Mexico is built on the traditions of pre-Columbian structures and institutions. They were not eliminated by the conquest but rather adapted to and were incorporated into European notions of absolutism and colonial subordination during a lengthy period of Spanish rule of some 300 years from 1521 until the early 19th century. Modern Mexico is also rooted in European Enlightenment thought and concepts of Western notions of popular sovereignty, albeit tempered by the "politics of place" and the reality of Mexico's dependence on its more

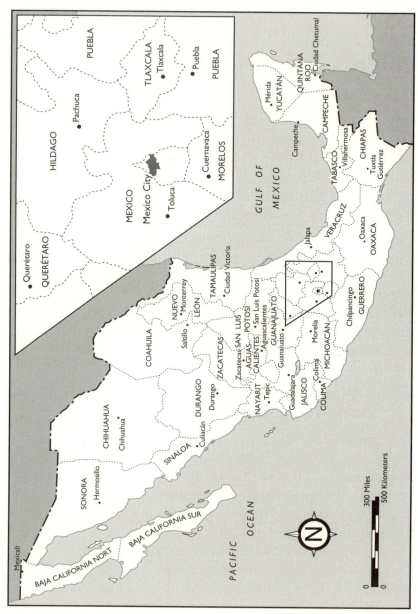

Mexico's current political divisions

powerful and influential northern neighbor. All of these realities have combined to create a unique Mexican political culture and system that has no comparable peer throughout the world.

Contemporary Mexican politics has its roots in four distinct periods of the country's history. The first is the pre-Columbian (indigenous) and Spanish colonial (European) period. The second is the postindependence 19th-century period. The third is the postrevolutionary period up until the 2000 election of President Vicente Fox. The final, current period is the post–Institutional Revolutionary Party (PRI) democratic period.

The pre-Columbian and Spanish colonial period, which stretches over a 300-plus-year period, laid deeply into the fabric of Mexican political culture a number of characteristics that were shared and reinforced by one another and that persist to the current day. One of the more important of these enduring characteristics is an authoritarianism that manifests itself in political absolutism. The pre-Columbian Aztec political system was an imperial monarchy that located authority in a hereditary nobility, which governed autocratically. Following the defeat of the Aztec empire in 1519, the Spanish took over the reins of the empire but continued to govern the region under the absolutism of the Spanish monarchy. The functional nature of both pre-Columbian Aztec governance and Spanish colonial governance included executive supremacy in managing affairs of state and a subordination of other branches of government to the all-powerful executive. A second enduring characteristic is the persistence of a rigid, hierarchical social structure that not only segregated Mexican society along class, race, and ethnic lines but also determined the nature and quality of public participation in politics on the basis of such classifications. A third characteristic is that of religious absolutism, or the idea of the fusion of church and state as opposed to the separation of church and state. Both the pre-Columbian political system and the Spanish colonial system of government were grounded in the belief that government was divinely authorized and that religious institutions and church leaders were central to statecraft. A fourth characteristic is the concept of personalism in politics. Personalism, as applied to politics, locates authority and conditions the process of formal social relations in the nature of personal connections and networks. Both pre-Columbian and Spanish colonial systems of government emphasized quite heavily intricate personal ties as a means to access power and rooted the public's perception of effective governance less in the institutions of state and more in the personalities of the people in power. And, finally, one might point to the concept of functional privilege as a fifth characteristic of politics in Mexico that is rooted in the pre-Columbian and Spanish colonial period. This concept basically affords special rights and duties to individuals according to their identification with a particular group. When discussing politics and political systems, functional privilege is often referred to as corporatism; it means not only that the state preserves and protects separate rights, privileges, and obligations to political actors but also that the state's natural role is to lead and coordinate the relationship between such actors, as well as to mediate any disputes arising between such actors. All of these characteristics were fundamental to the nature and operation of statecraft and politics in pre-Columbian and Spanish colonial Mexico. The pre-Columbian and Spanish colonial period represents a long, extended time frame in the creation of Mexico, and so the impact of this period is profound and deeply embedded in Mexican culture. Its characteristics cannot easily be extracted, modified, or removed from the contemporary realities of modern Mexico, and they continue to manifest themselves clearly in the contemporary Mexican political culture and system.

The postindependence period represents an often violent conflict between the premodern ideas and values of the pre-

Columbian and Spanish colonial period and the modern ideas and values of the post-Enlightenment period. In Mexico, this conflict manifested itself most clearly in the struggle between a progressive and secular liberalism and a reactionary and religious conservatism, especially regarding concepts of citizenship and government. It is here where the concepts of liberal democracy and orderly authoritarianism come into stark conflict and shape one of the fundamental modern ideological struggles in modern Mexican politics. Additionally, this period introduced the conflict between unbridled free market capitalism and the security of a patrimonial welfare state. Finally, this period represented the beginnings of the debate about the place of nonstate institutions in the public square—that is, business groups, the Catholic Church, international actors, and other functional interest groups. However, the 19th-century period represented more a struggle between differing elite concepts of state and society and did not really challenge the efficacy of a premodern social order.

The revolutionary period addressed this latter concern, especially as it impacted the construction and function of government. The Mexican Revolution transformed modern Mexican politics by inserting concepts of nationalism, *indigenismo, mestizaje* (i.e., Mexicanization), a virulent secularism, and racial/social/ethnic egalitarianism. In the postrevolutionary period, the Mexican state became the engine for a radical restructuring of social and economic patterns of concentrated landownership, foreign ownership and control over the national patrimony, and the incorporation of previously excluded social classes directly in the process of governing—albeit through some innovative modifications and retentions of past traditions.

The Mexican Constitution

Contemporary Mexican politics has as its legal foundation the 1917 Constitution. This constitution, a product of the reformist impulses of the Mexican Revolution, embraced some important principles that have since become ingrained into the Mexican political culture. It was produced at a national constitutional convention held in the state of Querétaro and was ratified by a Congress called specifically for the purpose in February 1917. The 1917 Constitution continues to serve as the foundational document of Mexican political, social, and economic life, even though it has been modified and amended in significant ways over the 90-plus years of its existence.

The Mexican Constitution of 1917 is clearly rooted in the values of 19th-century Mexican liberalism, especially in terms of its provisions regarding the role of the Catholic Church in public life. Its most important articles also reflected the inclusion of a revolutionary nationalism and antiforeign sentiment into the formal apparatus of government. For instance, Article 3 of the 1917 Constitution addresses the subject of education and declares not only that every Mexican has the right to a free education financed by the state but that all state-financed education in Mexico be completely secular and free from any religious orientation. Furthermore, the state reserved the right to sanction and approve the curriculum of all educational institutions, including private institutions, to ensure its conformity to national educational standards and principles. This was an important change for Mexico because, until that point, religious institutions operated the vast majority of schools throughout the country with minimal state intervention or oversight. Article 3, when coupled with Article 130, which addressed the question of separation of church and state and mandated state regulation of the public activities of religious institutions and clerics, was perceived by religious authorities as an attack on its traditional rights and prerogatives.

The 1917 Constitution was also unique for its provisions regarding its treatment and discussion of labor. Article 123 of the Constitution protected the rights of labor by mandating an eight-hour workday, a six-day workweek, and a minimum wage and by guaranteeing the right of workers to unionize and to strike. With regard to Mexico's relationship with foreign interests, Article 27 was perhaps the most radical and controversial of the Constitution's provisions. It declared that only Mexican nationals or private companies with majority Mexican ownership could hold title to national territory or its subsoil resources, all of which pertained exclusively to the state. Article 27 would serve as the constitutional basis for Mexican President Lázaro Cárdenas's nationalization of the petroleum industry in 1938, an effort that represented a major moment in Mexico's relationship to private foreign capital and a huge psychological victory for Mexico's revolutionary nationalism.

The Mexican Constitution of 1917 has been amended over the years as it served the interests of the ruling party, but it still stands as one of the pillars of Mexico's revolutionary consciousness and as a hallmark of the stability of Mexico's political system as well as the social purpose of government.

MODERN MEXICAN POLITICS: A CONCEPTUAL NOTE

The modern Mexican political system is a hybrid of sorts. It is not fully a democracy as commonly understood, and it has particular authoritarian characteristics. Thus, one of the fundamental debates in any study of Mexican politics is the degree to which Mexico is a democratic country and the degree to which it is authoritarian. One way to measure this is to look at the political culture of Mexico and to see what kinds of values Mexicans express with regard to their political system, their political processes, and their political leaders. Included in this notion of political culture is how individual Mexicans view their own role in the political system and process of government. Do Mexicans feel as if their participation in government matters? Do Mexicans trust

*The National Palace in Mexico City, the seat of Mexico's federal
government. In the foreground is the Plaza de la Constitución, also
called the Zócalo, a popular site for public demonstrations. (Andres
Balcazar)*

their governing institutions and political leaders? Do Mexicans have confidence in their neighbors as fellow citizens
working toward the common cause of advancing the national interest? Do Mexicans encourage and expect themselves and their fellow citizens to become involved in the
civic life of their local communities, their states, and the
country? All of these questions try to get at the heart of how
Mexicans view politics and their own roles in the political
life of the nation.

In addition to looking at the values, attitudes, and behaviors that Mexicans exhibit regarding politics and government, another way to evaluate and understand Mexican
politics and government is to look at the country's formal
political institutions and the formal mechanisms that regulate the political system and Mexican citizens' participation

in this system. For instance, the nature and design of Mexican governing institutions such as the executive, the legislature, and the judiciary, and the relationships between them, can help us to understand not only how Mexican politics works concretely but also how perhaps Mexican political culture is either reflected in or conditioned by such governing institutions.

The way public needs and interests are articulated to the Mexican governing apparatus is another meaningful way to understand Mexican politics. Some of these means include participation in elections. But electoral competition is by no means the only way the public participates in the political life of the nation. Corporate interest groups that have a special relationship to government are also an important vehicle for citizen participation in the political life of the country to articulate needs, desires, and aspirations to the state.

Another important way that Mexicans articulate their concerns to governing authorities and express their desires is through informal channels such as the lobbying of grassroots civic organizations, peaceful demonstrations and protests, and even, at times, armed uprisings and rebellions. While some Mexicans view certain of these avenues of political participation as unacceptable under any conditions, many Mexicans understand and accept the legitimacy of some of the more radical measures when circumstances might warrant them.

CENTRALISM, PRESIDENTIALISM, AND PERSONALISM

At the level of national politics, the Mexican political system can be characterized as both presidentialist and centralist. It is presidentialist in two ways. At the most basic level, the Mexican political system is presidentialist in the sense that executive authority is held by a popularly elected president, who serves as the country's head of state and head of government. Unlike a parliamentary political system, in which executive authority is constituted by the political party winning the majority of seats in parliament (or through a process of multiparty coalition formation if no single party wins a majority of parliamentary seats), a presidentialist political system determines its executive authority by direct popular election to the office of the president. The Mexican political system is also presidentialist in the sense that governing authority is centralized in the office and person of the president and the executive branch of government, at the expense of the legislative and judicial branches of government. The patterns of presidentialism and executive dominance at the level of the federal government are mirrored at the state and local levels of government, with power at those levels concentrated in the popularly elected governors and mayors, respectively, at the expense of state and municipal legislative and judicial bodies.

The Mexican political system at the national level is also centralist in the sense that power tends to be concentrated in the federal government at the expense of state and municipal governments, which are subordinate to and dependent upon the federal government in important ways. For most of its modern history, Mexico has had a very centralized political system, with authority concentrated in the federal government in Mexico City. This political centralism continues to define the Mexican political system today, but it is also clear that a trend is growing toward a decentralization of power that places more importance on municipal and state governments. This process of decentralization is not new to the Mexican political system. Since its independence, Mexico has had strong centrifugal federalist tendencies as well. Let us remember that the secession and independence of Texas from Mexico in the 1830s, which ultimately precipitated the U.S.-Mexican War, was primarily a reaction to efforts in Mexico City to centralize authority around the federal government and to restrict provincial autonomy. And in the first decade of the 20th century, provincial discontent with the centralized power of the Porfirio Díaz administration created an atmosphere in which calls for greater local autonomy from the central administration resonated with the peoples of the different provinces and fueled, in part, movements of rebellion against the Porfirian system that ultimately crystallized into the Mexican Revolution. Nevertheless, in spite of these considerable decentralization tendencies in Mexico's modern political history, the struggles between these two competing visions of government have tended to fall out in favor of centralized authority in the federal government.

Complementing the centralism and presidentialism in Mexican politics is the legacy of the personalization of power in the country's political history. Deeply rooted in Mexican political culture is the view that political authority and leadership rest more on the character of the individual holding public office than with the office itself. Furthermore, popular respect for and loyalty to a political leader reside not in the prestige of the office any leader holds but rather in such an individual leader's personal qualities outside of the office. Scholars sometimes refer to this element of Mexican political culture as the "cult of personalism." The personalization of power has been both a blessing and a curse for Mexico. It has permitted strong-willed, charismatic individuals to rally popular sentiment against external threats to the country (Benito Juárez), to maintain internal order and promote material progress (Porfirio Díaz), and even to lead revolutionary movements against autocratic dictators (Francisco Madero). But it has also encouraged narcissistic adventurism (Antonio López de Santa Anna), authoritarianism (Porfirio Díaz), and corruption (Carlos Salinas de Gortari) as leaders have succumbed to the temptations inherent in personalism to claim their offices as personal sinecures. In any event, personalism in Mexican politics still persists and, when combined with the traditions of centralism and presidentialism, offers a perspective on understanding the process and dynamic of Mexican politics that continues to merit attention.

Because of the predominance of centralism in the Mexican political system, the federal government has exercised considerable power and authority in conducting the affairs of the state. And within the federal government, power has concentrated even more completely in the executive branch of government, affording Mexican presidents an impressive and often unchallenged array of powers. In this sense, the Mexican political system has always been presidentialist, with the executive branch of government significantly more powerful than any other branch of government.

Given the centralized nature of the Mexican political system, power is concentrated particularly in the person of the president. Even though separate branches of government exist and function in Mexico, the balance of power among them clearly favors the executive; the legislative and judicial branches of government have often functioned as rubber stamp vehicles for legitimizing executive authority. However, since the presidential election of 2000, the Mexican political system has experienced a significant change that has challenged the nature of this relatively unchecked and disproportionately powerful presidentialism. The specific context of the 2000 elections and its impact on contemporary Mexican politics will be discussed more completely below. Suffice it to say here that, in spite of these significant recent changes in the Mexican political system, certain legacies and tendencies endure. The political culture of Mexico offers a glimpse into these persistent and enduring aspects of Mexican politics.

MEXICAN POLITICAL CULTURE
Nationalism

The political culture of any country consists basically of the values, attitudes, and beliefs that define and characterize the way individual citizens of a country view their government and their political system. Analysis of what constitutes Mexican political culture reaches back to the 1950s and continues to be a major point of debate among scholars of Mexican politics today. The crux of this debate concerns whether or not Mexican political culture is authoritarian or democratic; scholars have found convincing evidence in support of both, which makes the study of Mexican politics all the more interesting. An important component of Mexican political culture is the centrality of nationalism.

At a very basic level, the concept of the "nation" may be defined simply as the aggregation of a group of people on the basis of a shared cultural, historical, and linguistic identity that unifies them and distinguishes them from other groups of people. By extension, the concept of "nationalism" may be explained as pride in and devotion to the nation by its members. Additionally, nationalism is usually accompanied by the need both to celebrate the group's shared identity and to defend the integrity and the continued existence of this identity from external threats. Mexico and the United States are neighboring countries with very different conceptions of national identity; hence, nationalism in each country manifests itself in very different ways. But because the two countries share a border, the subject of nationalism is complicated even more by the existence of borderland communities and people whose identity is neither Mexican nor American, but rather a unique and distinctive combination of the two.

Mexican nationalism is rooted in two distinct phenomena. One is the recognition and promotion by Mexicans of a rich and exalted cultural legacy, and the other has to do with Mexico's self-perception as a marginalized participant in the community of nations. In the first instance, Mexican nationalism is an expression of confidence and pride in the glory of past greatness. But this expression of nationalism is also at times characterized by a reactive defensiveness, and even defiance, when faced with external attitudes that fail to acknowledge the relevance of this cultural legacy to Mexico's importance in the modern world.

By comparison, nationalism in the United States is almost exclusively connected to a sense of pride in the country's perceived political, economic, and military superiority in relation to other nations. As a "melting pot" country of multiple and diverse "nationalities," the United States does not imbue its nationalism with the exaltation of a common cultural legacy. Nor, by virtue of its position as a global hegemon, does the United States project a nationalism that is reactive and defensive. U.S. nationalism is often expressed in a proactive manner that comes across as aggressive and offensive. The geographical neighbors of the United States—Mexico and Canada—often feel the full weight of this nationalism with great poignancy. Anti-immigration sentiment, hostility to bilingualism, the exportation of American consumerism, and the "Hollywoodization" of popular culture are just some examples of both the expression and the impact of U.S. nationalism.

Partially to counter this impression of U.S. nationalism, contemporary Mexican nationalism has drawn profoundly on Mexico's history as one of the most important loci of civilization in the Western Hemisphere. Mexico was home to impressive pre-Columbian civilizations, not least among them the Aztecs and the Maya. Colonial Mexico, known then as New Spain, was the seat of perhaps the most important viceroyalty of Spain's colonial empire in the entire Western Hemisphere. And Mexico gave to Latin America its first successful social revolution of the 20th century. In fact,

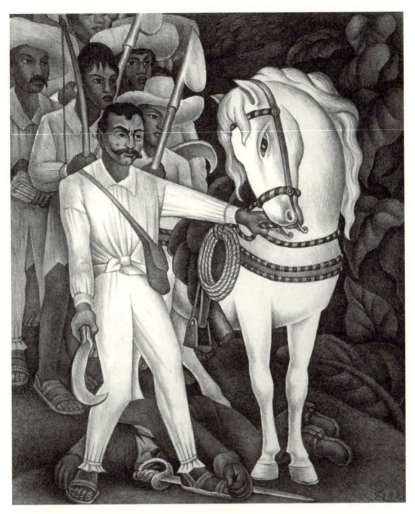

Mexican muralist Diego Rivera's portrait of national hero Emiliano Zapata, holding a sickle and standing over a fallen landowner; armed peasants stand in the background, ca. 1935. (Library of Congress)

Mexican nationalism in the postrevolutionary period is clearly manifest in the glorification of Mexico's indigenous past and through the stories of its modern, postindependence national leaders. The paintings and murals of Diego Rivera, José Clemente Orozco, David Alfaro Siqueiros, Frida

Kahlo, and other artists all make a point of portraying the splendor of Mexico's pre-Columbian civilizations and also of identifying and glorifying national heroes in public spaces for all to admire and from which to draw inspiration.

Additionally, the concept of the *raza cósmica,* or "cosmic race," forged by José Vasconcelos, exalted the Mexican mestizo as the repository of an even greater civilization. Contemporary Mexico continues to promote a nationalism wrapped in these cultural symbols as is evidenced by the popularity and omnipresence in all parts of Mexico of the ongoing Zapatista movement. In each of these examples, Mexican nationalism clearly emphasizes the country's cultural superiority and social progressiveness in ways that seek to elevate its position relative to the United States. The glorification of indigenous civilizations and the multifaceted progressiveness of a revolutionary social policy differentiate Mexican nationalism from what could be seen as the ethnocentrism, egotism, and materialism of the U.S. national identity.

However, Mexican nationalism also differs from that of the United States in less admirable ways not only in the sense that it represents a collective consciousness of shared cultural identity that binds all Mexicans together under a common sense of "nationhood," but also in the fact that it is an identity carefully and deliberately crafted by the postrevolutionary Mexican political elites for the purpose of maintaining the legitimacy of the single-party state. In essence, then, Mexican nationalism is a reflection of Mexico's cultural identity and the popular groundswell expression of such; however, it is also an identity that has been imagined, massaged, and shaped by the modern Mexican state. Mexican nationalism has consequently evolved into something more than pride in a shared cultural identity. Mexican nationalism, especially in the postrevolutionary period, has also functioned as a tool for muting public criticism of the state, for resolving social conflict, and for promoting a particular vision of the revolutionary society.

Clearly, then, what has come to be called Mexico's "revolutionary" nationalism has both a cultural and a political function. Its cultural dimension is centered around the forging of an identity linked to the country's indigenous roots and its cultural traditions. Its political dimension is linked to the creation of an independent, anti-imperialist, and revolutionary state. Thus, Mexican nationalism has the unique characteristic of being a positive expression of national culture and pride while at the same time being a reflection of a defensive and sometimes openly hostile xenophobia.

The political dimension of contemporary Mexican nationalism is mostly rooted in the success of the 1910 Revolution and its social, political, and cultural outcomes throughout the 20th century, but it is also to be found in the history of the country's struggles against external threats to its sovereignty throughout the 19th century. One cannot explain the vigor and passion of Mexico's desire to react against foreign interests in Mexico during and after the 1910 Revolution without reference to Mexico's humiliation in the physical dismantling of the Mexican "nation" by foreign interests in the 19th century, coupled with the sale of Mexico's patrimony to foreign financial interests in the late 19th and early 20th centuries during the Porfiriato.

The nationalism born out of these experiences demanded expression politically through the legal restrictions placed on foreign ownership of national resources and the subsequent nationalization of key strategic and symbolic industries. Though modern Mexican history is replete with such cases, perhaps the most important example is the nationalization of the petroleum industry carried out by Lázaro Cárdenas in 1938. This political aspect of Mexican nationalism also finds expression in Mexico's refusal to accept uncritically U.S. foreign policy, especially as it applies to the Western Hemisphere. From vigorously protesting the occupation of the port of Vera Cruz in 1914 to refusing to break relations with Cuba in the early 1960s to openly supporting the Sandinista government in Nicaragua in the 1980s to defending most recently Venezuela's besieged democracy, all in opposition to U.S. policy, Mexico has reiterated time and again that its sense of nationalism, as much as it means forging a unique Mexican identity, also means *not* being identified with the United States.

So, nationalism in Mexico, as an expression of shared cultural identity and revolutionary political ideology, is both a celebration of what Mexico is and a denunciation of what it is not. Mexican nationalism is defined by its indigenous and colonial legacies; by its struggles for independence and freedom not only from Spain but also from the hegemony of other imperial powers; by its 20th-century social revolution; and by all the attendant heroes, myths, and symbols associated with the forging of the cosmic race.

THE STRUCTURE OF THE MEXICAN GOVERNMENT

Like many constitutional democracies throughout the world, the Mexican political system is composed of three distinct branches of government: the executive, the legislative, and the judicial. Each branch of government manifests itself at federal, state, and local levels and is designed to function as a system of checks and balances. At the federal level, executive power is found in the office of the presidency. Legislative power is located in a bicameral legislature: the Chamber of Deputies and the Senate. The Mexican Supreme Court serves as the final authority on judicial matters. At the state level, governors exercise executive duties, and state legislatures, composed also of chambers of deputies and senates, exercise legislative functions at this local level.

The Executive Branch of Government

The executive branch of government in Mexico is headed by the president (currently Felípe Calderón of the Partido de Acción Nacional—PAN—or National Action Party) and is responsible for implementing laws passed by the legislature. The executive branch of government is also the principal representative of the country abroad and assumes primary responsibility for the conduct of the country's foreign relations. The president, who is elected to a six-year term of office and who is constitutionally ineligible to run for reelection, oversees a massive federal bureaucracy. This bureaucracy includes the various and myriad formal ministries of state that are the functional equivalents of the formal state ministries in other countries throughout the world. In Mexico, such ministries are called secretariats, and the heads of these secretariats, along with the attorney general and a select number of other department heads, comprise the president's cabinet. Common to most governments, the nature and structure of these executive secretariats change and evolve over time and through subsequent political administrations. Currently, there are 18 formal cabinet secretariats. In addition to these formal secretariats, the executive branch of government also supervises and manages agencies that are unique to the Mexican political system. These agencies, generally referred to as "parastatal" agencies, are semiautonomous, state-owned entities. Such entities include the state-owned petroleum monopoly, Petroleos Mexicanos, and the Federal Electricity Commission.

One of the interesting aspects of the structure of the federal executive branch of government in Mexico, and an example of the nature of Mexican presidentialism, is the minimal oversight exercised by any of the other branches of government over the executive in his choices for cabinet secretaries. For instance, with the singular exception of the

Felípe Calderón, Mexico's newly elected president, waves after taking the oath before the Congress of the Union in December 2006. (Marcos Delgado/epa/Corbis)

attorney general, not one of the president's choices to head up a cabinet-level secretariat requires confirmation by any other governmental body.

The Legislative Branch of Government

The dominance of the executive branch of government notwithstanding, the Mexican federal legislative body is an important actor in the Mexican political system, though one might argue that its principal importance is measured neither in its ability to craft legislation nor in its role as a counterbalance to executive authority.

The federal Congress is made up of two bodies: the Chamber of Deputies and the Senate. Due to a series of reforms that began in 1970, the Chamber of Deputies currently consists of 500 members and the Senate consists of 128 members. The term of a member of the Chamber of Deputies is three years, and the entire Chamber of Deputies is reconstituted every three years. Elections to the Chamber of Deputies are held in presidential election years and then again at the midterm of the six-year presidential cycle. The term of a senator is six years, and elections for the Senate are held concurrently with presidential elections. Each body of the federal Congress is constituted under a unique set of electoral rules.

In the Chamber of Deputies, 300 of the 500 seats are determined by plurality vote in electoral districts of approximately equal populations. In other words, for each district election, the candidate who receives the most votes wins the seat, even if that candidate does not win an absolute majority of the votes cast. Of the remaining 200 seats, five geographic electoral regions are each assigned 40 seats, which are then divided among various political parties based on a system of proportional representation, which allocates a percentage of seats to each political party based on the percentage of votes each party receives in each of the five geographic electoral regions. The particular individuals who end up occupying these seats (sometimes referred to as "at large" or "plurinominal" seats) are determined by rank order according to lists submitted by each party to the Federal Electoral Institute prior to the election. For example, if a political party receives 20 percent of the total vote in a particular region, then that party will be allocated 8 of the 40 plurinominal seats assigned to that region.

With regard to the Senate, each of Mexico's 31 states, plus the Federal District, is assigned two plurality vote seats, which add up to a total of 64 of the 128 Senate seats. Each party nominates a team of two candidates for these plurality vote seats, and whichever party's slate of candidates receives a plurality of votes in the election for a particular state wins both of that state's seats. The party whose slate of two candidates finishes second in the state senatorial election is awarded one Senate seat, which is filled according to a rank order list submitted by the party to the Federal Electoral Institute prior to the election. These "first minority seats" account for 32 of the remaining available 64 Senate seats. The final 32 Senate seats are then allocated by proportional representation to political parties based on the percentage of votes that each party receives at the national level.

The unique and complex set of rules that determines the total number of congressional seats and how these seats are filled was designed to guarantee minority party representation in the national Congress, thus ostensibly also strengthening the role of the Congress in the governing process relative to the executive. Yet, while such reforms may seem to address any potential imbalances in the representation of opposition minority voices in the governing process, we should remember that these reforms were initiated and implemented by a dominant executive in a presidentialist system and by a long-standing ruling party. Two other points about the federal legislature in the Mexican political context help to illuminate the overall effect of such reforms. First, Mexican legislators are also subject to the constitutional restrictions against consecutive term limits. Thus, with a constant and complete turnover in the Chamber of Deputies every three years, and in the Senate every six years, the ability of the federal Congress to emerge as an effective check and balance to a historically dominant executive is seriously compromised. Second, the continued salience of centralism, personalism, and presidentialism in Mexican politics tends to keep potential candidates to the legislature beholden to and focused on national as opposed to local politics, the charisma and guidance of their own party's presidential aspirants, and a disciplined subordination to the executive authority within their own parties.

In principle, the Mexican Constitution does afford the Congress appropriate powers of checks and balances relative to the executive that are typical for any liberal democracy. However, in practice, the Congress has rarely exercised its balancing function. Since the 2000 presidential elections, this is beginning to change. In those elections, Mexico witnessed for the first time in its modern, postrevolutionary history the election of a president whose party did not command a majority in either chamber of Congress.

Today, Mexicans are still coming to terms with the practice of divided government, and the Mexican legislature is still groping with how best to exercise its constitutional functions in the context of a divided government, a still-dominant executive, and a legislative framework hampered by the limitations imposed by constitutionally mandated term limits. Nevertheless, the Mexican Congress is asserting itself relative to the executive in significant ways. It is actually initiating legislation as opposed to awaiting suggestions for legislation from the executive. Or it is actually modifying or rejecting legislation originating with the executive. What is becoming more clear is that the Mexican Congress is no longer acting as the compliant legislative rubber stamp of

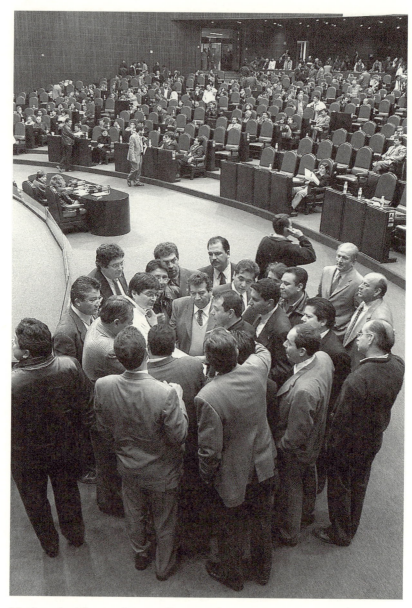

Mexican legislators discuss the 2002 federal budget in the Chamber of Deputies in Mexico City on December 30, 2001. (Reuters/Corbis)

presidential initiatives that once defined its exclusive purpose. The Mexican Congress is also exercising its oversight function in other ways, principally by calling in executive branch administrators and cabinet secretaries for regular policy briefings and testimony. It is even probing the waters of executive accountability by conducting congressional hearings on executive branch activities that it finds suspect, problematic, or lacking in adequate transparency.

The constitutionally mandated term limits for Congress, though, have had an unexpected negative consequence in this current environment of a greater congressional assertiveness. Without the prospect of reelection and with the corresponding accountability to the local electorate, congressional delegates are less inclined to view their purpose in terms of representing local constituent interests. While this problem existed prior to the 2000 elections, the voting public's hopes and expectations of its representatives has increased, and the perceived ineffectiveness of elected officials in providing for local constituent needs has magnified the public's sense of disillusionment with the effectiveness of all national political institutions, the federal Congress included. Additionally, congressional members have less incentive to compromise with the executive on policy initiatives dealing with pressing, but sticky, problems. In fact, the inability of Mexican President Vicente Fox to overcome congressional opposition to some of his initiatives and to find common ground that could lead to policy compromises not only eroded the public's expectation of clear, decisive, and authoritative executive authority, not to mention the president's personal leadership abilities, but it also negatively influenced the public's perceptions of Congress as unwilling to work with the president in finding solutions to the country's pressing problems.

Clearly, the Mexican federal Congress is undergoing a functional transformation that brings with it hopes as well as

challenges for the effective functioning of a Mexican political system accustomed to semiauthoritarian, presidentialist,
single-party rule. Yet, while the legislative branch of government at the federal, state, and local levels is emerging as a
counterweight of some substance to a long-standing pattern
of executive dominance, Mexico's third branch of government, the judiciary, is still fighting an uphill battle to assume
its place in the power triumvirate of the Mexican political
system.

The Judicial Branch of Government

The Mexican Judiciary is structured very similarly to the
way judicial systems are structured in other Western liberal
democracies. Courts exist at the local, state, and federal levels. At the national level, the highest judicial authority is the
Supreme Court, formally termed the Supreme Court of Justice of the Nation. An appellate court system also comprises
part of the federal judiciary of Mexico.

Currently, 11 jurists sit on the Supreme Court. Subject to
approval by two-thirds of the Senate, each Supreme Court
justice is appointed according to a staggered rotation by the
president for a limited term of 15 years. Justices are not eligible to serve a second term. The important point here is
that appointments to the Supreme Court are not lifetime appointments. The 11 Supreme Court justices elect one from
among themselves to serve as president of the body. The individual justice elected president serves a four-year term
and may serve more than one term as president, though not
consecutively. The Supreme Court is divided functionally
into two chambers, with the First Chamber dedicated to
civil and penal affairs and the Second Chamber dedicated to
administrative and technical affairs. Each chamber is composed of five Supreme Court justices.

Circuit and district court judges are appointed by the
seven-member Council of the Federal Judiciary, one of

whom is the president of the Supreme Court, who also serves as the de jure president of the Council. Three of the remaining six Council members are appointed by the full Supreme Court and must come from among the ranks of sitting circuit and district court judges. Of the remaining three council members, two are assigned by the Senate and one by the president. With the exception of the president of the Supreme Court, all members of the Council of the Federal Judiciary are appointed on a rotating schedule for a fixed five-year term and are ineligible for reappointment.

The ability of the judiciary to serve as an effective counterweight to the legislative and executive branches of government is heavily dependent upon its independence from each of the other branches. The fact that appointments to the Mexican Supreme Court are term-limited compromises the independence of the judiciary in its relationship with both the executive and legislative authorities, each of whom plays a determinative role in constituting the courts. One aspect of the Mexican judicial system that may be related to this structural condition is the reluctance of the judiciary to delve into legal matters that are primarily political in nature, such as the nature of political authority or the constitutionality of particular legislation or executive policy. The absence of judicial precedent in the functioning of the legal system also limits the scope and impact of the courts as an effective check and balance to the other branches of government. Finally, the chronic corruption and political manipulation that plague the lower levels of the Mexican justice system also may be rooted in the subordination of the judiciary as an unequal partner to the other branches of government in the balance of power.

Thus, it should come as no surprise that Mexicans generally view the Mexican legal system as broken and ineffectual. Average citizens have a deep distrust of the legal system and question the impartiality and fairness of the courts in administering justice, and this sentiment often translates into a lack of respect for the law. Episodes of vigilante justice being administered by agitated mobs, often with tragic outcomes, are not uncommon in smaller towns where the legacies of judicial corruption and abuse are deeply embedded and difficult to transform.

Since 1994, though, Mexican President Ernesto Zedillo Ponce de León and his successor, Vicente Fox, recognized the need to strengthen public perception of a nation committed to the rule of law and publicly bolstered the authority of the Supreme Court by emphasizing its impartiality and its independence. In fact, Zedillo presided over a series of reforms of the Mexican judicial system that not only gave the Mexican legislature more power in the selection of Supreme Court justices but also introduced a special kind of judicial review that, for the first time, gave the Supreme Court the power to rule on the constitutionality of administrative acts. Since 1994, within this new atmosphere, the Mexican Supreme Court has not only increasingly issued decisions on the constitutionality of controversial cases but it has also decided some cases that went against the Mexican executive. In this way, the Supreme Court of Mexico has begun to effectively exercise a real balance of power against the executive branch of government in the political system and thus strengthen public perceptions of the efficacy of the judicial system, at least at the federal level. This is not to say that the Mexican judicial system does not continue to face serious problems of corruption and a lack of public trust, but it does indicate that encouraging signs of movement are being seen within the area of reform of the judicial system that bode well for the consolidation of democracy in Mexico.

State and Local Governments

Politically, the country of Mexico is divided into 31 states and the Federal District, which is commonly referred to as the City of Mexico. Each state is a sovereign entity and is governed somewhat independently of the federal government. Each state has its own governor, elected to a six-year term of office, who exercises executive authority over the state, and each state has its own legislative authority in the form of state congresses. Judicial authority in the states is represented by a state court system, over which presides a state Supreme Court. One difference between the federal legislature and the state legislatures is that the federal legislature is a bicameral body, composed of both a Senate and a Chamber of Deputies, whereas state legislatures are unicameral bodies.

Each state is also subdivided further into municipalities, which can be considered the functional equivalent of counties in the structure of state government in the United States. Each municipality is governed by a municipal president in collaboration with a municipal council. Some municipalities subdivide further into smaller administrative units known as delegations.

The principle of no reelection applies equally to the executive authority at the state and municipal levels as it does at the federal level. In other words, state governors and municipal presidents are unable to be reelected to consecutive terms of office. However, whereas the national president and state governors are constitutionally prohibited from reelection, it is possible for municipal presidents to run again for the same office after sitting out a term.

The Federal District is the nation's capital city and is home to the federal government. It is divided into 16 distinct administrative units known as delegations. Because the Federal District pertains to the national citizenry, it has special administrative status within the structure of government in Mexico. With the exception of a few rare moments in the country's independent history, from 1824 to 1997, a regent appointed directly by the national president ran the local government of the Federal District itself. This regent, formally termed head of the Department of the Federal

District, traditionally constituted part of the presidential cabinet at the national level. This regent appointed, with presidential approval, the presiding heads of each of the Federal District's 16 delegations. In 1997, the Federal District became autonomous from the national government, and residents of the Federal District now not only elect both their head of government (formally called the head of Government of the Federal District) and their delegation representatives by direct popular vote, but they also elect members of a unicameral legislative assembly, which functions more or less as the equivalent of a state Congress.

Because political authority in Mexico has been concentrated and centralized in the federal executive office, state and local governments have been effectively subordinated to the will of the federal government. During the hegemony of the PRI over the 20th century, and even prior to that time under the dictatorship of Porfirio Díaz, the Mexican president has been able to manipulate state and local politics to conform to his vision for the political welfare of the country. One way that the president was able to do this was through the process of tax collection and budgetary allocations. Constitutionally, tax collection is the exclusive prerogative of the federal government. Thus, state and local budgets have been almost exclusively dependent on the federal government for receiving their share of tax revenues collected at the national level. Essentially, the federal government collects tax revenues, which are then reapportioned by the president to the individual state and local governing authorities. Recent reforms aimed at decentralizing control over tax collection and budgets have attempted to address this imbalance of power and control between the central government and state governments.

Another way that the president was able to influence local and state politics was through his de facto control over the party apparatus that nominated and supported candidates for state and local offices. This power was supplemented by the constitutional authority granted to the president to unilaterally remove elected officials from state and local office. The combination of these factors allowed the national president effectively to control virtually all aspects of state and local government.

Mexican Political Parties

As mentioned previously, Mexico has a unique electoral system that involves both direct majoritarian representation and proportional representation. The purpose of this hybrid electoral system is to ensure that Mexico's various multiple political parties secure some representation at the national, state, and local levels where their prominence and popular support is evident. This system of proportional representation has encouraged the proliferation of political parties, especially in recent years as elections have become more open and generally less corrupt.

Although there are many political parties, the most important three are the PRI (Partido Revolucionario Institucional, or Institutional Revolutionary Party); the PAN (Partido de Acción Nacional, or National Action Party); and the Partido de la Revolución Democrática, or Party of the Democratic Revolution (PRD). Other parties that have national reach are the Mexican Ecology/Green Party (PVEM), the Worker's Party (PT), the Convergence Party, and the New Alliance Party (PNA).

The PRD is a left-leaning party that emerged as a political force at the national level after the hotly contested 1988 presidential election. Its leadership came largely from the disaffected elements of the ruling PRI who felt that the official party had strayed too far to the right in adopting neoliberal economic reforms and dismantling many of the state's social welfare programs. The PRD also represented the "democratic" current among Mexicans who felt that the ossification of the ruling party and its lack of internal democratic practices had virtually locked out competing voices within the ruling party. The PRD's electoral strength lies mainly in the Federal District and in some south-central states, particularly in urban areas.

The PAN, which is Mexico's more traditional conservative opposition party, was founded in the 1930s and represents Mexico's business class. It also has maintained close ties to the Catholic Church, and its strength traditionally has been centered in the more conservative northern border states. The PAN, more than any other party, can be considered Mexico's traditional loyal opposition party. In the 2000 presidential elections, the PAN made history by capturing the presidency from the PRI. This victory by the PAN represented an end to more than 70 years of uninterrupted rule by the PRI and served as a turning point in Mexico's slow transition toward a more democratic political system.

The PRI is undoubtedly the political party that has had the greatest impact on the course of Mexican politics over the 20th century and into the 21st century. Though the PRI is currently experiencing its worst crisis and its popularity is at an all-time low, the party has always been resilient and adaptive, and one might expect that its current missteps and misfortunes will give way to a renewed relevance for Mexican politics. Certainly, the PRI's history as the country's long-standing and long-dominant ruling party affords it a strong base upon which to reform and rebuild itself as a contender once again in the dynamic of 21st-century Mexican politics. And the PRI still retains certain symbolic advantages over other parties in making claims to national loyalties. First, the PRI still retains its legacy as the party of the Revolution. It emerged as a unifying organization from the chaos of the Revolution, and it still can embrace the legacy of the Revolution and its accomplishments in ways the other political parties will never be able to do. For instance, the PRI is the only party that is associated with some of the strongest symbols of nationalism. Its colors are still the red, white, and green that represent the nation and appear on the Mexican flag. Its founding members are still revered individuals and national heroes in the postrevolutionary national consciousness. And its networks to corporate interest groups such as organized labor, peasants, and professional associations are still impressive and useful. Even though its long tenure as the unchallenged ruling party has contributed to part of its current problems, there is still the undeniable fact that the PRI has had, for better or for worse, extensive experience in governing. Because of this, one cannot but expect that the PRI will continue to adapt to the current environment and remain an active player in Mexican politics.

Elections and the Electoral System

Mexico holds presidential elections once every six years in the month of July. As of this writing, the last presidential election was held in July 2006. Elections for the national Senate follow the six-year presidential election cycle, with each of the Senate's 128 seats up for election in the same year Mexicans vote for their president. Elections for all 500 of the seats in the national Chamber of Deputies take place every three years and correspond with the six-year federal electoral cycle as well. In other words, Mexican citizens elect their federal congressional deputies in the same year that they vote for their president and their senators, and then again three years later at the midway point of the presidential and senatorial term.

Like the national president and federal senators, state governors are also elected to a six-year term of office, though their terms do not necessarily conform to the federal electoral cycle. The length of the terms of office for other state and local offices varies widely, however, and elections for these other state and local offices, like those for the state governorships, do not necessarily follow a schedule that corresponds to the federal election cycle.

The principle of no reelection, mentioned throughout this chapter, served an important function in curbing the legacy of personalist authoritarian regimes that plagued Mexico's 19th-century political history. However, the continued usefulness of this principle is a subject of debate as it relates to the continued consolidation of democratic change in Mexico with regard both to the process of government and to the general cultural environment supporting this process. On the one hand, the impossibility of reelection creates a lack of democratic accountability between elected officials and the voters. Without the possibility of an extended career in politics through reelection, there is nothing outside of goodwill binding the legislative agenda and the behavior of elected officials with the demands and interests of their local constituencies. Also, some argue that the principle of no reelection encourages political corruption, since the opportunities and perquisites that come with holding political office and exercising the power that comes with it are of limited duration. The thinking is that elected officials have a limited window to translate their political power into economic wealth, and so the quick and easy path of corruption becomes all the more tempting to them, especially since the deterrent effect of being voted out of office amidst allegations of corruption are a moot point. Additionally, the absence of the possibility of reelection serves as a disincentive for elected officials to work together toward compromise solutions to produce results that can then be brought back to their constituencies and upon which future campaigns can be conducted. In essence, every term of office for every elected official is a "lame duck" term in the Mexican political system, and lame duck administrations or officials are notorious both for their intractability and their relative powerlessness in influencing policy. For all these reasons, and in spite of its historical importance and its practical usefulness in maintaining political stability and a regular, generational transfer of power in the country, the hallowed principle of

Two Tzotzil Maya from the La Ormiga community of San Cristobal de las Casas, in the state of Chiapas, deposit their electoral ballots at their voting center on July 2, 2000. (Reuters/Corbis)

no reelection in Mexican politics has come under more intense scrutiny as Mexico's democratic consolidation proceeds apace and as Mexicans' level of trust in their elected officials to respect the democratic process grows.

Regardless, Mexico is one of the very few countries in the Latin American region that can boast a regular and predictable electoral cycle. This has given the Mexican political system a measure of stability and a well-established process of intergenerational political transition. However, elections in Mexico, until recently, have not truly been the determinative means for influencing policy outcomes and for determining political leadership. In fact, elections have simply been one means out of many by which the voting public can convey its values and preferences to governing authorities whose political positions are determined principally by nonelectoral processes. Elections have also served as a means to ratify or bolster the policy and the performance of governing authorities without necessarily challenging the authority structure itself. Conversely, elections have provided governing authorities a vehicle through which to publicize and propagandize their legitimacy and to rally popular support for the system. Furthermore, elections have served handily as a means through which individual loyalties to the system and to the ruling party were rewarded, as well as a means for the ruling party to distribute political patronage. Finally, elections were a vehicle through which the ruling party could offer programs of change or needed adjustments to policy in such a way that any social discontent with the government could be addressed and that the ruling party could avoid being perceived as out of touch or anachronistic.

Regardless of the purpose of elections in the context of the Mexican political system, what is uncontested in any study of the history of Mexico's modern, postrevolutionary electoral system is the presence of electoral fraud and the manipulation of the electoral system to produce a particular outcome. By the late 1960s and the early 1970s, the frustrations of average Mexican citizens, coupled with the growing disapproval of the international community, particularly of the world's liberal democracies, regarding the obviously fraudulent nature of Mexico's electoral system played no small part in goading Mexico's ruling party to initiate a series of electoral reforms (discussed in detail below). And over the past 30 years, given these pressures, Mexico has indeed experienced significant electoral reform.

Let us not forget, though, that these electoral reforms began within the framework of a semiauthoritarian political system and were dictated by the ruling party, and hence should be approached and evaluated cautiously and carefully. Since common sense dictates that no ruling party wants to write itself out of power, one cynical way to approach an evaluation of these electoral reforms in contemporary Mexico is to understand them primarily as a creative way to attempt to legitimize and perpetuate the continuation of single-party rule. In fact, some would argue that the long-time ruling party, the PRI, designed its various electoral reform initiatives in such a way so as to give the impression of an opening to opposition political parties within the electoral process and to remove the necessity for electoral fraud to ensure a particular electoral outcome, all the while further entrenching itself in power and making it even more difficult to unseat the ruling party via the electoral system. Indeed, a close evaluation of the electoral reforms initiated over the past 40 years seems to bear out this interpretation.

However, the electoral reforms, in spite of such designs, unleashed a Pandora's box of expectations for political change that the ruling party was unable to contain. In the end, these series of electoral reforms, begun in the 1960s and intended as a cosmetic concession to the opposition and a reputation-enhancing fix for the ruling party, led to the PRI's loss of its absolute majority in the federal Congress and eventually helped to bring an opposition party candidate to the presidency in the 2000 elections, thus effectively ending more than 70 years of single-party rule.

As mentioned, the PRI initiated a very modest and mostly cosmetic electoral reform project in the early 1960s. The need for such reforms emerged out of a nascent discontent with a governing party becoming ever more entrenched, and thus, seemingly, more and more unaccountable to the population at large. Furthermore, like many other Western countries throughout the world, Mexico was witnessing a growing sense of alienation with authority that defined a generation of people coming of age in the 1960s. The Mexican government and the ruling party that constituted it took note of this simmering discontent and, in a manner true to its very successful incorporating and co-optive strategy in handling dissent, initiated electoral reforms intended both to ameliorate these growing concerns and to improve the ruling party's image as a vanguard of reform according to popular will, all the while cementing the ruling party's continued hegemony over the political system and the Mexican social consciousness.

Mexican President Adolfo López Mateos (1958–1964), responding to the growing calls for democratic reforms of an electoral system that appeared to exclude any opposition voices, sponsored an amendment to the Mexican Constitution that would allow more opposition presence in the Chamber of Deputies. This new constitutional provision awarded any political party that won at least 2.5 percent of the national vote, even if none of its candidates won a direct electoral contest in any of the congressional districts, five guaranteed seats in the Chamber of Deputies as at-large representatives. Furthermore, for every additional half percentage of the vote above the minimum of 2.5 percent, each opposition party would earn an additional at-large seat in the federal Congress, not to exceed a total of 20 seats. Although this change in electoral law improved the representation of opposition parties in the federal Congress slightly, and thus seemed to indicate to the general Mexican population a democratically reform-minded government, it did nothing to address the corruption of the electoral process itself that still resulted in the ruling party capturing upwards of 90 percent of the national vote.

In spite of the existence of this modest and ultimately inconsequential electoral reform measure, its interpretation and application in subsequent elections over the next presidential administration of Gustavo Díaz Ordáz exposed the cynicism behind the government's intentions and stoked further the flames of discontent that were growing in Mexico regarding both the semiauthoritarianism of the political system and the failures of the economic development model to address the continuing problems of poverty and inequality. For example, the Díaz Ordáz administration ruled that opposition parties who did win a congressional seat through the direct district-level electoral contest would have that seat subtracted from the maximum number of 20 allocated under the new electoral reform code. Thus, no matter what the actual outcome of the direct elections was and no matter how much of a percentage of the total national vote any opposition party might obtain, the maximum number of seats any opposition party could claim would be 20.

Additionally, Díaz Ordáz, by intervening in a number of local elections in which opposition party candidates had apparently won and by declaring the election results voided because of "voting irregularities," indicated that the government could and would bypass the electoral system altogether to ensure the continuation of the hegemony of the ruling party in local, state, and federal government. Díaz Ordáz's ill-advised backtracking on even such minimal electoral reforms would help to create the conditions for a much more radical and aggressive protest movement against the regime, which would have tragic consequences in 1968 when government forces violently repressed a student-led protest gathering in Tlatelolco plaza. Furthermore, the lack of space within the established political and electoral system for opposition expression and representation pushed some elements of Mexican society to seek change through more radical means outside of the system. The emergence of revolutionary movements in the early 1970s, which engaged in kidnappings, armed uprisings, and urban insurgency, was simply one manifestation of popular frustration with the political system. The refusal by Mexico's most significant opposition party, the PAN, to field a candidate for the 1976 presidential election was another example of the frustration Mexicans felt with the electoral system.

The lessons to the ruling party were clear: In order to forge a public consensus of the governing model and to preserve the ruling party's continued dominant place in it, more substantive reforms of the electoral system had to occur. Thus, the presidential administration, this time that of José López Portillo, once again initiated a series of electoral reforms in the latter part of the 1970s, beginning with the expansion of the range of formally recognized political parties.

As in most electoral systems, candidates follow a formal process to have their names officially placed on an electoral ballot. In Mexico, candidates must be nominated by an officially registered political party. Therefore, elections in Mexico depend upon the prior existence of political parties, and the authority to approve a potential political party's petition for legal status rested in the executive branch of government. Until 1978, the only officially recognized political parties that could nominate individuals for election to any particular office were the ruling PRI, the Popular Socialist Party (PPS), the PARM, and the PAN. In fact, only the PAN represented a truly independent opposition party, since both the PPS and the PARM were essentially creations of the PRI to give at least the appearance of a competitive multiparty system.

In 1978, the government officially legitimized the expansion of the party system by permitting the formation of three new political parties: the Mexican Communist Party, the Socialist Worker's Party, and the Mexican Democratic Party. To ensure that this expansion of electoral competition would seem to produce concrete outcomes in diversifying representation in the political system, the government also added 100 seats to the federal congressional Chamber of Deputies that would be allocated on the basis of proportional representation. While these early electoral reforms had the effect of nominally increasing the presence of non-PRI legislators in the federal Congress, the changes had no practical impact on the hegemony exercised by the ruling party. State control of the television and print media was still firmly in place, as was the practice of using official government resources to support the candidacies of ruling party nominees to public office.

The next series of electoral reforms, undertaken over the 1986–1988 period, sought to expand on the previous reforms. During this time period, the new Federal Electoral Code was enacted and the federal Chamber of Deputies was expanded yet again, with the addition of 100 more seats to be allocated on the basis of proportional representation. Additionally, the reforms declared that the majority party would never assume more than 70 percent of the seats of the Chamber of Deputies. Thus, these reforms created an even greater presence of opposition party seats in Mexico's lower house of Congress, guaranteeing a minimum of opposition representation of 30 percent in this body.

Yet, these reforms also imposed limits on the ability of opposition parties to effectively challenge the hegemony of the ruling party. For instance, while the reforms assured that the majority party would never assume more than 70 percent of the seats of the Chamber of Deputies, the reforms also guaranteed that the party winning the greatest number of the 300 district seats would also be guaranteed an absolute majority through allocation of seats via the proportional vote mechanism. In effect, this guaranteed that the ruling party, which still controlled a significant block of the 300 district seats, would virtually always maintain control over the Chamber of Deputies. Furthermore, with the exception of determining that one-half of Senate seats would be elected every three years, instead of all Senate seats elected during the same year, no substantive alterations were made to the electoral process regarding the constitution of the upper house of Congress, the Mexican Senate. And all electoral reforms were designed exclusively to create opportunities for the opposition in the legislative branch of government, traditionally a subordinate and rubber stamp institution for the executive branch of government in the political system's balance of powers.

These electoral reforms, directed exclusively at the legislature, were predicated on the ruling party's continued dominance of the executive branch of government. In an ironic twist of fate, these modest electoral reforms had the effect of galvanizing and encouraging the opposition not only toward a greater presence in the legislature but also in challenging the ruling party's control over the executive branch of government, at both the state and national levels. In fact, these electoral reforms set the stage for a real opposition movement to challenge the PRI's hegemony over the presidency in the 1988 presidential elections.

The controversial presidential elections of 1988 created a broader crisis of legitimacy for the electoral system, in spite of the reforms undertaken to that date, in that the outcome of the presidential election and the way that it was managed by the state exposed clearly that the ruling party would not entertain or accept any threats to its hegemony via a free and untainted electoral competition. While the heavy-handedness of the ruling party in terms of manipulating the electoral system to its benefit was obvious, the 1988 presidential elections also marked a watershed in terms of instituting meaningful electoral reform that would ultimately create the possibility not only of opposition control over the Mexican Congress but also of opposition victory in elections to executive office.

The PRI's candidate in the 1988 presidential elections, Carlos Salinas de Gortari, won the election amidst demonstrable evidence of electoral fraud. Salinas assumed the presidency in December 1988 under this dark cloud, and his only recourse to establish the legitimacy of his executive authority was to commit himself to a process of reform that would address the nature of the very electoral fraud that brought him to office. Thus, his period of office, from 1988 to 1994, also known as a *sexenio,* witnessed the most wide-sweeping and substantive series of electoral reforms, setting the stage for Mexico's transition toward opposition party rule.

Early during his term of office, Salinas began a series of discussions with the opposition that resulted in constitutional amendments reforming the electoral process once again and, this time, establishing the basis for the new Federal Code for Electoral Institutions and Procedures (COFIPE). The COFIPE established an independent electoral authority in the Federal Electoral Institute (IFE) that would function separately from the executive. Reforms subsequent to the creation of the COFIPE included expanding opposition participation in the Senate, which was facilitated by the doubling of Senate seats, with the newly added seats to be allocated on the basis of proportional representation among opposition parties. Eventually, by 1994, these reforms would include the elimination of the "governability" provision of the electoral code regulating constitution of the federal Congress, which guaranteed the dominant party majority status in the Congress.

Other reforms during this period, and continuing through the 1994–2000 presidential *sexenio,* would seek to address the less tangible imbalances in the electoral process, especially regarding equal access to media, campaign finance reform, more liberal rules regulating the creation and registration of political parties, and revising the legal process for challenging electoral outcomes by placing authority to hear and decide on such challenges within an independent tribunal system specifically designed for the purpose. As a further punctuation of these reforms, the Mexican government invited independent external observers to monitor Mexican elections in order to be able to provide their own assessments of the fairness and transparency of the reformed electoral process.

The significance of these reforms is such that in the 1997 midterm congressional elections, the PRI lost, for the first time, its majority control over the Chamber of Deputies, with opposition parties winning 262 of the 500 seats. And in the subsequent presidential elections of 2000, the PRI relinquished its control over the executive branch of government by passing the presidency on to an opposition candidate, Vicente Fox, of the National Action Party, in a peaceful transition of power. Claims of electoral fraud surfaced again in the July 2006 presidential elections, only this time it was the opposition leftist party the PRD claiming electoral fraud by the ruling PAN party. Though the movement headed by the PRD's defeated candidate, Andrés Manuel López Obrador, challenged the legitimacy of the elections in ways that made for some good political theatre, the elections by and large were considered by most observers, both domestic and international, to be free, fair, and transparent. Mexico seems to have weathered this latest challenge to its electoral system, and whereas Mexicans less than 20 years ago thought of the electoral system as a farce and accepted electoral fraud as a matter of course, now Mexicans seem to think of the electoral system as quite legitimate, even if imperfect and requiring some adjustments.

Mexico's 2006 elections brought Felípe Calderón of the conservative PAN to the presidency and reconstituted the Mexican Congress. In the federal Chamber of Deputies, the PAN now holds a plurality of 206 seats, a left-leaning coalition of parties led by the PRD holds 160 seats, the PRI (in alliance with the PVEM) holds 121 seats, and two minor parties constitute the remaining 13 seats. In the Senate, the PAN occupies 52 seats, the PRD-led leftist coalition holds 36 seats, the PRI/PVEM alliance holds 39 seats, and the minor New Alliance Party occupies the remaining seat in the Senate. Thus, no single party holds a governing majority of seats in either chamber of Congress. Consequently, the current difficulties of effective governance and power sharing between the legislative and executive branches in contemporary Mexican politics are likely to continue, especially since the principle of no reelection still applies, which, as noted previously, greatly reduces incentives to compromise on policy matters.

Mexican presidential candidate Miguél Alemán surrounded by supporters at a campaign rally in Mexico City, 1946. (Library of Congress)

THE MEXICAN MILITARY

In the context of modern Latin American politics, the Mexican military is a unique institution. Unlike in most other Latin American countries, the Mexican military has not played a decisive role in contemporary Mexican politics. Since at least the 1940s, the Mexican military has refrained from intervening in the affairs of state and has never been a real threat to the constitutional order or to the authority of the civilian government. In fact, quite the opposite is true. During periods of economic crisis, natural disaster, or civilian regime transition, the Mexican military's political neutrality and its professionalism have played a critical role in maintaining a stability within the political system and in calming a society during periods of internal uncertainty or turmoil. This is not to say that the Mexican military has been an institution removed from the vagaries of politics and unaffected by the corruption inherent to a single-party dominant political system. The military has engaged, at times, in repression on behalf of the civilian authority, and its guns have been pointed at political and social dissidents. The massacre at Tlatelolco in 1968 and the military response to the Zapatista uprising in 1994 are but two examples of this. However, in each case the military was a reluctant participant and was, in fact, acting in accordance with the mandates of the civilian authority. In other words, the Mexican military's misbehaviors cannot be attributed to its internal workings or its internal institutional culture, but rather to the civilian authority exercising its powers over the military. In essence, even its misbehaviors are evidence of its effective subordination to civilian authority. Additionally, it is both impressive and significant that the Mexican military has neither attempted a coup nor intervened in other ways in the political process, even during those periods in Mexico's history when social discontent bubbled over into armed challenges against the state by guerrilla movements. At a time when the militaries of other Latin American states responded to such threats by taking over the reins of government from civilian authorities, the Mexican military responded with continued respect for and deference to civilian authority. Without a doubt, the depoliticization of the Mexican military and its subordination to civilian authority is a remarkable achievement, especially given the military's important role in Mexico's postindependence history. It is both interesting and somewhat ironic that the Mexican military's obedience to civilian leadership and its reluctance to intervene in the political arena is a consequence precisely of its incorporation into the governing apparatus and its early inclusion as a formal sector of the ruling party. The fascinating side story of the Mexican military in the larger story of the construction of the postrevolutionary single-party hegemonic state offers a lesson of sorts to other developing countries with a history of political instability and internal social discord.

Throughout the armed phase of the Mexican Revolution, leadership of the state demanded military experience and rank. Hence, all of Mexico's early revolutionary presidents from the time of Francisco Madero's overthrow and assassination in 1913 were high-ranking military officers. Even after the armed phase of the Mexican Revolution had ended, until the election of Miguél Alemán Valdés in 1946, the need to command authority over a still-emerging and unconsolidated state required that Mexican presidents have direct military experience. The critical moment in the transformation of the Mexican military in the postrevolutionary period as an institution subordinate to the state apparatus occurred during the administration of Lázaro Cárdenas (1933–1940). Cárdenas, himself a decorated and well-respected general in the revolutionary armed forces, incorporated the military into the new governing party apparatus as only one of its constituent branches. In doing so, Cárdenas accomplished two important things with regard to the military. First, he wed the military to the power of the ruling party, thus giving the official party control over the means of violence and the national security apparatus of the country. In a sense, he completely politicized the Mexican military by making it an official branch of a political party. However, in so doing, he made it possible for the military to become professionalized in the context of a dominant and hegemonic party/state apparatus. Second, by folding the military into a party structure that also had multiple civilian branches, he balanced out the political influence of the military with competing civilian organizations and interests. In essence, he appeased whatever concerns the military might have had in terms of its access to power by formalizing its integration into the ruling party apparatus, but he also mitigated its abilities to dominate or control the governing process by forcing it to share a voice in the government decision-making process with other civilian interest groups formally included in the governing party structure. In the process of doing so, Cárdenas began reducing the overall share of the federal budget that was allocated to the Mexican military relative to other state agencies or programs. This was another important step in reducing the military's effective strength as an actor within the political system.

Cárdenas's successor, Manuel Ávila Camacho, who was himself a revolutionary general, furthered the process of subordinating the military to the authority of the state, while also weaning it from its formal association with the ruling party. In a significant move, Ávila Camacho disassociated the military from the ruling party as one of its formal sectors and moved the locus of its authority firmly within the executive branch of the national government. Thus, Ávila Camacho transformed the military into an agency of the state rather than an agency of any particular party. Even though the state and the ruling party were virtually indistinguishable at the time, this move was nonetheless critical to the process of military professionalization and its institutional depoliticization. From that moment on, the Mexican military could develop a culture that demanded loyalty to the state, its citizens, and the constitution, no matter which party was in power.

When Ávila Camacho selected the civilian Miguél Alemán as his successor, the fact that Alemán did not have experience in the armed struggles of the Revolution was not anathema to the military's perception of him as an effective commander in chief. On the other hand, the fact that he had no military rank or training did not serve to condition the military's readiness to accept him as their commander in chief.

Surrounded by military officers, Mexican president Manuel Ávila Camacho delivers a radio address on the war against Japan in December, 1941. (Bettmann/Corbis)

The evolution of the military in Mexico as an apolitical institution that accepted the authority of civilian leadership was also supported by a number of other important factors. First, the absolute control by the ruling party over the electoral apparatus, and its ability to co-opt dissent through its corporatist structure, mitigated any tendency among disaffected elements of the civilian population to seek to forge an alliance against the government from among the ranks of the military. In other words, those who opposed the hegemony of the ruling party, and who refused to be co-opted by it, did not consider approaching the military as an avenue for challenging the political system. Essentially, even the opposition in postrevolutionary Mexico, where it existed, basically refrained from attempting to politicize the military against the system in any serious way, and this undoubtedly helped to consolidate the military's evolution as an independent, and ultimately apolitical, institution. Second, Mexico's civilian leadership, keeping fully in mind the historical legacy of military intervention in Mexico's politics, embraced a military education, socialization, and training process that emphasized the instilling of such values as respect for authority along the chain of command with the president as the ultimate authority as commander in chief, and a disciplined submission to such authority. On the one hand, from the point of view of a self-serving, hegemonic ruling party, this created a pliant and compliant military that would not question the governing authority, even in a semiauthoritarian context, and that could also be relied on to defend the authority against any challenges, should such arise. On the other hand, this instilled among the military the value of an apolitical and unquestioning deference to authority regardless of context that would create a reluctance on the part of the institution to become involved in efforts to defend the authority from a political threat to its claims to rule as opposed to a security threat to its claims to rule. When Vicente Fox defeated the PRI candidate, Francisco Labastida, in the presidential election in 2000, thus ending the hegemony of the PRI and transforming the nature of Mexican government, the Mexican military's response was instructive. Even though some worried about the loyalty of the armed forces to a non-PRI government, and even though a military coup plot was rumored, the Mexican military publicly declared that its loyalty was to the state and the constitution, and that it could just as easily fulfill its functions to the state and the constitution under a Fox administration as it could under any other administration. With this announcement, the Mexican military exemplified its exceptional status within the context of Latin America. Additionally, the PRI must also be credited with a creative approach to its handling of the military over time that made such an outcome possible.

Nevertheless, in spite of this significant aspect of the Mexican military, which has served the democratization process in Mexico quite admirably during the most recent years of significant political transformation away from hegemonic, single-party rule, the institution has also been conditioned by the functional missions civilian authorities have ascribed to it. While the primary purpose of any national military is the protection and defense of the nation and citizenry against external threats to its existence, the reality of Mexico's place in the global balance of power minimizes this military purpose. Mexico's military is logistically not capable of withstanding and defending against an assault by any of the world's major military powers. Furthermore, Mexico is quite aware that any challenges to its physical integrity or its sovereignty will elicit a response from the military powers of the world over which it exercises no control. Because of this, the Mexican military has defined its mission accordingly and has tended to focus its energies more as an internal police force, as an emergency readiness institution, and as a civic works organization. Not only has the Mexican military policed internal uprisings, such as the student protests of the 1960s and 1970s, but it has also engaged armed insurgencies that have cropped up from time to time. For instance, in the early 1970s, the Mexican military hunted down and engaged armed guerrilla movements, most notably the Revolutionary Armed Forces of the People, which operated in the state of Guerrero. In 1994, the Mexican military responded with force against the armed Zapatista uprising in the state of Chiapas. More recently, in the summer of 2006, the armed forces were called in to engage and disband armed protestors in the state of Oaxaca. But the military also has functioned as an emergency readiness response institution. Its most notable work in this arena followed the 1984 Mexico City earthquake, in which the military's rapid mobilization and its organized and efficient work in saving lives and creating calm stood in stark contrast to the inadequacies of the civilian agencies of the government in responding to the crisis.

The use of the military as a domestic policing force has also produced its share of problems and challenges for both the mission and the integrity of the institution. The most visible example of this is in the Mexican military's involvement in the war on drugs. Involvement of the armed forces in Mexico's fight against drug trafficking and in its drug production interdiction efforts has introduced a level of corruption to the institution that has not only damaged the institution's reputation in the minds of the Mexican population but also severely compromised the professionalization and traditional apoliticization of the military. It has led to a breakdown in the respect for civilian authority and has encouraged a resistance to adhere even to the institutional chain of command within the military structure itself.

Thus, while the Mexican military has been exceptional in many ways relative to its other Latin American counterparts, and while it has been a critical component in securing the environment that has permitted Mexico's democratic transformation away from a single-party dominant state, this very success has also removed the military from subordination to a system that could manage it effectively and demand its compliance. As its ties to the civilian authority become further loosened within the democratic process and as its institutional independence from the state becomes more consolidated, the temptations for the armed forces to operate outside of the state and civilian regulation will likely grow. How the military evolves in this new environment will be a testament not only to the way the Mexican military has been constructed by civilian leadership in the context of Mexico's postrevolutionary history but also to the manner in which the military perceives itself as an actor in the Mexican national context, both socially and politically.

MEXICO'S INTERNATIONAL RELATIONS

Mexico has a unique place in the world system. Part of its prominence is due to its physical size, the extensiveness and diversity of its natural resources, and the corresponding strength of its economy. However, Mexico's unique role in the international system is primarily conditioned by the fact that it borders the United States.

In the broader global environment, Mexico functions as a second-tier country in terms of its abilities to influence the course of international events. It primarily reacts and responds to major events that affect the global system and must always consider what its regional hegemon's position is before it takes any kind of decisive action.

However, as a second-tier country with a certain level of capability, Mexico has been able to pursue a foreign policy that is unique from other countries in the Western Hemisphere. It has been able to formulate a foreign policy that embraces principles such as the respect for national sovereignty and nonintervention, and has been able to exercise these principles in the face of pressure by stronger world powers because of its greater capabilities in the global system. This foreign policy independence is also a product of the strong nationalist, anti-interventionist sentiment that came out of the Revolution.

Patterns from the Past: History and Foreign Policy in Mexico

Colonial Mexico, more than any other Spanish new world colony with the possible exception of Peru, was Spain's wealthiest overseas possession. Consequently, Spain jealously guarded its prize colony and strictly controlled and limited foreign activity in colonial Mexico's economic and political life. As previously noted, contact with the outside world was filtered through the Spanish mercantilist system, which sought to regulate trade to the advantage of Spain and at the exclusion of other world powers. When colonial Mexico did experience contact with the outside world, it usually came in the unpleasant form of piracy. What evolved over the long 300-year history of colonial Mexico under such circumstances was, in essence, suspicion, fear, and a tendency toward defensive isolation on the part of the colonists with regard to the outside world, attitudes that were nurtured by Spanish colonial authorities. Mexico's postindependence distrust and suspicion of all things foreign have their roots in this colonial legacy; this psychological attitude toward external relations is difficult to overcome in less than 200 years.

Like that of any other sovereign state, Mexican foreign policy has undergone gradual transformation. Indeed, Mexican foreign policy today handles substantially different issues than it did 30 years ago, much less 100-plus years ago, and the orientation of Mexico's foreign policy elites has likewise also undergone substantial revision. Yet, one could point to certain historical consistencies in a country's foreign policy that traverse different periods in the country's independent life and encompass markedly different global circumstances. In U.S. foreign policy toward Latin America, for example, one might point to the overriding goal of keeping extra-hemispheric powers out of Latin America as a historical constant, regardless of the particular historical context. Likewise, for Mexico there are historical roots to the country's foreign policy goals that have lasted over time, regardless of the nature and type of political regime ruling the country, and that still factor into the contemporary foreign policy process. Of these roots, three defining concepts in Mexico's postindependence history have come to form the ideological backbone of Mexico's contemporary foreign policy: (1) preservation of the country's territorial integrity; (2) a virulent, antiforeign (specifically anti-U.S.)

revolutionary nationalism; and (3) the country's inevitable economic dependence on the United States.

From the standpoint of international relations theory, it is only natural that an independent, sovereign nation orients its foreign policy toward the goal of national self-preservation through the defense of its territory. The very viability of the independent nation-state is dependent upon that nation-state's ability to exercise sovereign political control over the land, natural resources, and population of a demarcated and bounded geographical region. For the most part, however, this goal is pursued by states at various levels given their military defense capabilities. For the United States and other advanced military powers, the actual loss of control over national territory to a hostile foreign power is usually not an immediate and direct threat. Instead, for such countries, the foreign policy goal of preserving territorial integrity is usually expressed more in terms of relative increases or decreases in power potential rather than in actual, physical assaults on the countries themselves. And frequently, when an active competition for power does occur among these nation-states, it takes place outside of the geographical confines of the nation-state. Hence, with the possible exception of the Japanese attack on Pearl Harbor, Hawaii, on December 7, 1941 (and even this is a debatable example), the United States has never experienced in its national history the imminent loss of national territory, even temporarily, to a global power rival.

However, for nation-states that are not highly advanced militarily, the concern with protecting their national territory from direct intervention by stronger powers is much more urgent and predominant in their foreign policy. This is especially true for weaker countries that share a border with a comparatively much stronger neighbor. The foreign intervention and territorial dismemberment of Mexico at various moments in its history serve as an illustrative example of this condition. Although protecting the territorial integrity of the state is a fundamental foreign policy goal of all sovereign countries, for Mexicans it is singularly important. Perhaps no other country in the Western Hemisphere has had the issue of sovereignty over territory, resources, and people so thoroughly challenged and tested than has Mexico. It is no wonder, then, that the issue of preserving the country's territorial integrity in the face of potential external intervention is a fanatic obsession of Mexicans and has predominated in Mexican international relations and foreign policy.

Mexican foreign policy at the time of the country's independence from Spain was especially directed toward securing the protection of its territorial integrity from a potential Spanish military effort at reconquest. Mexico's principal foreign policy strategy in addressing this concern was to earn diplomatic recognition from already established foreign powers, foremost among them the United States and Great Britain. The hope was that such recognition on the part of the preeminent global power of the moment (Great Britain) and the budding hemispheric leader (the United States) would not only confer a certain legitimacy on Mexico as a sovereign state in the international system but also serve as a protective shield against Spain and her allies.

Yet, more importantly for Mexico's future, diplomatic recognition was seen as carrying with it a certain respect for its rights as the legitimate inheritor of Spanish territorial claims pertaining to the former viceroyalty of New Spain. Consequently, independent Mexico's establishment of formal diplomatic relations also served as a vehicle for ironing out territorial disputes with countries that supposedly professed a mutual respect, by the simple fact of their formal recognition, of Mexico's self-defined interests as an equal and independent partner in the relationship. The concern in Mexican foreign policy with protecting the country's territorial integrity became even more of an issue throughout the 19th century as the external assault on the country did not diminish, but instead intensified. Jorge

Castañeda, a prominent Mexican diplomat and statesman who served for a short while as President José López Portillo's secretary of Foreign Relations from 1979 to 1982 once commented, "The first fifty years of independent life were in the main a sequence of foreign onslaughts. It is not to be wondered that the country's international stand became hermetic, nationalistic, distrustful, and defensive; the 'outside world' meant only a source of nameless troubles for the country" (Castañeda 1969, 138–139).

What Castañeda is referring to, and what any sensitive student of Mexico must constantly remember, is that Mexico suffered through the loss of nearly half of its national territory to the United States in the U.S.-Mexican War of 1846–1848. In addition, Mexico suffered the humiliation of numerous foreign interventions that resulted in the loss of political control over all or parts of the country. The U.S. military occupation of Mexico City in 1847–1848 and the French intervention of the 1860s, followed by the externally imposed Maximilian empire, are perhaps the two most dramatic episodes of the many foreign interventions that Mexico, as a sovereign nation, has experienced.

Yet, the preservation of territorial integrity was not only a foreign policy objective of 19th-century Mexico; the issue was still very much alive throughout the 20th century as well. For instance, the loss of sovereign control over national territory to foreigners continued to be a problem, and a source of resentment, for Mexican leaders during the course of the Mexican Revolution as the U.S. militarily occupied the port of Vera Cruz in 1914. In addition, during this very turbulent time in Mexico's history, the territorial integrity of the nation was also compromised by the punitive expedition of General John J. Pershing, which was both sanctioned and launched by the U.S. government in pursuit of Pancho Villa across Mexican territory.

One might argue that the political instability resulting from the Revolution, and the lack of adequate safeguards for

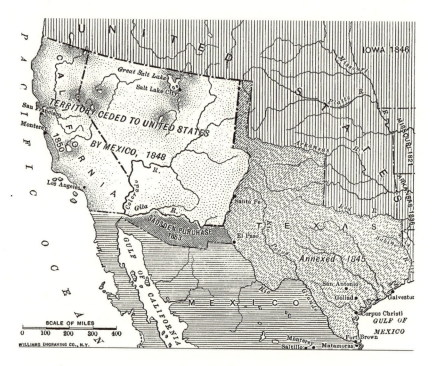

Map of territory ceded to the United States by Mexico following the Mexican-American War. The United States took possession of the territory north of the Gila River (shown on map) according to the Treaty of Guadalupe Hidalgo following the Mexican-American War in 1848. In 1853, the Gadsden Purchase (Treaty of La Mesilla) added the territory south of the Gila River. (North Wind Picture Archives)

the protection of foreign lives and property that was a product of this instability, justified U.S. behavior in these instances. Yet, the simple fact is that the historical quest to keep Mexican territory inviolable and sovereign has even factored into Mexican international politics during periods of obvious political stability. For instance, Mexico has complained that its territorial sovereignty was violated by the extraterritorial abduction of two of its national citizens by U.S. Drug Enforcement Agency agents, one in 1986 and another in 1990. These are just a few pertinent examples of direct foreign intervention in the country. Mexicans have taken them to heart and have made them part of this foreign policy bedrock.

On a more subtle, though no less important, level, the relinquishment of the national patrimony to foreign investors, most notable during the Porfiriato (see chapter 1), served to emphasize the inability or lack of desire on the part of Mexico's leaders to preserve and maintain control over national lands and resources. Consequently, modern Mexican interpretations of sovereignty include the natural and irrevocable ownership of the physical, material resources that fall within the territorial boundaries of the state. Other historical examples of this issue abound. Among some 19th-century examples are included, for example, Santa Anna's ignominious sale of the Gadsden territory to the United States in 1854 as well as Sebastian Lerdo de Tejada's offer of the Isthmus of Tehuantepec to foreign transportation interests during the reform period. In the 20th century, the question of territorial sovereignty also created tensions in U.S.-Mexico relations regarding possession of the Chamizal, a tract of land located between the cities of El Paso, Texas (United States), and Ciudad Juárez (Mexico), whose ownership was a matter of dispute following a natural change in the pattern of the Rio Grande that had served as the territorial boundary between the two countries.

Unfortunately, in nearly every instance, Mexico has been unable to withstand or prevent the temporal loss of sovereignty over its territory, national resources, and even national citizenry to stronger outside forces, whether to foreign troops or foreign investors. This sad fact has only compounded the passion with which Mexicans strive to advance the cause of preserving their country's territorial integrity and national sovereignty in their foreign policy. It is also important to note that the most blatant incidences of direct foreign military intervention in Mexico have almost always followed a period of internal political instability and disorder. As noted previously, the United States prepared for war with Mexico in the mid-19th century as Mexican politicians and generals squabbled amongst themselves over political control of the country. Likewise, the French intervention in Mexico and the installation of the Maximilian empire came sharply on the heels of the War of the Reforms, and the U.S. military occupation of Vera Cruz and the Pershing expedition came amidst the confusion of the Mexican Revolution. In fact, the reasons most often given by foreign powers for intervention have been the perceived inability of Mexican governments to meet their international obligations or to preserve internal order and, consequently, the inability to adequately ensure the protection of the lives and property of foreigners. As a result, Mexican leaders have come to associate internal political and social stability as a necessary prerequisite for the prevention of foreign intervention and the loss of sovereignty, either permanently or temporarily, over national territory.

Hence, a corollary to this need to preserve the country's territorial integrity in its foreign policy orientation is the equally important need to demonstrate to the world the ability to maintain an orderly and stable internal political system. This fact of Mexico's historical weakness in the face of foreign intervention and its subsequent xenophobia, coupled with the nationalist emphasis of the Mexican Revolution of 1910 and the need to maintain internal political stability, has particularly penetrated the postrevolutionary international relations and foreign policy of the country.

This points to a second important facet of Mexican political culture that has been a historical constant in the country's contemporary foreign policy: a virulent antiforeign, revolutionary nationalism that sprung out of the bloody social revolution of the early 1900s.

Indeed, the Mexican Revolution was born partially out of the social and economic injustices caused by the Porfiriato's economic policy of cozying up to foreign interests as well as the political alienation of the majority of Mexicans who found themselves outside of the tightly strung, exclusive, and overwhelmingly proforeign Porfirian political machine. One of the principal aims of the Revolution in terms of its impact on Mexican foreign policy and international relations was to dismantle and undermine the foreign policy orientation of the Porfirian regime. In essence, this meant a rejection of foreign penetration and control over vital sectors of the Mexican economy. A concrete effort to realize this aim was to reclaim the Mexican patrimony from its foreign usurpers, to exercise maximum control over the nature and degree of future foreign economic involvement in Mexican development, and to develop a passionate defense of an international legal code that would adhere to the following principles: (1) a mutual respect for the absolute sovereignty of all independent states in the world system in determining the nature and structure of internal and external political regimes; (2) a concurrent recognition of the juridical equality of sovereign states within the international system regardless of the levels of economic development or military strength; (3) a legal prohibition against any form of economic, political, or military intervention in the internal affairs of sovereign states by other states for any reason whatever; (4) and a common defense of the sovereign rights of states to pursue a course of national social, economic, and political development along lines determined exclusively by itself without the least bit of outside interference. This ideological nationalism has pervaded the thinking of Mexican society in general, and Mexican leaders in particular. Since the Revolution, moreover, this nationalism has received its most determined and impassioned expression in the country's postrevolutionary foreign policy.

The xenophobic nationalism that came out of the Mexican Revolution and found expression in the country's foreign policy cannot be divorced from the nature of Mexico's economic relationship with the United States. It is Mexico's inevitable economic dependence on the United States against which Mexico's revolutionary nationalism is most frequently directed. Consequently, the third, and perhaps most important, historical root to contemporary Mexican foreign relations has been and continues to be this profound economic dependence on the United States.

Because of its unalterable geographical position in which it shares an extensive land border with the United States, Mexico always has a cautious eye on the international attitudes and behavior of the United States, whether it be conciliatory or contradictory to the interests of the United States. Consequently, Mexican foreign policy, while never exactly parallel to that of the United States, is more accurately described as a reactive policy rather than a proactive policy because of this unique and unequal relationship.

The Revolution of 1910 dramatically changed fundamental perceptions in Mexico about its relationship with the United States. One of the consequences of the Mexican Revolution for the country's foreign policy was the formal resistance to external attempts to influence internal developments. Throughout the 19th century, Mexico's internal political problems could not be separated from the aspirations or the desires of external actors. The same tendencies of foreign involvement emerged during the years of the Revolution in which the United States, as well as other global powers, attempted to work the internal struggles of Mexico to its own national advantage. Mexicans reacted very strongly against this persistent tendency of foreign intervention or interference in their internal politics and consequently incorporated this reaction into the country's revolutionary mythology through a strong nationalism.

The periods during and following the revolutionary upheaval thus marked a time of conflict and challenge in U.S.-Mexican relations. Mexican foreign policy of the time produced such novel concepts as the Estrada doctrine, which repudiated the use of the tool of diplomatic recognition as a measure to exert influence over a country's internal political development. In U.S.-Mexican relations, this period was also marked by the tendency for Mexico to exercise control over its natural resources and to challenge foreign ownership of those resources. The nationalization of the petroleum industry in 1938, carried through during the administration of Lázaro Cárdenas, is a perfect example of this change in how the country approached its international relations.

With the institutionalization of the Revolution, however, the Mexican state began to concentrate much more intensively on promoting internal economic development, and, in the realm of international relations, Mexico began to assume an ambivalent policy. This policy was one of active cooperation with the United States over issues related to economic development, but also one of passive distance from the more polemical and polarizing political issues facing the international community. It is during this phase of Mexico's historical development that we begin to see the emergence of a discordant bilateral/multilateral foreign policy process.

Finally, with the breakdown of Mexico's developmental model in the late 1960s and the need for Mexico to seek alternative options outside of its national borders, Mexican foreign policy entered a phase of intense activism, though not without the sacrifice of its postrevolutionary foreign policy principles. The debt crisis did not end Mexico's foreign policy activism, but instead transformed this activism from one of traditional revolutionary principles to one of pragmatic realism.

In essence, this period marks the collapse of the discordant process, the closure of alternative foreign policy options, the reemergence of U.S. global military and regional economic hegemony, and Salinas's pragmatic response (integration) in the face of internal political and economic crises (crises of internal stability). In this latter phase, Mexico's foreign policy has become a by-product of its bilateral relationship with the United States. In fact, the singular importance of the United States in all aspects of Mexican politics, both national and international, is much more a product of Mexican creation than it is a product of U.S. pressures and influence.

Thus, these three elements in Mexico's national history— (1) the historical inability coupled with the psychological need to preserve national territorial integrity from foreign intervention and the corresponding reality of maintaining a stable internal political system as a defensive precaution against foreign intervention; (2) the institutionalization over time of a xenophobic nationalism in the Mexican postindependence political system and the congelation of this nationalism on the country's collective consciousness as a consequence of the Mexican Revolution of 1910; and (3) the historical economic dependence of Mexico on the United States—have predominated both in the Mexican foreign policy process and in the country's overall patterns of international relations.

Sources of Mexican Foreign Policy

It has been argued that Latin American nations often take recourse to the typical tactics of the developing world in their foreign policies. Most often, Latin American countries resort to the use of international law, nonalignment, and issues of respect for national sovereignty and economic development. In the face of their relatively weak international position, the developing nations of Latin America relegate the issues of global security and strategic balances of power to a level of secondary importance in their foreign policies. Mexico, as a developing country, has been representative of this position in its foreign policy. However, Mexico's unique opportunities for economic growth, its proximity to the United States, and its relative political stability for the past 50 years have placed Mexico in a distinct position with regard to both the developed and the developing communities, most particularly in its foreign policy orientation.

As indicated earlier, the geographic proximity of the United States to Mexico as an influencing factor in Mexican foreign policy cannot be overlooked. Yet, as we have also seen, the current Mexican political system is also a product of a national revolution whose basic tenets were the redistribution of wealth and power internally as well as an antiforeign (specifically anti-U.S.) sentiment projected outward into the world community. Therefore, in order to consolidate its rule, institutionalize the Revolution, and stabilize the polity, Mexico's revolutionary leaders forged a unique coalition of elements of the political left, center, and right in its governing process. This coalition, coupled with a "special" relationship with the United States, has given direction to Mexico's foreign policy initiatives. But maintaining the coalition has also placed limits on such initiatives.

These various considerations have influenced the course of Mexican foreign policy in significant ways, regardless of the different means of expression and implementation of foreign policy. Nevertheless, the combination of these considerations has produced a consistency in Mexican foreign policy that has spanned the entire range of Mexican government administrations, regardless of the differing ideological orientations that these administrations may have manifested. Furthermore, this consistency across political administrations also helps to explain why Mexico's foreign policy is still very much a dependent one, despite its recent activism in one ideological direction or another.

Since 1910, Mexican foreign policy has been based upon a single underlying, yet often contradictory, purpose: to secure the Revolution by ensuring the economic, social, and political stability of the nation. In the context of Mexican history, there have been two basic and constant conditions that any Mexican government must meet in order to achieve this end. The first of these conditions is to find the means, whether internally or externally, to sustain the national economic growth necessary for economic development. Because Mexico is still a relatively underdeveloped nation, Mexican governments have recognized the need for external investment in the country's economy in order to continually support a national economic development strategy. Consequently, Mexican governments have continually sought to attract such investment, especially since 1940, from wherever possible. In post-1970 Mexican administrations, where an activist foreign policy began to emerge, the struggle to meet this particular economic condition can be seen in Luís Echeverría's stubborn lobbying at the United Nations (UN) for international acceptance of an economic charter on the rights and duties of states; in López Portillo's extravagant and reckless use of petroleum reserves as a source of securing both investment capital and foreign loans; in Miguel de la Madrid's tentative steps toward successful debt renegotiations by agreeing to dismantle the protective barriers surrounding the Mexican economy and to join the General Agreement on Tariffs and Trade (GATT) as a symbol of this agreement; and by Salinas's neoliberal economic experiment, the culmination of which is best noted in his surprising proposal for the creation of a North American free trade area.

Unsurprisingly, in each of these specific instances, as well as previously, the United States has been and continues to be the single most important source of external investment, either through loans or private capital investment, in the Mexican economy. What has resulted in the process, in spite of the ideological rhetoric surrounding Mexican administrations, is Mexico's overwhelming dependence on the United States to finance its economic development. This has remained true despite any Mexican administration's aggressive efforts to obtain foreign investment from other sources. Even President Salinas, who offered foreign investors perhaps the most appealing opportunities, came up short in his

The North American Free Trade Agreement was initialed in San Antonio, Texas, with President Bush (center), Mexican president Carlos Salinas de Gortari (left), and Canadian prime minister Brian Mulroney (right) in attendance, October 7, 1992. (Bettmann/Corbis)

efforts to bring about some sort of economic diversification and consequently resigned himself to the United States as the only real option and used the North American Free Trade Agreement (NAFTA) as a way to cement the relationship in an economically uncertain world.

On the other hand, the second of these conditions is deeply rooted in the revolutionary nationalism that formed the ideological cornerstone of the Revolution. Simply stated, another fundamental aspect of Mexico's foreign policy is to protect Mexico's national sovereignty and independence in the face of foreign aggression by stronger world powers and to stand up for the right of other nations of the world to do the same. In light of the fact that Mexico lost half its national territory to the United States, suffered through humiliating periods of foreign intervention since its independence from

Spain, and struggled against the persistent manipulations of entrenched foreign interests during and after the nationalistic revolution of 1910, this foreign policy goal is understandable. Naturally, the United States has been the most frequent object of criticism and attack by Mexico in its foreign policy on this front.

Herein lies the essential paradox of Mexican foreign policy. Mexico projects a foreign policy that is independent, and often critical, of the United States yet, at the same time, engages in a foreign policy that serves to heighten the country's economic dependence on the United States. Therefore, in order to perpetuate and to actualize the mythology of the Revolution, every Mexican government must satisfy each of these necessary, and yet contradictory, foreign policy conditions.

Given the Mexican political system's remarkable ability to manage conflict, it is not surprising that it should discover a way to meet both conditions effectively. What this has meant historically, on the one hand, is an accommodationist and dependent foreign policy by Mexico in its more secretive bilateral relations with the United States, upon which the health of its economy ultimately depends. On the other hand, Mexico has been able to satisfy the demands of its revolutionary nationalism by following a nonaccommodationist and seemingly independent foreign policy in the more public multilateral international arena.

When these two goals cannot be pursued independently, however, the more important foreign policy goal of the two becomes evident. A healthy economy with high levels of growth is viewed by the Mexican political leadership as the only way possible to ensure the national strength necessary to maintain internal political and social stability and thus be able to successfully perpetuate the nationalistic principles of the Revolution and to prevent foreign interference in this process. Consequently, when it is impossible to pursue both goals independently, Mexico's foreign policy of challenging great power hegemony and actively supporting the sovereign rights of other nations becomes subordinated to the policy of national economic development. Hence, the special (asymmetrical and dependent) relationship that Mexico has with the United States with regard to its economy is always favored in Mexico's foreign policy, regardless of whether it is an aggressive and active foreign policy, as initiated and practiced by Echeverría and subsequent administrations, or a passive and isolated foreign policy of the manner of pre-Echeverría administrations. The foreign policy of the Salinas administration falls squarely within the activist foreign policy camp. For instance, Salinas traveled extensively to many foreign countries on official state business, he surprised the international community by his proactive pursuit of international commercial agreements, he himself (as opposed to U.S. officials) suggested to the United States that preliminary discussions for the North American Free Trade Agreement be undertaken, and he committed Mexico to a foreign policy of active "insertion" into the global community. This latter policy goal resulted in Mexico's serious consideration of accepting a seat on the UN Security Council, which would have contradicted a long history of resistance to this course of action; it characterized Mexico's outspoken role in the GATT negotiations; and it further expressed itself in Mexico's leadership in Latin American regional associations.

Salinas's foreign policy activism mirrored that of his recent predecessors. As a consequence, it is necessary to understand the nature of this foreign policy activism as it evolved in order to understand the base upon which the Salinas foreign policy emerged. In spite of this activism, nevertheless, the foreign policy of the Salinas administration also diverges from the past in a way that differentiates it from its recent predecessors. In a sense, this differentiation in foreign policy parallels the manner in which the foreign policy activism of the post-1970 administrations differed from the foreign policy passivism of pre-1970 regimes.

On the one hand, the activist foreign policy of Echeverría and López Portillo, in order to mask the ever-increasing economic dependence of Mexico on the United States, tended to exacerbate the dichotomy of Mexico's foreign policy paradox. As will be demonstrated below, the administrations of Echeverría and López Portillo sought to assert publicly and vociferously an active and aggressive foreign policy, which confronted and challenged the foreign policy of the United States. At the same time, however, these administrations quietly pursued an accommodationist and subordinate foreign policy in its bilateral relations with the United States in order not to jeopardize its principal guarantee for continued economic development. Hence, a precarious balance of extremes characterized the foreign policy activism of these post-1970 administrations. The Salinas administration made no pretense of what was the most important condition in its foreign policy process. It accepted the fact that a publicly confrontational foreign policy limited the possibilities for economic growth and development. Forthwith, Salinas abandoned the former in order to pursue the latter, only this time utilizing an activist and visibly public foreign policy to this end. The difference between the foreign policy activism of the Salinas administration and that of both the Echeverría and López Portillo administrations is simply a question of direction. Salinas's was directed publicly toward integration and accommodation with the first world economic powers, as opposed to a foreign policy activism that was publicly confrontational and protective against these very first world economic powers upon which the success of the Mexican economy depended. In essence, Salinas attempted to eliminate the paradox from Mexican foreign policy, but as a consequence, the price he had to pay was in some respects a compromise on the traditional understanding in Mexico of the revolutionary principles that had for so long guided Mexican foreign policy.

Explaining Mexico's Foreign Policy Activism

Mexican foreign policy in the multilateral arena has traditionally served as the means to showcase Mexico's independence from the United States. Although this has been modified somewhat in the foreign policy activism of recent years, the intent is still very much the same. To give a historical example, Mexico refused to enter into any bilateral military arrangements with the United States during World War II (and immediately afterward) that called for the establishment of U.S. military bases on Mexican soil. Although the demands of wartime and an overall feeling of goodwill in hemispheric relations propelled many other Latin American nations to lease temporarily certain strategic areas of their national territory for the war effort, Mexico clung to its foreign policy principles and resisted this tendency. Although Mexico was one of the few Latin American countries to send troops into the war on behalf of the Allied cause, Mexico perceived such lend-lease arrangements as contrary to the goals of the Revolution and as inherently threatening to its national sovereignty. After the Cuban Revolution of 1959, the Mexican government stubbornly refused to follow U.S. initiatives in the Organization of American States (OAS) for expelling Cuba from the OAS and later for breaking diplomatic relations with the Cuban government of Fidel Castro. Also, Mexico would not accede to the use of the OAS to sanction a U.S.-backed invasion of Guatemala in 1954 and to legitimate the 1965 U.S.-led invasion of the Dominican Republic. Furthermore, Mexico was one of only three Western Hemisphere nations to maintain diplomatic ties with Moscow at the height of the Cold War.

By confronting the United States in these arenas and by nominally supporting revolutionary efforts throughout the hemisphere, Mexico was able to live up to its traditional foreign policy principles and to fulfill its commitment to its own revolutionary history. On a more pragmatic level, Mexico's left-leaning foreign policy and its public support for reformist or revolutionary regimes prevented attempts at interference in its internal affairs by any externally based revolutionary movements that could threaten the internal hegemony of the PRI in Mexican politics or the political stability necessary to attract foreign (i.e., U.S.) investment. The United States, for its part, was more than willing to accept a Mexican foreign policy that nominally conflicted with its own if it managed to keep revolution at bay in Mexico and away from its southern doorstep.

Mexico, though, was never as bold an actor as the rhetoric of its leadership might suggest. For instance, the continuance of regularly scheduled flights to and from Cuba served as a concrete symbol of Mexico's refusal to break relations with Cuba at the behest of the United States. Yet, Mexico also allowed the U.S. Central Intelligence Agency (CIA) to monitor and photograph all persons on such flights. Moreover, Mexico aided the CIA in wiretapping the phones of the Cuban embassy. At the same time, Mexico's economic development strategy during these years consolidated and deepened the nation's financial and overall economic dependence on the United States, which later would play a significant part in the social crises of the 1960s and the economic crises of the 1980s. This dependence would, in turn, be reflected in the shifts in foreign policy orientation of the regimes following these crises.

Perhaps the greatest challenge to the legitimacy of the Revolution occurred in 1968. In that year, the massacre of hundreds of student protestors by government troops at Tlatelolco threw the Mexican political system into its greatest legitimacy crisis since 1910. The administration of

Gustavo Díaz Ordáz was responsible for brutally repressing a student demonstration in Tlatelolco. Luís Echeverría, as Díaz Ordáz's minister of the Interior, was implicated in the crisis. Hence, as Echeverría assumed the Mexican presidency in 1970, he had to not only reestablish the integrity of the political system but also vindicate his own reputation for his part in the student massacre. Echeverría's predicament upon assuming the mantel of the presidency in 1970 was not unlike that faced by Salinas following the 1988 election scandal. In each case, the legitimacy of the political system was questioned and an unpopular president was faced with the uphill battle of winning back public confidence not only in the system but also in his personal ability to lead the nation. In both instances, it may be argued, an activist foreign policy was a critical component in the effort to stabilize the country politically, socially, and economically.

Luís Echeverría chose to pursue an activist and left-leaning foreign policy. He sought to placate the disaffected groups to the left, which were ideologically behind the 1968 student demonstrations and, consequently, were the symbolic targets of the repression of 1968. His efforts toward this end included addressing the domestic issues that spurred the student protests, promoting a foreign policy that rallied around Mexico's revolutionary nationalism, and aligning himself with the leftist and progressive forces in Mexico and elsewhere. In attempting to reestablish regime legitimacy at home by projecting a leftist and activist foreign policy, he necessarily changed Mexico's governmental institutions responsible for deciding and implementing foreign policy and for guiding Mexico's international relations. Mexico under Echeverría asserted itself in the international community at a level unprecedented in Mexico's independent history and broadened the scope and content of Mexico's participation in international organizations and bodies. In fact, Mexico's role as a leader in Third World issues during this time can be considered second only to that of Cuba in the entire Latin American region. Echeverría initiated diplomatic contact with other nations of the world that had previously been considered unimportant and irrelevant to Mexico's interests. Echeverría managed this personally through extensive official visits to other countries and institutionally by expanding Mexican diplomatic and consular services. During his six-year term, Echeverría established formal diplomatic relations for the first time with 62 nations. Mexico under Echeverría also hosted numerous international conferences and often led the nations of Latin America in the formation of various regional economic integration programs such as the Economic System of Latin America and the Latin American Free Trade Association. A flurry of such international activity, although with a markedly different tenor, would not again be seen to such a degree until the administration of Salinas in the late 1980s.

Nevertheless, perhaps the best known and most significant example of this activism in foreign policy was Echeverría's formulation and promotion within the United Nations of a charter on the economic rights and duties of states. Ideologically, Echeverría's foreign policy activism tended to highlight and focus upon the complaints levied by the developing nations of the world against the activities of their military and industrial powers, which were deemed exploitative or interventionist in the affairs of the developing states. Hence, Echeverría's foreign policy activism was not one of integration and insertion into the mainstream of international relations led by the economic and military powers of the world, but a reaction against this very process.

However, as subsequent research into the domestic sources of Echeverría's foreign policy activism has revealed, Echeverría's foreign policy was as much an attempt at finding ways to restructure an imbalanced economic system as it was a measure of securing internal political legitimacy from Mexico's political left. For instance, the crisis of 1968 was basically a product of a failing economic

Mexican president Luís Echeverría talks to reporters during a press conference held at the Palace of Congresses in Rome after he spoke to representatives of more than 100 countries at the UN World Food Conference on November 11, 1979. (Bettmann/Corbis)

development strategy, an inequitable economic distribution policy, and a perceived political unwillingness to deal with such severe structural distortions in the economy. Hence, an obvious, but often overlooked, dimension of Echeverría's foreign policy activism was its central focus on economic issues. For any political considerations in Echeverría's foreign policy, economic issues were the causative dimension. For Echeverría, therefore, in order to "secure" the Revolution, a foreign policy that appeased Mexico's political left with its nationalistic rhetoric and its call for an end to international economic dependency had to be tempered by a more pragmatic policy of economic restructuring that sought not to reduce Mexico's economic dependence on the United States, but to change the nature of this dependence by diversifying it. In actuality, Echeverría's foreign policy continued to fall into line within the greater context of U.S.-Mexican economic relations. While Echeverría searched for investment alternatives abroad, U.S. public and private investment in Mexico continued unabated and even reached levels that surpassed U.S. investment during any previous administration. Mexico's indebtedness to U.S. creditors increased dramatically, and its economic dependence on the United States was further consolidated.

Also, while Echeverría was searching for ways to appease the domestic political left, to diversify the country's economic dependence, and to reestablish the PRI's commitment to the fundamental ideology of the 1910 Revolution, he was careful not to disrupt U.S.-Mexican economic relations nor to contradict the United States on sensitive foreign policy issues. For instance, Echeverría was reluctant to join either the Organization of the Petroleum Exporting Countries (OPEC) or the Non-Aligned Movement because of how each of these forces approached the United States. Also, when the U.S. Jewish community's tourist boycott of Mexico because of its anti-Zionist vote in the United Nations caused a 20 percent drop in tourism revenue during the late 1975 holiday season, Echeverría sent his foreign minister to Israel to, in effect, retract its United Nations vote. The visit to Israel resulted in the foreign minister's eventual resignation and merely highlighted the predominant concern in Mexico's foreign policy not to disrupt further its already weakened economy. In the end, Mexico's economic dependency on U.S. tourism was worth the sacrifice of Mexico's highest foreign policy official.

Therefore, the foreign policy of Echeverría can be explained easily within the context of Mexico's economically dependent relationship with the United States. As previously noted, the resolution of Mexico's internal political crisis and the reestablishment of internal stability demanded a nationalistic and left-leaning posture by the Echeverría government. Because the conditions for following this course of action in his domestic policy were too difficult to meet and the political costs of following such a course too high to risk an attempt at it, especially considering Mexico's economic dependence on the United States, Echeverría was forced to rely almost completely on foreign policy as a vehicle for placating Mexico's disaffected left. Considering its own desire for internal stability in Mexico, the United States was willing to accept Echeverría's left-leaning foreign policy posture, but only under three conditions: first, that it be limited to the multilateral forum; second, that it cooperate with, or at least avoid confrontation with, the United States on politically sensitive issues that presented themselves in the international arena; and third, that it not jeopardize the natural course of U.S.-Mexican bilateral relations traditionally characterized by a sensible pragmatism rather than an intransigent nationalism. Echeverría was extremely careful to adhere to these conditions. On the few occasions when he did not, his government was forced to reformulate its position and was obligated to pay a high political price for its transgression.

This foreign policy activism was continued under the López Portillo administration. Moreover, the discovery of vast petroleum deposits gave the López Portillo administration some breathing room with regard to continuing the more activist and independent foreign policy direction begun by López Portillo's predecessor. This is evident in Mexico's stance regarding Central America and its active participation in the Contadora Group. Yet, Mexico often viewed itself as a mediator between the United States and Central America, representing both interests without repudiating its ties with the United States. Furthermore, Mexico's support for the Sandinistas in Nicaragua and the Farabundo Martí National Liberation Front (FMLN) in El Salvador was effectively countered by its lack of support for the revolutionary movement in Guatemala. This indicates that Mexico's overall policy in the region was not as dissimilar and contradictory with U.S. policy toward the region as it at first might appear.

Therefore, because Mexico's actions with regard to Guatemala and the recognition that ensured stability in Mexico is, in part, dependent on a posture supportive of revolutionary movements in Central America, the United States was willing to tolerate the foreign policy of López Portillo. López Portillo, for his part, was always careful to demonstrate to the United States that he would not take his Central American policy too far. The fact that Mexico agreed at the request of the United States not to invite Cuba to the October 1981 North-South Summit in Cancún serves as a striking example of this implicit agreement.

The economic crisis of 1982 and the subsequent problems associated with Mexico's external debt effectively closed the doors on Mexico's maneuverability in the international arena. The withdrawal of Mexico from that arena; its subsequent redefinition of its Central American policy and its role in the Contadora peace process as a reactive one; and the reestablishment of the primacy of the United States in its foreign relations has further supported the notion of a dependent Mexican foreign policy.

One might ask why the United States was prepared to accept the activism of both Echeverría and López Portillo in the multilateral forum, even, as in the case of the López Portillo administration, beyond reestablishing regime legitimacy within Mexico. A few comments on the global situation in which their activism occurred provide the beginnings of a rational explanation. During Echeverría's *sexenio* there was an overall "global warming" of relations between the countries of the world. It was a time in which U.S.-Soviet relations were entering into a period of detente and the U.S. began exploring the possibilities of reestablishing relations with China. U.S. involvement in Vietnam was winding down and Cuba's activity in the region had been tempered by Soviet pressures. Hence, the rigidity of the international system due to Cold War tensions was becoming more flexible. This development consequently offered a limited avenue for increased Third World activism at the formal international level. Echeverría benefited from this environment, and his foreign policy activism was more readily tolerated in Washington in the context of this environment.

During López Portillo's tenure in office, the situation was very similar. At the beginning of his administration, López Portillo benefited from U.S. president Jimmy Carter's more tolerant and permissive approach to the region. Within this conciliatory and hands-off environment fostered by Carter, López Portillo sought to stretch the influence of Mexico in the region. López Portillo began to distance Mexico more fully from the United States by asserting a more independent and confrontational stance in the country's bilateral relations with its northern neighbor. López Portillo utilized the Central American regional context as the testing ground for the expression of a more independent foreign policy orientation. For example, the Carter administration, in keeping with its noninterventionist platform, hesitated in taking definitive action with regard to the Sandinista Revolution in Nicaragua in 1979. Carter vacillated between acquiescence and criticism of the revolutionary impulse in Nicaragua and the rest of Central America, and his foreign policy toward the region was ambiguous. Mexico's open and hostile break with the Somoza regime and its subsequent support for the Sandinistas in Nicaragua and for the FMLN in El Salvador were realized in the wake of this U.S. ambiguity.

Additionally, López Portillo was able to use Mexico's petroleum wealth to back up materially its position in Central America in the wake of mounting U.S. criticism. Also, following so nearly on the heels of the OPEC oil embargo, López Portillo was able to capitalize on the U.S. need for secured access to Mexico's petroleum reserves both as a bargaining chip in its Central American policy and as a means to increase Mexico's level of international borrowing. Yet, the mismanagement of petroleum funds, the miscalculation of future earnings from increased petroleum production, a massive indebtedness to U.S. public and private sources of credit at levels even greater than those under Echeverría, and the ideological repolarization of the region after Ronald Reagan assumed the U.S. presidency in 1980 all contributed to the withdrawal of Mexico as a leading player in the Central American crisis and from an outspoken activism in its foreign policy in general. Despite Mexico's continued interest in the region, the problems of its economic dependence on the United States and the need to restructure its economy forced Mexico into a foreign policy posture more aligned and less confrontational with that of Washington.

One of the most successful aspects of the Mexican political system has been its remarkable adaptability to changes in internal and international conditions in order to maintain the nation's social and political equilibrium. By so doing, Mexican governments have been able to guarantee the condition of internal stability that is so crucial to both the United States and to the Mexican government. In order to maintain such stability, however, the Mexican government must consistently address the important nationalistic and anti-U.S. sentiment that sprung from the social revolution of 1910. Likewise, the United States, for its part, has recognized the need to permit a certain degree of nationalism and anti-U.S. rhetoric in Mexican politics in order to keep Mexico stable and thus to defend its own national security. The traditional left in the United States as well as Mexico has accepted a more radical foreign policy rhetoric as a necessary response to these contradictory demands. However, a more radical foreign policy rhetoric does not signal an independent foreign policy reality.

Although most scholars note the complexity of the Mexican situation, both internally and externally, the overriding consensus is that Mexican foreign policy is generally defined and determined by the country's dependent relationship with the United States. Yet, the U.S. desire for continued economic and political stability in Mexico has allowed Mexico a certain degree of maneuverability and independent posturing within this essentially dependent relationship.

Mexican foreign policy, despite its sometimes ideological and anti-U.S. framework, is nearly always pursued with an eye toward U.S. reaction and response. As has been noted, Mexico pursued a foreign policy relatively independent of the United States only when the international situation allowed for a greater degree of foreign policy maneuverability. But even in the context of a more flexible global environment, Mexico's ability is limited further by its economic needs. Given the opportunity to assume a more active and independent role in foreign policy, Mexico has been able to take advantage of such an opportunity only when its economic position either demanded it or permitted it. Echeverría used an activist foreign policy stance to seek diversification of its economic dependence. López Portillo's foreign policy activism was possible in the wake of an economic boom (though short lived) spurred by its vast petroleum finds. Salinas, unlike López Portillo, did not have the benefit of an economic windfall to support a more independent foreign policy posture. Although both Salinas and Echeverría did have to respond personally to political crises of legitimacy, Echeverría, unlike Salinas, had the benefit of an ideologically polarized global environment within which to maneuver his foreign policy. Salinas had to operate under the recognition that the United States, following the collapse of the Soviet Union, was an uncontested global hegemon.

In addition to the external political limitations placed upon Salinas's ability to conduct an anti-U.S., nationalistic foreign policy, the economic problems of the country closed other potential avenues to expressing nominal independence in terms of its international relations. Nevertheless, because of the importance of history and tradition in shaping the Mexican national consciousness, even Salinas did not abandon completely the fundamental elements of postrevolutionary Mexican foreign policy.

Though the traditions are present in the foreign policy of Salinas, the overt activism in promoting them is not. It is true that Salinas limited his foreign policy options by following a program aimed at relinquishing state control over various sectors of the economy, by relaxing restrictions on direct foreign investment, and by moving toward an integrated economy with the United States and Canada through participation in NAFTA. But it should be noted that internal stability, as well as substantive economic growth, demanded such a foreign policy posture. Salinas's personal popularity throughout his tenure in office and the initial economic success of his program seemed to have borne this out. Therefore, with regard to the most fundamental goal of Mexican foreign policy, that of ensuring a healthy economy and a stable polity, the only major exception in Salinas's foreign policy compared with that of his predecessors is that Salinas, to a much greater degree, demonstrated a willingness to publicly acknowledge the close ties and the historical dependence that have always existed between the United States and Mexico and that have always been an extremely significant factor in Mexican national and international politics. More importantly, Salinas accepted this fact and tried to capitalize on it. The evidence seems to bear this out. Mexico under Salinas experienced a remarkable transformation in foreign policy posturing, although the consequences of Salinas's foreign policy direction are still hotly debated and sometimes openly criticized. Nevertheless, it is important to recognize that the criticism faced by Salinas in pursuing this course of action, be it from internal or external sources, placed important restrictions and limitations on the ability of Salinas to generate a fundamentally "new" foreign policy that was less ideologically motivated and more openly pragmatic.

The United States, for its part, was willing to accept a certain degree of independent posturing by Mexico in the foreign policy arena, even by Salinas, as it was fully aware that such activity was still an important requisite for the maintenance of internal political stability in Mexico, especially since the Mexican political system under Salinas began to take its first tentative steps out of semiauthoritarianism and toward democratic liberalization. Yet, the economic dependence of Mexico on the United States, always a dominating factor in pursuing any course of policy in any administration, effectively limited a truly independent foreign policy.

Since the Salinas years, Mexico's foreign policy, and its international relations with the United States particularly, have continued to reflect Mexico's foreign policy traditions, but within the context of the new globalizing environment. Carlos Salinas propelled Mexico into the global arena as a proactive and engaged participant, shedding the country's traditional reluctance and hesitations about international engagement. The subsequent administrations of Ernesto Zedillo and Vicente Fox continued down the foreign policy path forged by Salinas, and Mexico's current president, Felípe Calderón, appears poised to do the same.

In the case of Zedillo, his administration's foreign policy activism was tempered both by the domestic political turmoil he inherited from Salinas and by the economic crisis related to the crash of the Mexican peso in December 1994. Each of these factors contributed to Zedillo's assuming an accommodating, nonconfrontational posture in the country's international relations. Nevertheless, Zedillo's commitment to deepening Mexico's participation in the global project of neoliberal reform and strengthening its economic bonds with its NAFTA trading partners is unquestioned.

Vicente Fox promised a new manifestation of Mexico's place in the world and the possibilities of an even more influential leadership role in it. The peaceful transition from a

President George W. Bush and Mexican president Vicente Fox shake hands during a visit to Savage Hall at the University of Toledo in Toledo, Ohio, on September 6, 2001. Fox pressed his case for immigration overhaul to the U.S. Congress earlier in the day, urging greater trust between neighbors as the basis for "a new partnership in North America." (AP/Wide World Photos)

PRI government to a PAN government bolstered Mexico's democratic credentials and thus enhanced its reputation among the global community. Perhaps more importantly, the relative stability of Mexico's democratic transition gave it renewed leadership within the Western Hemisphere. The fact that Fox came from the PAN also gave Mexico an opportunity to reevaluate many of its postrevolutionary foreign policy traditions, and even the chance to break with some of the more anachronistic manifestations of this tradition. For instance, Fox was able to negotiate with the United States on traditionally contentious issues such as immigration reform, border control, and drug trafficking in a spirit characterized more by a cooperative internationalism rather than by polite, but cautious and defensive, nationalism. Also, Fox was able to reorient the debate regarding such traditionally nationalistic foreign policy matters as foreign investment and foreign ownership of property within Mexico, and Mexico's relationship with Cuba and other revolutionary or populist governments in the Americas. With regard to the latter case, the Fox administration, in fact, moved away from its traditionally uncritical support of the Castro government to a posture more in line with the U.S. position on Cuba as it related to the need for democratic transformation in Cuba. Although Fox neither broke off relations with Cuba nor embraced the U.S. economic embargo with Cuba, he also did not shy away from leveling pointed criticism at Cuba's antidemocratic and repressive government, which represented a shift away from Mexico's traditional postrevolution foreign policy of a nonjudgmental and impartial noninvolvement in criticizing the nature of any other country's domestic politics.

Being from the north of Mexico, and representing the probusiness and pro-U.S. inclination of his National Action Party, Fox clearly approached the United States in a spirit of enthusiastic collaboration and partnership. For its part, the United States, at that time led by George W. Bush, a Texas conservative, welcomed a new era of positive collaboration with Mexico. And for a brief period, the positive predisposition of both countries toward the other, complemented by the personal expressions of solidarity and friendship between the two countries' leaders, seemed to be inaugurating a new phase in the bilateral relationship, even to the point of a breakthrough in the traditionally contentious issues of border control and immigration reform. However, this changed following the terrorist attacks in the United States on September 11, 2001. After this event, the budding possibilities for a new relationship that had blossomed in the new environment withered under the weight of traditional suspicions and antagonisms. The Bush administration, responding to the new threats, placed its relationship with Mexico on the backburner, reemphasizing to Mexico that its subordinate status in the relationship was still the operational norm. For the remainder of his term, and in the context of the renewed xenophobia that the 9/11 attacks produced in the United States, Fox was unable to get the United States to consider an immigration reform agenda that reflected a willingness to accommodate Mexico's concerns. Further, when the United States tried to pressure Mexico, then sitting on the UN Security Council, into supporting the UN resolution authorizing the use of force in Iraq against the Saddam Hussein regime—implicitly threatening Mexico in the process with negative consequences should it refuse to support the resolution—the old charges of U.S. interventionism and disrespect for Mexico's sovereignty emerged in the context of Mexico's foreign policy, and particularly in its relations with the United States. Not only was the Iraq War very unpopular in Mexico, but America's heavy-handedness in twisting arms to garner international support tapped into the basest elements of traditional Mexican suspicions regarding U.S. intentions toward the country.

Fox never abandoned his public posture of friendship and collaboration with the United States, but the opportunity for a significant transformation of Mexican foreign policy from the traditions of its postrevolution past were lost. And the open position of the United States against the candidacy of the populist PRD candidate, Andrés Manuel López Obrador, in the 2006 presidential elections, and popular Mexican reactions to the United States on this front, merely confirmed the continued persistence of foreign policy traditions in Mexico and the contentious dimensions of U.S.-Mexican bilateral relations, which continue to define Mexican foreign policy and U.S.-Mexican relations under the current Mexican administration of Felípe Calderón.

Concluding Remarks.   As this chapter has demonstrated, Mexico has a fascinating and unique political system and foreign policy. Mexico clearly comes out of the Western political tradition that emphasizes democratic government, popular sovereignty, and global engagement. Its political system and governing institutions attest to this tradition. However, Mexico's geographic location neighboring the United States has produced some interesting dimensions to Mexico's political and institutional development. The historical threats to Mexican independence and sovereignty posed by sharing a border with a country that has historically demonstrated expansionist ambitions has produced a political system that demands a strong and stable government, capable of defending the country's territorial integrity in front of the world. Its need to contain destabilizing forces within the country that might compromise the state's ability to defend its national sovereignty have also produced a political system prone to co-optation and control within the context of a revolutionary history. For instance, the Mexican military has been successfully subordinated to civilian authority, social revolutions have been contained, and mechanisms for incorporating popular views into a relatively closed political system have been built into the functional structure of Mexico's governing apparatus. The outcome seems to have been a semiauthoritarian political system, which succeeded in creating domestic institutions and structures that have perhaps made the gradual and continual transition to a more open and democratic system feasible and stable. Surely, the unique elements of Mexico's political system will remain as factors in its evolution, but the traditional adaptability built into this unique system should serve Mexico well as it continues to reform and transform itself on the path to democratic reform and consolidation.

References
Bailey, John. *Governing Mexico: The Statecraft of Crisis Management.* New York: St. Martin's Press, 1988.

Camp, Roderic Ai. *Mexico's Mandarins: Crafting a Power Elite for the Twenty-First Century.* Berkeley: University of California Press, 2002.

Camp, Roderic Ai. *Mexico's Military on the Democratic Stage.* Washington, D.C.: Center for Strategic and International Studies, 2005.

Camp, Roderic Ai. *Politics in Mexico: The Democratic Consolidation,* 5th edition. New York: Oxford University Press, 2007.

Castañeda, Jorge. "Revolution and Foreign Policy: Mexico's Experience," In *Latin American International Politics: Ambitions, Capabilities and the National Interest of Mexico, Brazil, and Argentina,* ed. Carlos A. Astiz. Notre Dame, IN: Notre Dame University Press, 1969.

Castañeda, Jorge G. *Perpetuating Power: How Mexican Presidents Were Chosen.* Translated by Padraic Arthur Smithies. New York: New York Press, 2000.

Centeno, Miguel Angel. *Democracy within Reason: Technocratic Revolution in Mexico,* 2nd ed. University Park: Pennsylvania State University Press, 1997.

Chand, Vikram K. *Mexico's Political Awakening.* South Bend, IN: University of Notre Dame Press, 2001.

Davidow, Jeffrey. *The Bear and the Porcupine: The U.S. and Mexico.* Princeton, NJ: Markus Weiner Publishers, 2007.

Domínguez, Jorge I., and Rafael Fernández de Castro. *The United States and Mexico: Between Partnership and Conflict.* New York: Routledge, 2001.

Eisenstadt, Todd A. *Courting Democracy in Mexico: Party Strategies and Electoral Institutions.* New York: Cambridge University Press, 2007.

Erfani, Julie A. *The Paradox of the Mexican State: Rereading Sovereignty from Independence to NAFTA.* Boulder, CO: Lynne Rienner, 1995.

Grayson, George W. *Mexican Messiah: Andrés Manuel López Obrador.* University Park: Pennsylvania State University Press, 2007.

Hughes, Sallie. *Newsrooms in Conflict: Journalism and the Democratization of Mexico.* Pittsburgh: University of Pittsburgh Press, 2006.

Lawson, Chappell H. *Building the Fourth Estate: Democratization and the Rise of a Free Press in Mexico.* Berkeley: University of California Press, 2002.

Levy, Daniel, and Kathleen Bruhn. *Mexico: The Struggle for Democratic Development.* Berkeley: University of California Press, 2001.

Mora, Frank O., and Jeanne A. K. Hey, eds., *Latin American and Caribbean Foreign Policy.* New York: Rowman and Littlefield, 2003.

Peschard-Sverdrup, Armand B., and Sara R. Rioff, eds. *Mexican Governance: From Single-Party Rule to Divided Government.* Washington, D.C.: Center for Strategic and International Studies, 2005.

Rodríguez, Victoria, ed. *Women's Political Participation in Mexican Political Life.* Boulder, CO: Westview, 1998.
Roett, Riordan, ed. *The Challenge of Institutional Reform in Mexico.* Boulder, CO: Lynne Rienner, 1995.
Tulchin, Joseph S., and Andrew D. Selee, eds. *Mexico's Politics and Society in Transition.* Boulder, CO: Lynne Rienner, 2003.

CHAPTER FOUR
Society and Culture

This chapter explores some of the more salient aspects of Mexican society, arts, and culture. If there is one theme that binds this section together, it is the complexity of Mexican identity and the quest to uncover this identity, define it, refine it, and promote it through social, cultural, and artistic media and production. But this has not been an easy project for Mexicans to undertake. The question of what constitutes the Mexican identity is one that has engulfed Mexico in many ways. It has troubled Mexicans of all different socio-economic classes and ethnic backgrounds, and it is loaded with contradictions, both real and imagined. Mexico's social and cultural institutions have evolved in ways that have vacillated between different notions of Mexican identity, and Mexicans continue to grapple with this question as they celebrate who they are in the process.

MEXICAN IDENTITY AND THE IMPORTANCE OF "MESTIZAJE"

Mexico and Mexicans are a country and a people in search of an identity. Mexican writer Octavio Paz wrote about this aspect of Mexico in his classic work entitled *The Labyrinth of Solitude*. Mexico, Paz argues, struggles with its identity because the country and its people are born out of a series of paradoxes and contradictions, which have a tendency to emphasize the least common denominator. Mexico and Mexicans also embrace a kind of resigned fatalism about their reality, which further complicates the question of identity and conditions attitudes regarding aspirations and hopes for the future. Mexico is a country that possesses

many wonderful and beautiful traditions and cultural artifacts that go back thousands of years. But modern Mexico
is a country born out of violence, born out of forced integration and racial mixing, born out of conquest and pillage
and subjugation. It has suffered indignities of chronic interventions by stronger forces throughout the world. And it
continues to be a country where indicators of success are
measured by how well the country, and particularly its
economy, compares with its disproportionately stronger
and more wealthy northern neighbor, the United States.

In spite of this, Mexicans have managed to forge a sense
of common identity out of this history. Mexico's troubled
history has not only offered a kind of shared experience that
all Mexicans can call their own, but it has also produced a
richness of culture and a pride among Mexicans about this
culture and its impact on the larger world around them.

One of the main features of this common identity is the
concept of "mestizaje." Mestizaje refers primarily to an ethnic and cultural blending, or mixture, of elements of the
country's pre-Columbian indigenous peoples and cultures
with those of the Spanish colonizers. In modern Mexico, this
concept also can refer to the assimilation of modern, West-
ernized cultural norms with both the colonial and indigenous traditions that have evolved over the years.

José Vasconcelos, a prominent Mexican intellectual and
educator during Mexico's early 20th-century revolutionary
period, coined the concept of *la raza cósmica,* or the cosmic race, not only to capture the uniqueness of this process
of mestizaje but also to celebrate the magnificence and even
superiority of the Mexican people. Vasconcelos's conception
of the cosmic race was partly in reaction to a current of
thought that promoted the idea that racial and ethnic mixture between culturally inferior indigenous peoples and
their culturally superior European colonizers diluted and
weakened the national character. Vasconcelos attempted to
stand this thinking on its head and to propose that the

blending of cultures and peoples strengthened national character and further enriched Mexico's and its citizens' standing in the world. In other words, out of the Conquest of Mexico and the subjugation of the country's indigenous populations to the hegemony of the Spanish colonizer was born a mestizo nation that manifested the best of both the indigenous and the European peoples and cultures, all bundled into that one, enigmatic identity of the Mexican.

Mexican Concepts of Family and Marriage

The institutions of marriage and family in Mexico are central to Mexican life, for many reasons. On the one hand, marriage and family are inextricably linked. Marriage, in a sense, both expands the family unit and binds this extended family unit together. And it is the family in Mexico that provides a shelter of sorts against an uncertain and hostile external environment.

Octavio Paz, in his *The Labyrinth of Solitude,* discusses this aspect of the Mexican psyche, which views the world outside of the family with suspicion and trepidation. He argues that Mexicans live their lives in society hiding behind masks that both protect and isolate Mexicans from one another. The logical consequence of this internal and self-reflective element of the Mexican condition is to elevate the family to a status of primary importance in the private as well as public lives of Mexicans. And threats to the family are thus perceived as threats to the very fabric of social stability and personal security and well-being. However, because Mexicans consider the family to be the main institution through which interpersonal relations and trust between one another can be obtained, elaborate and complex social rituals and cultural activities center around the family.

Marriages become the vehicle through which families can join forces in front of the larger world and through which individual opportunities and expanded social networks can take form.

The compadrazgo system is another way beyond the institutions of marriage that families can be broadened and cross-class social networks formed. Through compadrazgo, or "godparenting," Mexican families can forge alliances that even transcend blood relations. The compadrazgo relationship is often built upon a patron-client model, and many times with one partner in the relationship generally socially or economically disadvantaged relative to the other partner. The compadre, who is usually the more powerful or wealthy partner in the relationship, assumes some responsibility for the well-being of his godson or goddaughter, and by extension the larger family. In return for his patronage, often expressed by providing career or educational opportunities, the compadre can expect the family to be a loyal ally and supporter in the compadre's larger political, social, or economic ambitions.

SOCIAL STRUCTURES AND CLASS/ ETHNIC RELATIONS

It would be inaccurate and unjust to think of Mexico unreflectively as a society of a vast majority of extremely poor Indians from the countryside contrasted with a very few extremely wealthy and cosmopolitan elites of European descent, with very little in between. Certainly there are very poor indigenous Mexicans who are subject to crushing discrimination and minimal access to opportunity for social advancement. And there are also extremely wealthy Mexicans whose global power and influence are considerable. But as any visitor to Mexico realizes, the country also has a very considerable middle class and the majority of Mexicans fall somewhere in between the very rich and the very poor. Nevertheless, Mexico is a deeply divided society, and the divisions are stark. Income inequality can be dramatic, especially between rural Mexico and urban Mexico, and structural impediments to social mobility are real and entrenched, and they affect many people. What is also clear, though, is that the inequality and lack of access to opportunity that does exist in Mexico are connected to race, ethnicity, and even gender in Mexican society. What is the nature of Mexican society? And how do the racial, class, and ethnic dimensions of Mexican society shape Mexico's history and its contemporary reality?

Mexican society is a blend of very culturally and ethnically distinct peoples. The existence of large, settled, and complex pre-Columbian indigenous civilizations and peoples prior to the Spanish conquest has not only made the process of racial and ethnic mixture difficult and troublesome but also complicated the process of constructing a unique national identity. Many Mexicans still identify less as members of some kind of national community and more in terms of their local or ethnic communities. And efforts to bridge the stark differences that often separate the different peoples of Mexico have been a major part of public policy and intellectual debate.

In fact, during the colonial period, the European settlers and administrators believed that the best way to manage these differences was simply to recognize that they existed and, instead of trying to encourage a process of either aggressive social integration or elimination, to create two parallel worlds that existed side by side that were governed primarily by their own conditions and practices. Thus, colonial Mexico evolved as a place where the concept of different worlds defined by ethnicity, region, cultural practices, or economic status was actively encouraged and accepted, or at least not questioned.

Evidence of this was the creation, for instance, of hospitals, schools, and convents that separated Mexicans according to ethnic identity. Social conventions such as the institutions of marriage or property ownership also varied according to the different worlds in which people lived. And while the Spanish colonial authorities established Roman Catholicism as the only officially tolerated form of religious expression, the practice of indigenous and other non-Catholic religious beliefs and rituals continued with minimal interference by the enforcers of religious orthodoxy. The replication of these worlds, differentiated by racial, ethnic, and class lines throughout the colonial period and even up through the present day, have led some to speak of Mexico not in the singular, but in the plural. The phrase "many Mexicos," coined by the Mexicanist scholar Lesley Byrd Simpson, captures this sentiment.

Evidence of the continuing importance and relevance of class and ethnic identity in Mexican society is also present in the country's modern, postindependence society. The independence movement of 1810 was led by the criollo priest Miguel Hidalgo y Costilla and continued by the mestizo priest José María Morelos, but it was a movement that not only represented a quest for political separation from Spain but also captured the voice of Mexico's lower classes and indigenous peoples. In the middle of the 19th century, Mexico's first and only full-blood indigenous president, Benito Juárez, seemed to have broken through the confines that kept indigenous Mexico apart from Spanish and mestizo Mexico; but whatever chance this presented in the forging of a unified nation was shattered first by the French intervention and occupation of the country and later by the racist and classist elements of positivism espoused by Porfirio Díaz that thrived on the conceptual discriminations inherent to the notion of "many Mexicos."

And even in the 20th century, the Mexican Revolution divided along the lines of racial, ethnic, and class identity. The agrarian, peasant-based movement of Emiliano Zapata, which resonated with Mexico's indigenous peoples, clashed with the more nonindigenous, popular class faction that constituted the bulk of support for Pancho Villa. And both of these groups

*Masked Zapatista rebel women walk near the village of San José la
Esperanza August 26, 1999, following a clash a day earlier between
Zapatista supporters and the army troops near Mexico's southern
border with Guatemala. Chiapas, which borders Guatemala and is
one of Mexico's poorest states, has been the scene of simmering
tensions since the Zapatistas launched an uprising in 1994 for Indian
rights. (Reuters/Corbis)*

clashed with the ultimately victorious revolutionary faction
dominated by criollo ranching elites from the north in collaboration with the urban working and professional classes.

Yet, the governing consensus that emerged out of the Revolution, and that found expression even in an embrace of
Mexico's rich and varied ethnic diversity through the *indi-
genista* movement, could not overcome the ethnic, linguistic, and cultural divisions inherent to Mexico. The 1994
Zapatista uprising, which claimed to speak on behalf of all of
Mexico's oppressed indigenous peoples and poor underclass,
is simply a modern, contemporary manifestation of the different ethnic, class, and socioeconomic elements that continue to define the country's reality.

Mexico's cultural and ethnic diversity is a source of cultural richness and national pride, but it is also a regular and continuous source of social conflict. Such conflict is likely to remain present in Mexico in the years to come, with occasional outbursts of protest and violence among and between Mexico's different ethnic populations. Nevertheless, nearly all Mexicans understand that their existence as a nation depends upon finding a way to continue to embrace and celebrate the multicultural and multiethnic identities that define them as they also continue to work through the lingering sociopolitical structures that divide them along class and ethnic lines.

GENDER RELATIONS AND THE CONCEPTS OF MACHISMO/ *MARIANISMO*

In Mexico, male identity is wrapped up in the notion of machismo, which is most often associated with virility, power, and authority. An image very commonly associated with the Mexican male is that of the Latin lover, who is seductive, charming, smooth, and chivalrous on the one hand but also deceptive, unfaithful, and morally suspect on the other. Certainly, these characteristics do make up one part of what can be observed in the attitudes and behaviors of men in Mexican society. However, there are other components of the stereotype that may apply equally and that often are overlooked. For instance, male identity in Mexico also centers around a strong commitment to the family, both as its material provider and as its defender.

Female identity in Mexico, however, is a more complex subject. Women are often held up to the ideals of moral purity, subordination to the male authority, and an ideal of virtue that is almost impossible for any human being to live up to. People who study gender identity in Mexico often refer to the concept of *marianismo* as an explanation of the place that the woman occupies in Mexican society. This concept is placed both in opposition to and complementary to the notion of machismo as applied to the Mexican male identity. *Marianismo* explains female identity in Mexico as the equivalent of all the features of the Virgin Mary. She is a long-suffering, sinless mother who is venerated as the repository of family values in the face of a hostile world and untrustworthy and morally inferior men. She is the glue of the family unit who not only keeps the moral standing of the family intact but also assumes the primary role as family caretaker in its day-to-day existence. While the *marianismo* image affords the Mexican woman a privileged space within Mexican culture and society, and especially within the family unit, it also can be very limiting and constraining at the same time. Much like the image of the Virgin Mary, there is very little, if any, social space or tolerance for human failing on the part of the woman. While the Mexican man who cavorts and philanders lives up to an expectation of the machismo ideal, the Mexican woman can brook no such moral laxity in her own life without damaging not only her reputation but also, worse, the integrity of her family. Further, Mexican women who fail to live up to the ideals of *marianismo* may be categorized by another, less flattering image of female identity that is particular to Mexico: *malinchismo.*

Malinchismo is a term that is derived from the name of one of Mexico's most notorious females, Malinche. Malinche was the Aztec woman given to the Spanish conqueror Hernán Cortés by a group of Maya defeated by the Spaniards during the early phases of the Conquest of Mexico. Malinche became both personal concubine and translator for Cortés throughout the Conquest of Mexico. History has not been kind to Malinche, and she has long been maligned by many in Mexico as a traitor to her people for assisting Cortés and the Spanish as they went about defeating the Aztecs. Furthermore, Malinche bore an illegitimate son to Cortés. This individual, the product of the illegitimate union between the European conqueror and the native woman, is the symbolic face of modern Mexico today. And so the role of Malinche as both mistress and translator to Cortés embodies all of those aspects of female identity that bear the scars of a nation built on the ashes of conquest and forced miscegenation. A woman who fails to live up to the ideals of moral purity, virtue, and the family betrays not only the ideal of womanhood but also the notion of Mexican national identity itself.

MEXICAN MUSIC, SONG, AND DANCE

In the realm of popular culture, music and dance are very much a part of Mexican daily life. Mexico is home to many folkloric dance traditions that combine the colorful costumes and dances of the indigenous peoples of the region with those brought over originally from Spain and later from the United States. Opportunities are plentiful throughout Mexico to partake of its vibrant music and dance culture.

The traditional music most associated with Mexico is the mariachi. Mariachi music today is characterized by players dressed in vibrant and colorful costumes that look like a cross between ranching clothes and frilly tuxedos. Also unmistakable in the mariachi attire is the large sombrero, or what many call the 10-gallon cowboy hat, that matches in color and style the rest of the mariachi costume. Mariachi bands are generally ensemble groups composed of anywhere from a handful of players to groups of a dozen or more. Although the instruments, sounds, tempos, and melodies of mariachi music have evolved over the years, what most today know as mariachi music includes trumpets, violins, and a mixture of different guitar types. Chief among them are the typical six-string guitar; the five-string vihuela, which keeps the rhythm of the music; and the larger, six-string *guitarrón,* which is used for bass sounds and plays at the lower pitches. The vihuela and the *guitarrón* are musical instruments unique to the mariachi band. Occasionally, for larger mariachi bands, the harp might also be included as a throwback to the origins and traditions of the genre, when the harp was a more common presence.

One might trace mariachi music back in Mexican history all the way to the colonial period, with the arrival of the folk guitarist among the Spanish exports to its American colonies. However, what we know as mariachi music today really has its roots in the late 19th century and emerges out of the central western regions of the country, particularly from the traditionally ranching states of Jalisco and Guanajuato. The first recordings of mariachi music took place toward the end of the first decade of the 20th century, on the cusp of the Mexican Revolution. Mariachi music, rooted in the Mexican countryside, was a contrast both to the cosmopolitanism of the Porfirian regime and to the popular perception of the Porfirian regime's preference for foreign culture and ideas. For this reason, following the Mexican Revolution, many Mexicans embraced mariachi music as a symbol of the country's unique identity and a source of nationalist pride. And it was at this time that mariachi music, while continuing to express traditional elements of the folk life and culture of rural Mexico, also began to embrace more fully themes of social and revolutionary consciousness in the lyrics of the songs its musicians composed, played, and sang.

Today, one can hear mariachi music incorporating elements of almost every musical genre on the market, from classical to jazz to pop. For instance, mariachi bands have recently been heard to incorporate hip-hop beats and classic rock-and-roll tunes in their repertoire. But there are a few types of music that the mariachi sound typifies and that are most often associated with the style. The most important historically among these types of mariachi music is perhaps the *son*. However, other styles of music are also closely associated with mariachi style: These are the *canción ranchera,* the *bolero ranchero,* the *huapango,* and the mariachi polka. Each type varies in terms of tempo, rhythm, and melody, but the instrumentation and basic orchestration of each type remain distinctly within an identifiable mariachi sound. For instance, the *canción ranchera* has a festive, up-tempo swing, whereas the *bolero ranchero* has a slower and more deliberate rhythmic quality that is more conducive to the mood of languorous ballads.

The mariachi band and the mariachi style of music have become so completely identified with Mexican folk culture that in just about every major city one can find a section of town where mariachi bands congregate and offer their services on the spot to anyone passing by willing to contract out a song. In fact, in many places, all one needs to do is to seek out the *Plaza de los Mariachis* and he or she will find the full expression of a thriving mariachi music and folk culture, one that is eager and ready to entertain. Needless to say, mariachi bands are staples at many traditional cultural events such as wedding receptions, birthdays, *quinceañeras,* or any other festive social occasion. And one can regularly find mariachi bands in full regalia roaming around the floors of local restaurants enticing the patrons to order table-side musical entertainment along with their meals.

Corridos

Corridos are a part of another folk musical and storytelling tradition in Mexico. Popularized during the Mexican Revolution, corridos are essentially stories of national heroes or mythological figures in Mexican history told through the medium of an oral musical tradition. It would not be too far of a stretch to liken the Mexican corrido to the oral traditions of ancient Greek and Roman epic poetry; in a sense, the purpose and intent of the Mexican corrido is the same: to pass along in song and verse in front of popular audiences the mythologized stories of the great icons or characters representative of the epic of the Mexican Revolution or other notable moments and individuals in Mexico's history.

Although mostly associated with the 1910 Revolution, the corrido in Mexico has its roots in the romance ballads that Spanish conquistadors brought with them from Europe as early as the 16th century. These ballads generally chart, as do the contemporary corridos of Mexico today, the exploits of a brave and valiant individual in the midst of very difficult or trying circumstances. Sometimes, the outcome for the hero is not positive, but even in failure, the hero retains his honor and virtue. This remains true even within the contemporary tradition of the *narco-corrido,* which glorifies the lives and the often violent deaths of drug traffickers and criminals. Yet, other corridos speak of romantic conquests or of unrequited love. And all of them provide social and political commentary in the context of a nationalistic medium of cultural expression.

Mexicans continue to create and sing corridos for the same reasons that they always have: to express frustrations with the social and political realities that govern their lives and communities, to criticize and mock politicians and other public figures, to glorify local achievements or cultural greatness, and to keep alive the memory of important moments in Mexico's social or political history. They are also a very enjoyable pastime for Mexicans when they gather at parties or in local saloons (cantinas). Unfortunately, many people associate corridos with drunken men singing in the tavern. And while the corrido certainly is a staple of barroom camaraderie in Mexico, its reach and cultural relevance go well beyond that stereotype. It has been, and continues to be, an important part of popular oral history traditions in Mexico; the popular knowledge of national historical events and icons can be directly attributed to the stories told in corridos.

Very often, the same story will be told in many different ways and by many different performers with the intent of embellishing or elaborating upon yet another element of the protagonist's character or the context. In this way, corridos can even be continuously reshaped to address themes that may be more relevant to the environment and social conditions of the moment in which it is recast and retold.

The corrido can be accompanied by musical instruments, which are usually one or two guitars, and maybe a fiddle or an accordion; however, it is very common for Mexicans to belt out corridos a capella, or without accompaniment. In terms of lyrical composition, the corrido itself follows a very structured pattern. Usually, a corrido is composed of four-line stanzas and follows a rhyme scheme of ABCB. There is no limit to the length of a corrido or its number of stanzas, which can vary greatly depending on the type of story told and the detail with which the composer and lyricist want to provide. But the presentation and format of the content are fairly standard. In the first few lines of the corrido, the singer (*corridista*) introduces the subject of the song and issues a personal invitation to sit down and to listen to the story about to be told. In the next segment of the song, the singer provides the particular context and gives the listener all the relevant details: who the main protagonist is, where the story took place, when it happened, and the other parties involved. Then the song proceeds to tell the story of the specific event, primarily addressing the reality of the protagonist's situation and his or her goals or concerns as they relate to the event. Eventually, the singer reveals the story's outcome and points to its moral. Finally, with the lesson provided, the balladeer ends the song by bidding the listener farewell, usually exhorting the listener to remember the story and to take it to heart.

Some of Mexico's most famous corridos came out of the Mexican Revolution, which is quite understandable since the convulsiveness of the experience was so profound and far reaching and the characters so plentiful and colorful.

One of the most famous corridos is *"La Cucaracha,"* or "The Cockroach," the tempo and refrain of which are nearly universally recognized. There are dozens of versions of this corrido, nearly all of them containing verses that refer to the different warring factions and prominent personalities of the Mexican Revolution. Corridos of Mexico's most colorful revolutionary, Pancho Villa, also abound. And many other corridos tell the stories of famous battles of the Revolution. An interesting contemporary phenomenon regarding the corrido has been its recent resurgence in popularity among Mexico's youth culture. Traditionally, the corrido is associated with old themes, traditions, and characters in the country's history that Mexico's modern youth tend to associate with bygone days and past glories. However, the corrido format and style have merged with popular street culture, and particularly youth gang and drug-trafficking activities, to create a revision of the genre that many now refer to as the *narco-corrido*.

The *narco-corrido* is most associated with a performer named Chalino Sánchez, who popularized the corrido by writing stories and singing about some of Mexico's most notorious contemporary drug dealers and traffickers. In these *narco-corridos,* the drug traffickers are often presented as modern day Robin Hoods, who give back to their communities and whose intentions are noble and good. Of course, the heroes of these *narco-corridos* are also examples of individuals who challenge and defy authority, which is a theme that always resonates among the youth of every generation. Some have even spoken of these *narco-corridos* as Mexico's cultural equivalent of hip-hop music in the United States, playing the same countercultural role, only using the traditional style and format of the corrido instead. Nevertheless, while this new type of corrido speaks of very different characters in very different contemporary contexts, the basic thrust of them is the same. They still, as always, tell stories of bravery and courage in the face of difficult circumstances, and they provide commentary on the social context and issues facing the youth of Mexico today.

SOCCER IN MEXICO

The national sport of Mexico, as in most other Latin American countries, is soccer, or *fútbol* (football). Today, Mexicans are passionate soccer fans and the country fields a national team comprised of the best players throughout the country. The Mexican national team is formally called the Selección Nacional Mexicana; informally, it is known as "El Tri" for the three colors of the uniform (red, green, and white), which, naturally, also constitute Mexico's national colors as represented in the nation's flag. The national team represents Mexico at the major international soccer competitions such as the World Cup, the Americas Cup, and the Gold Cup, among others.

Like the National Football League or Major League Baseball in the United States, a national professional soccer league, called the Federación Mexicana de Fútbol Asociación (Mexican Federation of Soccer Association) exists in Mexico. The national professional soccer league in Mexico is divided into four divisions, which can be thought of as roughly the equivalents of a major league and three minor leagues. And, of course, many other amateur, school, and community recreation leagues exist all throughout the country. Needless to say, the sport is widespread and popular, with soccer matches taking place year-round.

According to the Mexican Federation of Soccer Association, soccer in its current form was brought to Mexico by English mine workers in the late 19th century. Until the early 1920s, the sport was dominated primarily by foreigners in the country. In 1923, Mexico fielded its first national team, and its first international competition took place at the 1928 Amsterdam Olympics. In 1930, the Mexican

Mexico's Francisco Rodríguez (right) beats United States' Landon Donovan to the ball during a World Cup qualifier on September 3, 2005. (International Sports Images/Corbis)

national team participated in the first World Cup Competition in Montevideo, Uruguay, losing all three of its initial round matches. Not until the mid-1940s did soccer explode as a national phenomenon that resulted in the creation of a national professional soccer league. Since then, soccer has been and continues to be the leading Mexican national sport.

Although the Mexican national team has never risen to the level of global competitiveness of either Brazil or Argentina, Mexico has become an important and respected actor in the international soccer community. In fact, Mexico has hosted two World Cup competitions, one in 1970 and one in 1986. Of the 18 World Cup matches held since the 1930 inaugural competition, the Mexican national team competed in 13; the Mexican national team failed to qualify for three World Cup competitions and boycotted another competition (1938). Perhaps the lowest point for the sport of soccer in Mexico at the national level occurred in 1990, when the International Soccer Federation sanctioned Mexico for having fielded ineligible players in the classification rounds for the 1988 Olympic games. For this infraction, Mexico was subsequently banned from competing in all international competitions for a period of two years, including the 1990 World Cup. The Mexican national team has rebounded thereafter and has qualified for every World Cup competition since then, making it to the second round in each of these subsequent World Cup competitions.

MEXICAN LITERARY TRADITIONS

Mexico's postindependence literary tradition began with the production of the picaresque novel, which was a stylistic import from Spain. Interestingly, the first major literary worked produced in the entire Spanish American region following independence came from a Mexican intellectual and man of letters, José Joaquín Fernández de Lizardi. His famous picaresque novel, *El periquillo sarniento,* was published in 1816. In this work, Fernández de Lizardi crafted a story that satirized the venality and corruption that could be found throughout the country at the time. His work also marked the first time that the structure and the values of Mexican society were put under a critical microscope of inquiry. Because Mexico was wracked by violence, war, and foreign occupation for most of the 19th century, its literary production was limited and replicative.

But when the Mexican Revolution got underway, a Mexican writer by the name of Mariano Azuela published a novel, *Los de Abajo,* or *The Underdogs,* which ushered in a completely new genre of fiction for the Latin American region. Azuela's novel told the story of the Mexican Revolution from the perspective of peasants in the countryside caught up in the ever-shifting winds of the movement. In the novel, the hero, Demetrio Macías, is a reserved peasant who enlists in the Revolutionary Army of Pancho Villa and follows a circuitous path of fighting, during the course of which the ideological purposes of the war are swallowed up and lost. The only purpose left to Macías in the struggle is the fight itself. In the last scene of the novel, Macías finds himself subject to an ambush in the very place where he first enjoined the struggle, and his life comes to an unceremonious end as simply another casualty in what appeared to be an endless and ultimately purposeless civil war. In the process of narrating the story, Mariano Azuela portrays in vivid detail the contradictions of revolutionary Mexico that pit the simple peasant against the cultured urban intellectual, the sleepiness and routine nature of rural village life against the chaos and tumultuousness of life in the big cities and on the battlefields, and tradition against an unfolding modernity. This novel was the first and perhaps the greatest representative of the genre of revolutionary fiction that more or less continued to dominate the content and style of the national literary production of Mexico until the magical realism genre swept over the entire Western Hemisphere.

This period in Latin American literature is often referred to as the "boom period" because it witnessed an explosion of creativity in the magical realist tradition that was unique to Latin America and that influenced literary trends throughout the world. Mexico did not escape the region's consumption with magical realism and produced a rich tradition of its own within the genre. Some Mexican authors whose works can be located within this tradition include writers such as Juan Rulfo, with his classic work *Pedro Páramo* (1955), Carlos Fuentes, *La muerte de Artemio Cruz (The Death of Artemio Cruz)* (1962), and even the contemporary female novelist Laura Esquivel, *Como agua para chocolate (Like Water for Chocolate)* (1994).

A few other notable Mexican authors and intellectuals merit some attention in the discussion of Mexico's contemporary literary tradition. Octavio Paz is perhaps Mexico's most famous, prolific, and influential 20th-century writer and public intellectual. His career spanned almost the entire latter part of the century and included work not only as a writer but also as a statesman. In terms of his literary contributions, Paz produced over the course of his life a solid body of poetry, but he is mostly known for his work as an essayist. His 1950 publication of *El laberinto de la soledad (The Labyrinth of Solitude)* is considered one of the finest and most provocative essays on the Mexican psyche and character ever written. His penetrating insight into the identity of the Mexican remains relevant to this day, almost 60 years after its initial publication. For his singular accomplishments as a poet and an essayist, Octavio Paz was awarded the Nobel Prize for Literature in 1990 in recognition of a lifetime of literary production. Another figure important to Mexico's contemporary literary tradition and culture is Elena Poniatowska. Poniatowska emigrated as a child from France to Mexico, where she took up a career as a journalist. Her writing style reflects her journalistic training and made her a pioneering author in a genre some refer to as the documentary narrative. In 1971, Poniatowska published *La noche de Tlatelolco,* which was a collection of testimonials from people directly involved in the infamous government-ordered massacre of student demonstrators in Tlatelolco plaza in 1968. Later, in 1988, Poniatowska published *Nada, nadie,* which collected the poignant reactions and direct, firsthand commentary of people involved in the 1985 Mexico City earthquake. This work again reflected the documentary narrative style that she used in her earlier work on the Tlatelolco massacre. Poniatowska continues to be a productive author, social commentator, and public intellectual in Mexico today, and she continues to serve as an inspiration and role model for women writers in Mexico.

MEXICAN VISUAL ARTS

Mexico also has a rich visual art tradition that includes sculpture, painting, architecture, photography, and cinematic expression. In the pre-Columbian period, visual art within the indigenous communities is represented in the beautiful pictorial manuscripts, the pottery, and the impressive architectural structures of the great pre-Columbian civilizations of Mexico. Even then, visual artistic production had more than simply an aesthetic purpose. Mexican visual art chronicled the history of the indigenous civilizations and functioned as a main educational tool for the inhabitants of the region on the important religious, social, and political rituals, myths, and institutions of the times. Ever since, Mexico and Mexicans have continued to embrace the social, political, and religious function of the visual arts.

During the colonial period, for example, the visual arts in Mexico deepened the cultural syncretism of the Western aesthetic traditions with those of the indigenous peoples. The styles and methods of the European schools of art and architecture migrated to Mexico, where they both combined with and were sometimes superimposed over native traditions. Undoubtedly, the production and distribution of ornate sculpture, paintings, and other icons during this period also contributed to the socialization of Mexicans to the empire and their places within it. One very concrete manifestation of this syncretic process as it related to patterns of socialization and imperialism appears in the realm of colonial architecture. Often, European-style churches and altars were built around pre-Columbian temple sites, and the designs of these new churches often incorporated not only the actual stones used to construct the temples but also pre-Columbian design traditions of open-air ceremonial worship spaces.

During the independence and early national periods, the visual arts were critical in developing an independent national consciousness and in forging representative imagery of this new national identity. Mexican artists during this period generally employed neoclassical styles in portraits, landscape paintings, sculpture, and architecture, but usually in commemoration of independence and national heroes or important national events. However, often lacking in this immediate postindependence period was an embrace of indigenous culture as represented in all forms of the visual arts. For example, the National Academy of San Carlos, reestablished in 1847 by Mexican President Antonio López de Santa Anna, privileged artists trained in European styles and traditions and marginalized those working in the traditions and styles native to Mexico. Mexican visual culture during this period tended to celebrate the creation of a new Mexico and a new national identity, but the new Mexico in these visual artistic productions looked less like Mexico, even when the subjects and themes were native to the country. Instead, this classical style made Mexico look a lot more like ancient Greece and Rome. Nevertheless, the social and political dimensions of the visual arts in 19th-century Mexico are clear. Yet, perhaps nowhere in Mexico's history of the visual arts was the blending of a unique aesthetics of art with the sociopolitical purpose of visual expression as evident and as powerful as in the muralist movement that emerged out of the revolutionary experience.

As an artistic movement, Mexican muralism may be traced back to the early artistic vision and work of two main individuals: Gerardo Murillo and José Guadalupe Posada. Both individuals did not produce muralist artwork themselves, but each, in his own way, cultivated and nurtured into the mainstream art world the idea that art should be both popular and political. Posada was a graphic artist who had his satirical and wildly popular woodcut prints published primarily in Mexico's newspapers during the period of the Porfiriato, mostly in the form of what might today be referred to as political cartoons. He produced his work for

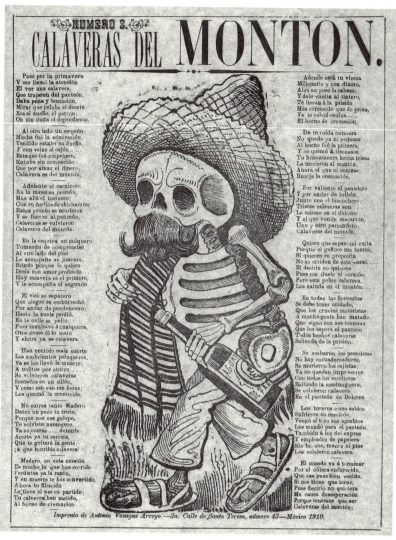

*Illustration by Mexican artist José Guadalupe Posada entitled Cala-
veras from the heap, 1910. The broadside shows the skeleton of a
drunken peasant holding a bottle of Aguardiente de Parras—
a reference to Franciso Madero's family's maguey plantation and
distillery operation. (Library of Congress)*

popular consumption, and the themes of his artwork were almost exclusively related to popular culture, current fashions, and contemporary social and political issues. His prints were detailed, refined, and haunting, and his artistic techniques, in spite of having almost no formal artistic training, were irreproachable. Through his prints, Posada caricaturized and lampooned Mexico's political and social elites, and he unapologetically produced biting commentary of the social conventions of his day. Posada, perhaps more so than any other visual artist up to that moment in Mexico's history, transformed the perception of visual art as being the privilege of the cultured few, to one that was popular, socially relevant, connected to the average Mexican's daily experiences, and politically engaged.

The Mexican muralists built squarely on the groundwork laid out by Posada, albeit on a much grander scale. These muralists launched a major artistic movement that would transform worldwide the concept of a public visual art that was politically engaged and civic minded, that was easily and readily accessible to all, and that drew upon and celebrated recognizable elements of popular culture. On the other hand, Gerardo Murillo's influence in shaping the muralist movement in Mexico was more intellectual and inspirational. Unlike Posada, Murillo, also known as Dr. Atl, was an arts culture insider. He was a classically trained artist who learned his craft in the salons and studios of Europe's famous artistic centers. He rubbed elbows with some of the more famous and internationally recognized artists of the time. And his own artwork tended to reflect the studio conventions that guided the creation of the artistic production of his day. But he was never fully comfortable in the confines of this classical and insular world, and he articulated a vision of artistic production that hoped to break down the walls of this narrow space and bring into the world of visual art the energy and vibrancy, not to mention the social and political ideas, of the environment and the people in the actual world surrounding it. Dr. Atl was an ardent nationalist, and the Mexico that he observed surrounding him on a daily basis contrasted starkly with the insularity and the pretensions of the Mexico of Porfirio Díaz, which he also associated with the stuffiness of the classical artistic traditions and culture of Mexico's premier art school, the Academy of San Carlos. As a critique of both the artistic conventions and the Porfirian system, and animated by the revolutionary impulses bubbling up throughout the country, Dr. Atl organized a dissident arts exhibition as part of the 1910 centennial festivities celebrating Mexico's independence movements of 1810. The artists that Dr. Atl gathered around him for this early nationalist exhibition ended up forming the nucleus of the muralist movement that the revolutionary governments of the 1920s and 1930s would inaugurate and promote as official state policy.

The public official who catalyzed the muralist movement and who brought these revolutionary and radicalized artists into the orbit of the revolutionary state was none other than Mexico's dynamic educational reformer and intellectual, José Vasconcelos. Upon his appointment as secretary of Education in 1921, Vasconcelos put the full weight of the Mexican government and the federal treasury behind the muralist movement. Vasconcelos outlined his objectives of a public art that would be imbued with the themes and principles of the Revolution, that would educate Mexicans in the richness of their national history and culture, that would be monumental and expansive in scope and coverage, and that would be available and accessible to all regardless of race, class, or socioeconomic status. The intent was to create not only an informed and engaged citizenry but a cultured and virtuous one. Vasconcelos gave the walls, halls, and ceilings of the Mexican patrimony to socially conscious artists as their canvasses.

Hundreds of artists embraced the bold vision of Vasconcelos to transform the nature and intent of the visual arts in

*Mexican artist Diego Rivera was known for his expansive and
politically radical murals. (Library of Congress)*

Mexico; but three artists in particular stood out among
them: Diego Rivera, José Clemente Orozco, and David Alfaro Siqueiros. Known as the "big three," these artists, colorful as much in their social and political lives as in their
artistic productions, embodied the spirit and the energy of

the muralist movement. Diego Rivera, born in Guanajuato and classically trained in the visual arts at the Academy of San Carlos, is perhaps the most famous of the three great Mexican muralists throughout the world. His murals adorn the walls in the Ministry of Education building and the National Palace in Mexico City, as well as the National School of Agriculture in Chapingo, among many others. Although he produced a rich body of individual portraits, Rivera is best known for his impressive murals. The Rivera murals are distinguished from those of the other two great muralists of the period by their soft, pleasant tones and by the epic dimensions of the stories of Mexican history and culture that he told through his paintings. It is principally through the work of Diego Rivera that the richness and idealization of Mexico's indigenous heritage and culture in Mexico's postrevolutionary national identity emerged forcefully within Mexico's visual arts. Rivera often presented an idyllic, albeit an oversimplified and perhaps even overglorified, picture of Mexico's indigenous peoples. But this emphasis on resuscitating the central place of Mexico's indigenous heritage in the public consciousness was central to the muralist movement and to Rivera's work in particular.

For his part, José Clemente Orozco was more subdued and contemplative in his work. Born in the state of Jalisco and most comfortable in the provinces, Orozco produced works that reflected a subdued and more austere tone. While Orozco did not shy away from reflecting the goals and aspirations of the Mexican Revolution in his artistic creations, his paintings revealed a more realistic and perhaps more balanced representation of the complexity of Mexican history than the works of either Rivera or Siqueiros. Some of Orozco's most impressive works are located in the Government Palace and the Hospicio Cabañas in Guadalajara, the capital city of his home state of Jalisco. David Alfaro Siqueiros rounded out this famous trio of muralists. Siqueiros was undoubtedly the most politically active and radicalized of the three. For him, the Revolution was a living movement and one that required expression and realization in more than just paint on walls or on canvasses. The political activity of Siqueiros landed him behind bars on many occasions, and even involved him in politically motivated assassination plots and intrigues. And though one might argue that Siqueiros lived a brash and irresponsible life, this experience surely contributed to the breathtaking boldness and emotionally charged themes that came through in his artwork. Siqueiros used bright colors and sharp edges in his paintings, and the scenes he portrayed were usually extremely melodramatic and visually exaggerated. His most impressive and well-known murals portray the stoic heroism or triumphalism of revolutionary values in the face of a crushing oppression. Representative of this tendency are his works found on the walls of the Fine Arts Palace in Mexico City.

In the end, Mexican muralism succeeded for the most part in blending the popular political art tradition of Posada, the passionate advocacy of Dr. Atl for the establishment of a radical national art, and the educational vision of Vasconcelos in using the visual arts as a vehicle for building a national revolutionary consciousness across the country. To this day, contemporary Mexican visual arts reflect the values, techniques, and social purpose that characterized the muralist movement. Visual artists still produce excellent mural paintings, and the style has even filtered down to the local levels in the well-established tradition of graffiti wall art.

While the muralist movement tends to dominate the discussion of Mexican visual arts because of its singular importance, a number of other modern Mexican artists who moved beyond the muralist tradition and have made important contributions of their own to Mexico's visual arts culture deserve mention. The first is the enigmatic and fascinating surrealist painter Frida Kahlo, who is undoubtedly Mexico's most recognizable female artist. Although

Kahlo, through her relationship with Diego Rivera, her on-again, off-again husband, was intimately involved with the muralist movement as a supporter and as an activist, her own art occupied a place all to itself. Her most famous paintings are very intimate, personal, and often graphically violent self-portraits that represented her own troubled and pain-filled life. As a young, teenage college student, Kahlo was involved in a serious trolley-car crash that nearly took her life. In the course of the accident, a steel handrail from the trolley car impaled Kahlo and pierced through her abdomen and her reproductive organs. Though she survived the accident, she was never able to bear children and she lived the remainder of her life in constant pain, often confined to her bed. Her portraits, often haunting and disturbing, are clear manifestations of these unhappy conditions of her life. She also fully embraced the revolutionary valoration of the country's indigenous past, particularly in terms of its dress and fashion, and she celebrated such aspects of Mexico's indigenous legacy both in her paintings and in her own grooming habits and customs. She died in 1954 at only 47 years of age.

Another artist deserving mention is Rufino Tamayo, a contemporary of the famous muralists whose best works are his easel canvas portraits. Unlike his muralist counterparts, Tamayo did not embrace the overtly political purpose of artistic production envisioned by José Vasconcelos and Dr. Atl, even though he did paint a number of murals in service to the state. He preferred to keep his personal politics and his art distinct from one another as much as possible. Consequently, much of his work sought to depict the mundane, everyday life of Mexicans, and his style was much more in line with the European modernism, cubism, and abstract art movements.

Mexican artists continue to produce quality paintings, borrowing heavily from the traditions of the muralists and the other early 20th-century artists; but there has not been a replication of the intensity and vibrancy of artistic production that compares with these early decades of the 20th century.

MEXICAN MEDIA

The media in Mexico has always been an interesting and fascinating case study for students of Mexican state-society relations. For most of Mexico's history as an independent country, the national media in Mexico has had a symbiotic and intimate love-hate relationship with the state system. At various moments in the country's modern history, the state has attempted to co-opt the media and to use it toward its own exclusive purposes, often through the use of force and against the will of the media itself. Yet the media has also resisted the restrictive pretensions of the state and has been able to maintain some semblance of critical independence from it. In the postrevolutionary period of contemporary Mexico, these conflicting tendencies simply intensified. The postrevolutionary political elites who constructed the single-party state apparatus were never fully able to co-opt the media as a functional interest group of either the state or the ruling party; however, the media did allow itself informally to be manipulated and used by the state and ruling-party elites through a variety of mechanisms. The Mexican media, like most other social institutions, found itself subject to the corporatist nature of the postrevolution single-party state system.

In the context of the unique semiauthoritarian/ semidemocratic political system that characterized Mexico for most of the 20th century, the Mexican media, both print and broadcast, walked a fine line between being an independent and critical voice of the people in relationship to authority and being an official propaganda and public relations vehicle for the authority. It has never been fully controlled or owned by the state and thus has maintained some distance from the authority. But it has also been very reluctant to assume its role as a critical watchdog of the state, often compromising its own independence in relation to the state through a process of selective self-censorship. Any truly democratic society demands the existence of a vibrant and independent media, which is necessary both for holding the political authority accountable for its actions and for providing objective and transparent information to the national citizenry about the state of affairs of the country and the world within a national, free, and protected public space. In Mexico, the media, both print and broadcast, has been relatively free, albeit within clear constraints and limitations imposed by the state.

Mexican print media, which includes newspapers, magazines, and other periodical and popular literature, has traditionally depended on the state both for its advertising revenue as well as for its access to newsprint, the production, sale, and distribution of which the state controlled. In the realm of broadcast media, which includes television and radio, the relationship of the media industry to the state was and continues to be even more dependent. Mexican broadcast companies depend on the state and its regulatory agencies for broadcast licenses as well as for access to the significant technological and financial resources needed to produce television and radio programming. And the entry costs for establishing new radio or television broadcast enterprises in Mexico are enormous, with technical and financial support from the state being really the only viable means through which new broadcast media ventures can be launched and nurtured. Perhaps the best way to exemplify the Mexican media's social function as well as its relationship to the state is to take a look at the history, the institutional evolution, and the media content of Mexico's most important and largest media organizations.

Televisa is Mexico's largest media conglomerate, with operations and interests ranging from its television broadcast network to newspapers, radio stations, cable and satellite services, magazines, film production companies, among many others. Its reach transcends Mexico and has made Televisa the best-known, most-recognized, and ubiquitous Spanish language media corporation in the world. Its programs reach into homes across the world, and its famous telenovelas, or soap operas, have been consumed fanatically by people in every country of the world.

In 1955, at the dawn of Mexico's television age, a pioneering entrepreneur in Mexican radio broadcasting by the name of Emilio Azcárraga, who had been granted one of the very first television licenses by the probusiness government of Miguél Alemán, and who had used this license to set up one of Mexico's first television stations, Canal 2, in 1951, merged his successful media operation with those of the owners of Mexico's two other competing television stations. The product of the merger was Telesistema Mexicana, Televisa's corporate forebear, and it established a formidable television monopoly. This monopoly lasted until 1968 when two independent networks were created to compete with Telesistema Mexicana and to diversify the television market. In spite of this nominal competition, Telesistema Mexicana continued and even expanded its dominance of the market. In 1972, Telesistema Mexicana merged with the most serious of its two competitors, Televisión Independiente, to form the company that bears the current name of Televisa. Televisa would continue to dominate the media market, particularly the broadcast media market, until the early 1990s, when the Mexican administration of Carlos Salinas de Gortari privatized the state-owned television network, Instituto Mexicano de la Televisión (Imevisión) and thus birthed TV Azteca.

From the beginning, the Azcarraga family and Televisa maintained intimate relations with the Institutional Revolutionary Party (PRI). Although Televisa has always been functionally independent of both the party and the government, the company has never tried to play down its collusion with and loyalty to the PRI, and it has served unabashedly as a mouthpiece in defense of the state.

Telenovelas

A fascinating element of Mexico's television media culture is the telenovela. The telenovela, which is a kind of television soap opera, is not unique to Mexico, but the Mexican television media industry has been one of the forerunners and leaders in developing the genre and in distributing the shows. The telenovela reaches millions of Mexican viewers, and it has served both as commentary on and as dissemination of Mexican popular values and cultural beliefs.

Perhaps more so than any other cultural export, Mexican telenovelas have had a widespread reach and impact globally. Mexican telenovela stars have developed loyal fans as far away as Japan and Russia, and the Mexican telenovelas themselves have even determined the shape and timing of wars in other parts of the world. For instance, as Sam Quinones reports in his book *True Tales of Another Mexico,* the different ethnic factions involved in the civil wars of the former Yugoslavia would observe an informal ceasefire during airings of episodes of Mexican telenovelas, so that everyone would be able to tune in to the latest dramatic happenings in the lives of the shows' principle characters without being distracted by the noises of exploding mortar shells and gunfire.

Within Mexico during the period of PRI hegemony of the political system, the close relationship between the government and the official media outlets, such as Televisa, would collaborate to produce telenovelas that would serve as propaganda either in support of the regime or in defense of particular social values that the government thought important to disseminate among the citizenry.

Yet in almost every case, the basic plotline of a telenovela would follow a fairly standard formula. Usually, the struggles and sufferings of a poor and socially disadvantaged, but beautiful woman from the lower classes, perhaps even from a nonwhite ethnic background, would form the basic substance of the story. Such struggles and sufferings would often involve a socially unacceptable love affair with a man from outside of her class, which would ultimately be resolved in the young woman's favor after a roller-coaster ride of rejection and redemption through various intrigues and deceptions. In essence, such telenovelas would present a kind of rags-to-riches, happily-ever-after Cinderella story involving characters typical of the Mexican socioeconomic environment.

Perhaps the major difference between a Mexican telenovela and the typical daytime soap opera in the United States is that the Mexican telenovela has a clear beginning and end. Another difference is that most telenovelas are broadcast during primetime evening hours so as to attract an audience of both males and females from among the working and professional classes who would not be able to view the telenovelas if shown during the hours of the regular workday.

Cinema

In the realm of cinema, Mexico boasts a rich tradition extending all the way back into the era of the silent films of the early decades of the 20th century. There is only a sketchy historical record of these early pioneering years in Mexican cinema; however, Mexican cinema experienced a flourishing in the 1930s and 1940s during what has come to be known as the "golden age" of Mexican film. In this period, a fair number of Mexican actors and actresses, such as Dolores del Rio, María Félix, Lupe Vélez, and Pedro Infante, crossed over into international audiences.

As in many areas of Mexican culture, the golden age of Mexican cinema corresponds to the period of the institutionalization of the Mexican Revolution; the stories told on

Mexican film star Dolores del Rio, about 1930. (Library of Congress)

the silver screen in Mexico during the golden age are typical
of the new revolutionary consciousness. Indigenous civilization and culture were idealized, peasant life was contrasted
with urban life, and the heroism and bravery of the icons of
the early phases of the armed revolutionary conflicts were
common themes. In fact, the Revolution itself often provided the backdrop to many of the stories, and Mexico's
most prominent directors of the period, Emilio "El Indio"
Fernández and Fernando de Fuentes, established themselves via the production of such films in a genre that cinema scholar John King refers to as the "melodrama of the
Revolution," which tried to explain and contextualize the
chaos, motivations, and accomplishments of the revolutionary struggle.

Today, the interests of the Mexican cinema industry are
represented and promoted by the Mexican Academy of Film
Arts and Sciences (Academia Mexicana de Ciencias y Artes
Cinemáticas). The Mexican Academy of Film Arts and Sciences is the functional equivalent of the Academy of Motion
Picture Arts and Sciences in the United States. The Mexican
Academy's recognition award, known as the Ariel, is similar
to the Oscar and is bestowed on the most significant accomplishments among Mexican filmmakers, producers, and
actors every year. Currently, led by the talented work of directors Alfonso Cuarón (*Y tu mamá tambien, Harry Potter
and the Prisoner of Azcaban, Children of Men*), Guillermo
del Toro (*Doña Lupe, El espinazo del Diablo, El laberinto
del fauno*), and Alejandro González Iñárritu (*Amores perros, 21 Grams, Babel*), and actors Gael García Bernal (*The
Motorcycle Diaries, Amores Perros*), Diego Luna (*Y tu
mamá tambien, Dirty Dancing: Havana Nights*), and Salma
Hayek (*Frida, Once Upon a Time in Mexico*), the Mexican
national film industry is thriving and Mexican cinema professionals are having a tremendous influence in the global
film industry.

EDUCATION IN MEXICO

Article 3 of the 1917 Constitution guarantees that all Mexican citizens will have access to a secular and free public education. Although the Mexican Constitution does not specify whether this right applies to every level of education, from basic elementary schooling to the university, most Mexicans interpret this constitutional right in the broadest and most expansive way possible. As such, there is an extensive network of free, public primary and secondary schools, as well as a substantial contingent of free, public vocational schools, colleges, and universities, that Mexican citizens may access. However, in spite of this, most Mexicans are unable to take advantage of this constitutional guarantee beyond the mandatory six years of primary education. The fact that primary education is mandatory and that the government does provide access to education at the primary level for all citizens ensures that nearly all Mexicans achieve a basic level of functional literacy, even though only about half of Mexico's children make it all the way through these six years of primary schooling.

Although changing somewhat recently, the content and goals of education in the Mexican public school system have traditionally centered around not only the acquisition of basic knowledge and skills but also the creation of a sense of civic allegiance to the principles of the Mexican Revolution. The national secretary of Public Education formulates a standardized national curriculum that all public schools must follow. This curriculum extends beyond basic literacy and aptitude in the language arts (reading and writing), science, and mathematics to the subject areas of history, culture, and social studies.

Structurally and organizationally, the Mexican educational system is similar to that of the United States. Mexicans will begin their educational experience at the ages of five or six by attending the mandatory six years of primary education, which equate roughly to the kindergarten through fifth grade elementary school structure of the United States. Following completion of this mandatory primary education, Mexicans will advance to three years of middle school, or what is known as *secundaria,* in the Mexican educational system. It is during these middle school years that the Mexican educational system begins to sort through and prepare students for subsequent education in one of two tracks: (1) college preparatory schooling (the *preparatoria,* which is the equivalent of high school) followed by university attendance, or (2) vocational training education programs.

Although the Mexican government has made impressive strides in providing basic education to nearly all of its citizens, class, ethnicity, and locale still condition the quality of education and the ability of Mexicans to take advantage of educational opportunities. Mexicans who live in rural areas are much more likely to drop out of school at earlier ages than their urban counterparts, often not even completing the mandatory six years of primary education. A similar pattern can be observed among Mexico's substantial indigenous communities, whose levels of education lag behind Mexico's nonindigenous citizens. And, of course, Mexico's lower classes, whether urban or rural, also attain lower levels of education compared with middle- and upper-class citizens.

For those Mexicans able to acquire a postsecondary education, Mexico's college and university system is quite impressive. Its national public university, called the UNAM (Universidad Nacional Autónoma Mexicana) and located in Mexico City, is one of the oldest and most prestigious national universities throughout all of Latin America. Founded in 1521, the UNAM today enrolls more than 250,000 students and offers the full range of degree programs from the liberal arts to the professional trades. Consistent with the constitutional right to free, public, and secular education,

The library at Universidad Nacional Autónoma Mexicana, with a statue of former president Miguel Alemán. (Bettmann/Corbis)

most of Mexico's institutions of higher learning are secular and state supported; however, the past 20 years have witnessed extraordinary growth in the number of private institutions offering some form of postsecondary education. These private colleges and universities have selective admissions procedures and often assess tuitions that are beyond the range of most Mexicans to afford. Nevertheless, for any Mexican who completes the required preparatory education and would like to continue studies at the college level, admission to one of Mexico's public universities is guaranteed and essentially free, perhaps with only a token tuition fee assessed.

Mexican university education, both public and private, tends to be organized along the European model in which students select a particular career path (or *carrera*) and then enroll in the corresponding school associated with this career track. Within universities and colleges, these schools are quite distinct from each other, each with its own faculty and its own curriculum. The notion of a shared core liberal arts curriculum, or the general Bachelor of Arts or Science degree that most university students in the United States obtain, is foreign to the Mexican system of postsecondary education. Thus, Mexican undergraduate college students will often identify themselves as a student in the various faculties and whose terminal degrees will be awarded in that particular career. Essentially, students enter directly into law schools, business schools, medical schools, or schools of letters and arts right out of high school (or *preparatoria*) and will earn the corresponding professional degree upon graduation. Once a student graduates, he or she earns what is called a *licenciatura*, or a license, which allows the graduate to practice officially the career in which he or she is educated. Students must generally study at the university or college level for at least five years to earn a *licenciatura*, which requires more work than the traditional bachelor's degree in the United States, but not quite enough work to earn the graduate master's degree.

Until recently, it was uncommon for Mexican universities to offer graduate doctoral degree programs, but as Mexico's university and college system has grown, especially its private institutions, the opportunities for advanced graduate study have also increased.

Since the 1910 Revolution, an important goal of the Mexican educational system has been to create a sense of national identity that could foster a sense of unity among Mexico's diverse populations and engender a sense of nationalist pride that would cross class and ethnic boundaries. Thus, from the very early stages of Mexico's educational curriculum, students are taught to embrace and celebrate the indigenous as well as the European origins of the modern Mexican nation. The hope was to encourage marginalized indigenous peoples to feel integrally connected to the Mexican nation and to encourage their continued assimilation into Mexico's dominant mestizo culture. Likewise, this goal intended to engender an appreciation among Mexico's non-indigenous citizens to embrace their fellow indigenous Mexicans as full members of the Mexican nation. This has been a controversial aspect of Mexico's educational system as critics point out that the politically dominant nonindigenous peoples of Mexico were the ones who unilaterally identified and declared Mexico's national identity as a mestizo identity and who formalized an educational curriculum and school structure based upon an image of Mexican national identity that did not actively incorporate all Mexican voices into the process.

Another important aspect of the Mexican educational system is its role in political recruitment, upward social mobility, and economic opportunity. The clientelistic nature of the Mexican social, political, and economic systems is such that personal networks are often the most important criteria for success and career advancement in government service and business. For most of Mexico's social, political, and economic elite, networks are forged and solidified during their college or university years; thus, being able to take advantage of college or university education is generally a firm prerequisite for access to economic or political power. Those who are unable to attend university or college, and to take advantage of such important networking, run into a glass ceiling that serves to further divide Mexico along socioeconomic and ethnic lines.

DRUGS AND DRUG TRAFFICKING

Because Mexico shares a long and relatively porous land border with the United States, the country has found itself caught in the international drug-trafficking phenomenon. Most illegal narcotics that enter the United States do so through the U.S.-Mexican border, and the impact of this flow of drugs on Mexican society, economy, and politics has been unavoidable and substantial.

Although there has been a steady flow of illegal drugs from Mexico into the United States since the 19th century, cross-border drug trafficking was minimal until the 1960s. In the 1960s, demand for illegal narcotics in the United States began its steady upward climb. However, collaborative binational efforts to contain illegal drug trafficking from the 1960s to the 1980s were fairly successful, although not without controversy. For instance, in 1969, the United States, without consulting the Mexican authorities, launched a drug-trafficking counteroffensive program on the U.S.-Mexican border called Operation Intercept. The main element of this program was the institution of a slow, individual, and thorough search for drugs on Mexicans crossing the border legally into the United States. The result of this unilateral policy move unsurprisingly heightened tensions on the border between Mexicans who regularly and legally crossed the border and suspicious U.S. law enforcement officials. Furthermore, the program slowed down the regular flow of cross-border traffic and disrupted commerce that negatively impacted businesses on both sides of the border. And the actual impact on containing the flow of drugs across the borders was insignificant, as traffickers found other routes into the United States. Following a brief and tense moment in the bilateral relationship, Mexican and U.S. authorities came together to resolve the issue and did so by replacing Operation Intercept with Operation Cooperation, which was a much more effective counternarcotics program since it involved the participation of both Mexican and U.S. law enforcement agencies. In spite of such occasional moments of tension and controversy surrounding the drug-trafficking problem, Mexico and the United States found ways to cooperate and to minimize the impact of the drug-trafficking problem on its relatively cordial bilateral relations.

In the 1980s, however, and continuing through the present day, the growing demand for drugs in the United States and the sophistication of the drug production and trafficking networks in meeting this demand outstripped both the Mexican government's and the U.S. government's efforts to contain it. In Mexico, the inability of law enforcement officials to keep up with the growing trafficking of drugs and the violence associated with it led to greater and more indiscriminate human rights abuses in the name of the drug war. And the Reagan administration's increased politicization of the drug issue, when coupled with Mexico's perceived inability to contain the growing flow of narcotics through Mexico across the border into the United States, increased the tensions between the countries. The situation reached a low point in 1985 with the grisly murder in Mexico of Enrique Camarena, a U.S. Drug Enforcement Agency agent for the United States working in Mexico out of the U.S. Consulate in Guadalajara. Camarena's murder was attributed to Mexico's drug traffickers, but the United States was dissatisfied with the Mexican government's response to solving it and bringing the perpetrators of the crime to justice. In the end, U.S. agents took matters into their own hands, captured a doctor who supposedly had participated in the torture of Camarena, and, with neither the knowledge nor the acquiescence of the Mexican government, transported him to the United States where he was put on trial for his alleged role in the torture and death of Camarena.

As we have seen in previous chapters, the neoliberal policies of the late 1980s and the 1990s, policies that included the North American Free Trade Agreement, significantly increased cross-border commercial activity, including, ironically, the commerce in illegal narcotics. Further, the economic benefits obtained by free trade are in many ways perhaps offset by the pernicious effects of the growth in the drug-producing and drug-trafficking business on Mexico's internal political system as well as in Mexico's relationship with the United States.

For instance, as the drug-trafficking problem intensified in Mexico throughout the 1990s, the country began to contend with its own increasing levels of drug consumption and addictions, and all the social problems that come along with this. Also, the destabilizing effects on Mexico's democratic process and on many of its most important institutions are obvious and troubling. In fact, some analysts suggest that the political violence and political assassinations at the highest levels of government and society in Mexico, including the brazen daytime murders of Cardinal Posadas, the catholic archbishop of Guadalajara, and Luis Donaldo Colosio, the PRI's initial presidential candidate for the 1994 elections, are attributable to the drug-production and drug-trafficking networks. Compounding this situation is the militarization of the drug problem in Mexico, which has transformed the Mexican military into a domestic policing agency in the war on drugs and has produced levels of drug-related corruption within the military that have serious ramifications for Mexico's defense and security apparatuses.

This chapter has presented a glimpse into the societal and cultural reality that is Mexico. There are certainly other interesting aspects of Mexico's national character, its cultural institutions and events, and the behaviors and attitudes of its people that would merit further exploration. Nevertheless, in the interests of space and time, this chapter pointed out some of the most important and formative aspects of Mexican society and culture.

References

Bethell, Leslie, ed. *A Cultural History of Latin America: Literature, Music and the Visual Arts in the 19th and 20th Centuries*. Cambridge: Cambridge University Press, 1998.

Bonfil Batalla, Guillermo. *México Profundo: Reclaiming a Civilization*. Translated by Philip A. Dennis. Austin: University of Texas Press, 1996.

Canak, William, and Laura Swanson. *Modern Mexico*. New York: McGraw-Hill, 1998.

Herrera-Sobek, María. *The Mexican Corrido: A Feminist Analysis*. Bloomington: Indiana University Press, 1990.

Joseph, Gilbert M., and Timothy J. Henderson, eds. *The Mexico Reader: History, Culture, Politics*. Durham, NC: Duke University Press, 2002.

Lewis, Oscar. *The Children of Sánchez: Autobiography of a Mexican Family*. New York: Vintage Books, 1961.

Lipp, Solomon. *Leopoldo Zea: From Mexicanidad to a Philosophy of History*. Waterloo, Ontario: Wilfrid Laurier University Press, 1980.

Orme, William A., Jr., ed. *A Culture of Collusion: An Inside Look at the Mexican Press*. Miami: North-South Center Press, 1997.

Oster, Patrick. *The Mexicans: A Personal Portrait of a People*, 2nd ed. New York: HarperCollins, 2002.

Paz, Octavio. *The Labyrinth of Solitude: The Other Mexico, Return to the Labyrinth of Solitude, Mexico and the United States, the Philanthropic Ogre*. New York: Grove Press, 1985.

Pilcher, Jeffrey M., ed. *The Human Tradition in Mexico*. Wilmington, DE: Scholarly Resources, 2003.

Quinones, Sam. *True Tales from Another Mexico*. Albuquerque: University of New Mexico Press, 2001.

Sheehy, Daniel. *Mariachi Music in America: Experiencing Music, Expressing Culture*. New York: Oxford University Press, 2006.

Scott, John F. *Latin American Art: Ancient to Modern*. Gainesville: University Press of Florida, 1999.

Taylor, Kathy. *The New Narrative of Mexico: Sub-versions of History in Mexican Fiction*. Lewisburg, PA: Bucknell University Press, 1994.

Zolov, Eric. *Refried Elvis: The Rise of the Mexican Counterculture*. Berkeley: University of California Press, 1999.

PART TWO
REFERENCE SECTION

Key Events in Mexican History

1519	Hernán Cortés encounters Mexico and the Aztec empire of Montezuma.
1521	The Spaniards, with their indigenous allies, topple the Aztec empire.
1535	Antonio de Mendoza is appointed the first Spanish viceroy of New Spain (Mexico).
1700	The Bourbons take over the Spanish empire from the Habsburgs and implement a series of "liberal" reforms.
1765	José de Gálvez arrives in Mexico as the Spanish Crown's visitor, and he spends five years at his comprehensive survey of colonial life and administration.
1767	The Jesuits are expelled from Mexico.
1808	Napoleon invades Spain, dethrones Charles IV, and installs his brother Joseph as Spain's regent.
1810	Miguel Hidalgo y Costilla declares Mexican independence on September 16. The Hidalgo uprising is not recognized by Spain, and Mexico's upper-class criollos and *peninsulares* remain committed to Spanish authority in the face of this grassroots popular rebellion.
1821	Agustín de Iturbide, a general in the Spanish colonial army, turns against Spain and sides

with the remnants of the rebels, and redeclares Mexican independence, which was recognized by the Spanish viceroy, Juan O'Donojú, in the 1821 Treaty of Córdoba.

1822 — Agustín de Iturbide is declared emperor of Mexico.

1823 — The first independent Mexican empire collapses, and Agustín de Iturbide abdicates his reign. Opposition to the empire is led by Antonio López de Santa Anna.

1824 — Mexico's first Federalist Constitution is promulgated.

1835 — Texas secedes from Mexico and declares its independence.

1836 — In March, the Mexican president, General Antonio López de Santa Anna, as part of his Texas campaign to forcefully reintegrate the wayward territory, engages and defeats a small contingent of fighters defending Texas's independence at the Battle of the Alamo.

In April, General Sam Houston defeats and captures Santa Anna at the San Jacinto River.

1845 — The U.S. Congress annexes Texas, which sets the stage for war between Mexico and the United States.

1846–1848 — In the U.S.-Mexican War, Mexico loses nearly one-half of its territory to the United States.

1854	The Gadsden Purchase is completed, in which more Mexican territory is acquired by the United States. This settles the current boundary between the United States and Mexico.
1855	Mexican dictator Antonio López de Santa Anna resigns his office following a liberal uprising based on the Plan de Ayutla.
1857	A liberal Mexican Constitution, incorporating very controversial provisions, is promulgated.
1857–1861	Civil war breaks out between liberals and conservatives, known as the War of the Reforms.
1861	The French invade and occupy Mexico.
1864	With the support of Mexico's conservatives and backed by French troops, Maximilian von Habsburg is installed as emperor of Mexico. Maximilian is joined by his wife, Carlota, and the second Mexican empire runs for approximately three years, from 1864 to 1867.
1867	The French withdraw from Mexico, and Maximilian is defeated by liberals and executed.
1876	Porfirio Díaz leads a coup and is installed as president, an office he controls until 1910.
1910	Francisco Madero, in his famous Plan of San Luís Potosí, leads a call to arms against the dictator Porfirio Díaz.

1911	In the face of the growing rebellion led by Francisco Madero, Porfirio Díaz renounces his office and goes into exile in France. Madero is first installed as president provisionally, and later wins election to the office.
1913	Mexican General Victoriano Huerta stages a counterrevolutionary coup. Madero and his vice-president, Pino Suárez, are executed.
1914	Victoriano Huerta resigns and the Carranza/Villa/Zapata revolutionary alliance succeeds him.
1917	The Mexican Constitution is promulgated.
1926–1929	The Cristero Rebellion takes place. During the rebellion, Catholic militant rebels battle the secular revolutionary government.
1929	The ruling party is formed, originally as the National Revolutionary Party (PNR), changing to the Mexican Revolutionary Party (PRM) in 1938, and then becoming the Institutional Revolutionary Party (PRI) in 1946.
1934–1940	Lázaro Cárdenas holds the presidency of Mexico.
1938	The petroleum industry is nationalized.
1940–1946	Manuel Ávila Camacho holds the presidency of Mexico.
1942–1964	The Bracero Program is instituted, whereby Mexican laborers are given legal status to work in the United States under the terms of

the program. It initiates migrant labor networks throughout the United States.

1945   Mexico sends troops to fight with the Allies in the Pacific Theater during the final stages of World War II.

1946–1952   Miguél Alemán Valdés is the first civilian president with no direct military experience in the Revolution.

1952–1958   Adolfo Ruiz Cortines holds the presidency of Mexico.

1958–1964   Adolfo López Mateos holds the presidency of Mexico.

1962   Mexico refuses to break diplomatic relations with Fidel Castro's revolutionary government in Cuba and opposes U.S. efforts to extend a sanctions regime against Cuba through the Organization of American States (OAS).

1964–1970   Gustavo Díaz Ordáz holds the presidency of Mexico.

1968   The Olympic Games are held in Mexico City. The Tlatelolco plaza student protest and massacre occur a month before the Olympics begin.

1970–1976   Luís Echeverría holds the presidency of Mexico.

1973   Mexico casts a controversial vote in the United Nations General Assembly declaring its support for a resolution equating zionism with racism.

1976–1982	José López Portillo holds the presidency of Mexico.
1978–1979	Vast petroleum reserves are discovered off the Gulf Coast of southern Mexico.
1982	Mexico defaults on its international debt, and the López Portillo administration nationalizes the banking industry.
1982–1988	Miguel de la Madrid holds the presidency of Mexico.
1985	Mexico joins the General Agreement on Tariffs and Trade (GATT) and embraces a neoliberal economic reform program.
1988	A contested election takes place between leftist ex-PRI candidate Cuauhtémoc Cárdenas (son of Lázaro Cárdenas) and Carlos Salinas. Carlos Salinas is declared the winner in murky circumstances.
1988–1994	Carlos Salinas holds the presidency of Mexico.
1994	The North American Free Trade Agreement goes into effect.
	The Zapatista uprising occurs.
	Carlos Salinas's handpicked presidential successor, Luis Donaldo Colosio, is assassinated on the campaign trail in March.
	The Mexican peso collapses in December.
1994–2000	Ernesto Zedillo holds the presidency of Mexico.
2000	Vicente Fox of the National Action Party (PAN) defeats Francisco Labastida of the PRI

and Cuauhtémoc Cárdenas of the Party of the Democratic Revolution (PRD) for the presidency, ending the PRI's dominance of the Mexican political system and the executive branch of government.

2000–2006   Vicente Fox holds the presidency of Mexico.

2003   The Mexican delegation on the Security Council of the United Nations refuses to support the Iraq War Resolution crafted and promoted by the United States and Great Britain.

2006   A contested election takes place between leftist PRD candidate Andrés Manuel López Obrador and PAN candidate Felípe Calderón. Calderón is declared the victor by less than half of 1 percent of the national popular vote. López Obrador refuses to accept the results and stages protests and occupations throughout the country, but centered in Mexico City. In December, Calderón is formally installed as president. Felípe Calderón assumes the presidency.

Significant People, Institutions, Places, and Events

Alamán, Lucas (1792–1853). Conservative Mexican states-man of the first years of Mexican independence. Alamán was known for his administrative brilliance and his intellectual acumen. Having witnessed as a child the evils of uncon-trolled mob violence in Guanajuato carried out by the un-principled and untrained masses that constituted what might be called Hidalgo's independence army, Alamán was very reluctant to embrace swift and radical social reform. He also was a staunch centralist who believed that Mexico's only hope for maintaining social order, constructing a uni-fied nation, and securing a modern economy depended upon a strong, unitary, central authority at the national level. In the later years of his life, Lucas Alamán published his fa-mous *History of the Mexican Republic*, which remains one of the most penetrating and observant studies of Mexico's first years as an independent country.

Aztecs. The ruling indigenous tribe in Mexico at the time of contact with the Spanish. The Aztecs were one of a number of Mexica tribes that competed for power and control in the Lake Texcoco region of the central valley of Mexico. There is no evidence that the Aztecs referred to themselves as such, preferring instead the use of the term "Mexica." The use of the name "Aztecs" became prominent in the 19th century and is generally thought to refer to the region of the tribe's origins, called Aztlán, which was located in the northern parts of contemporary Mexico and the southwest-ern United States. Today, the name "Aztecs" is the most commonly used and recognized name referring to these pre-Columbian peoples who lived in the central valley region of Mexico when the Spaniards arrived in the early 1500s. The Aztecs were a society guided by warfare, a polytheistic and fatalistic religion, and imperial expansion. The social and political structure of Aztec society was hierarchical, theocratic, and authoritarian. At the top of the political structure resided a hereditary nobility, led by an imperial monarch who was also imbued with divinity. The Aztecs spoke a language known as Nahuatl, which is still spoken among modern-day descendants of these indigenous peoples. Warfare was an integral part of the Aztec lifestyle, and human sacrifice was an established part of Aztec religious and political rituals. Modern-day Mexicans mostly embrace the cultural legacy of their Aztec indigenous past, take pride in its complexity and magnificence, and look to understand some of the more unseemly elements of the Aztec legacy as a product of the times.

Calderón, Felípe (1962–). The National Action Party's (PAN) candidate for the Mexican presidency in the 2006 national elections. Felípe Calderón was declared the official winner of the election by a slim margin. Amid protests levied by his defeated opponent in the election, Andrés Manuel López Obrador, of the left-leaning Party of the Democratic Revolution (PRD), and his supporters in the national Congress, Calderón took the oath of office as prescribed by the Mexican Constitution on the morning of December 1, 2006, thus officially assuming his position as the country's president until 2012.

Cárdenas, Lázaro (1895–1970). Perhaps Mexico's most famous postrevolutionary president and political leader. During his populist presidency, Lázaro Cárdenas initiated an ambitious agrarian reform program; improved the rights and protections for labor; and, in a bold move to assert Mexico's presence as an international power, expropriated and nationalized the petroleum industry. Cárdenas is often branded a socialist for his left-leaning social policies, but his dynamic and charismatic leadership made him one of Mexico's most beloved and most controversial 20th-century presidents.

Cinco de Mayo. The holiday commemorating the victory of Mexican forces over the invading French troops in the state of Puebla on May 5, 1862. It marks one of the few times when Mexican troops have successfully defeated a foreign invading force. Today, Cinco de Mayo is celebrated primarily among Mexican American communities in the southwestern United States and is usually associated with a festive party.

Cortés, Hernán (1485–1547). The astute and fearless Spanish conquistador who invaded Mexico with a small band of Spanish soldiers and who eventually, through deceit, bribery, cunning, and ability, defeated a much larger Aztec army. Hernán Cortés was born in the Extremadura region of Spain and sought his fortunes as an adventurer in the New World colonies of Spain. As a young man in his twenties, Cortés made the journey to the Spanish colony of Hispaniola and shortly thereafter to the island of Cuba, where he served under Diego Velázquez, then the royally appointed governor of the colony. In an act of insubordination, Cortés defied the orders of Diego Velázquez and embarked on a conquest expedition to the Mexican mainland where rumors indicated there existed an advanced civilization that possessed significant caches of precious metals and other riches. Hernán Cortés is perhaps one of the most significant actors in the history of Mexico, yet he is generally reviled and despised by Mexicans today for his role in the conquest of the great indigenous civilizations of the region. It is interesting to note that there are almost no visible monuments or memorials to Hernán Cortés throughout the entire country that recognize this conquistador's contribution to the creation of modern Mexico.

Cuauhtémoc, the last Aztec emperor. Cuauhtémoc was cousin to the famed Aztec emperor Montezuma II, ruler of the Aztecs at the time the Spanish, under the leadership of Hernán Cortés, arrived in Mexico. In the turbulent few years from the moment of Cortés's arrival to the fall of Tenochtitlán, Cuautémoc would prove his worthiness as an Aztec warrior and would eventually be chosen to lead his people against the Spanish invaders. He did not immediately succeed Montezuma II as the Aztec emperor. Following Montezuma's death, Cuitláhuac, Montezuma II's brother, inherited the title of Aztec emperor. However, Cuitláhuac fell victim to the smallpox disease rampaging through the defenseless Aztec population and died a short four months after taking power. Cuauhtémoc, apparently at the young age of 18, succeeded Cuitláhuac and mounted a valiant, but ultimately futile, final defense against the onslaught of the Spaniards and their indigenous allies. On August 13, 1521, in Tenochtitlán's neighboring city of Tlatelolco, Cuauhtémoc, while attempting to flee to seek reinforcements, was captured by the Spaniards. History records that Cuauhtémoc was tortured during his captivity by having his feet burned off for refusing to divulge the location of treasure deposits, which Cuauhtémoc insisted did not exist. Some three years after the capture of Cuauhtémoc on the field of battle, Cortés apparently ordered the execution of Cuauhtémoc. Today, Cuauhtémoc is revered in Mexico for his bravery and his opposition to foreign invasion. He is a symbol of the strong nationalist and antiforeign sentiment that characterizes this important aspect of Mexico's national culture.

Díaz, Porfirio (1830–1915). Mexico's president from 1876 until 1910. His long tenure in office, known as the Porfiriato, witnessed remarkable but uneven growth in Mexico's economic development. He maintained power through a combination of repression and co-optation, but as the population of the country grew, his authoritarian and elitist regime elicited criticism and protest from the growing numbers of disaffected Mexican citizens. This brewing disaffection burst into open revolt in 1910 after Porfirio Díaz reneged on his promises to uphold democratic elections. The resulting revolution forced Díaz into European exile, where he died in 1915.

Díaz del Castillo, Bernal (1496–1584). A Spanish conquistador and soldier who participated in the conquest of Mexico as a member of the expeditionary force assembled and led by Hernán Cortés. Bernal Díaz del Castillo is perhaps one of the most important chroniclers of the events of the conquest of Mexico from the perspective of a foot soldier. Díaz del Castillo began writing his firsthand chronicle of the conquest in 1568 in response to an account of the conquest written by Francisco López de Gómara, Hernán Cortés's biographer. Bernal Díaz del Castillo claimed that López de Gómara, who had never actually been to the Americas and had relied exclusively on the testimony of Córtes and a few other participants, had written a grossly inaccurate history of the events of the conquest. Díaz del Castillo's work is titled *True History of the Conquest of New Spain,* and it pretends to set the historical record of the conquest straight. It was published in 1632 and describes in particular detail, and in clear, simple language, many of the battles and personalities of the conquest. While his account cannot itself be held out as an impartial representation of the conquest of Mexico, it is still perhaps one of the most engaging and readable works of a contemporary eyewitness of the events.

Fernández de Lizardi, José Joaquín (1776–1827). A Mexican intellectual, journalist, and fiction writer of the late 18th and early 19th centuries. With the publication of *El Periquillo Sarniento,* or *The Mangy Parrot,* Fernández de Lizardi can be considered one of Mexico's first novelists. His writings, in the best of the picaresque tradition, poked fun at colonial authority, inefficient bureaucracy, and the unenlightened traditions of Mexican culture.

Fox Quesada, Vicente (1942–present). Mexican president from 2000 to 2006. He is the first opposition president to win election and govern Mexico in more than 70 years, putting an end to the traditional ruling party's predominance in Mexican politics and helping to consolidate the process of democratic transition. Vicente Fox was born in Mexico City in 1942, but was raised on the family ranch in the northern state of Guanajuato. Fox studied business administration in college and worked for the Coca-Cola Company's operations in Mexico. In 1975, Fox was promoted to chief executive of the corporation's Mexico division. Fox later left the company and started successful business ventures of his own. In 1987, Fox formally joined the conservative opposition National Action Party (PAN), and in 1988 he won election to a seat in the federal Congress representing his home state of Guanajuato. After his three-year term in the federal Congress expired in 1991, Vicente Fox ran as the PAN candidate for the governorship of the state of Guanajuato. Fox lost the election, but when the election was nullified by the president due to charges of electoral fraud, Fox ran again as his party's candidate in the subsequent special election in 1995 and won. Using the visibility of his governor's office, Fox catapulted himself into Mexico's national politics and eventually won his party's nomination to be its presidential candidate for the 2000 elections. Capitalizing on the frustrations of the majority of Mexicans with the traditional ruling party, and positioning himself as a populist moderate willing to forge cross-party coalitions, Fox convincingly won the 2000 presidential elections. Keeping true to his campaign promises of collaborative government, Fox constructed a presidential cabinet that included not only members who were politically associated with his own party, the PAN, but also members associated with the PRD, the Green Party, and even the defeated Institutional Revolutionary Party (PRI). Although his administration was characterized by an attempt to build a coalition partnership among like-minded individuals across the partisan political spectrum, the Fox administration was a disappointment to many of his initial supporters. In essence, the old adage that efforts to please everyone will end up pleasing no one may be a useful way to understand the Fox administration. To his credit, Fox refused to abuse the authority of office to govern autocratically, in spite of the proclivities within Mexican political culture that expect and support a strong and decisive president. However, this very reluctance to act within the parameters of a strong presidentialist political culture created an impression of indecisiveness and weakness and bolstered the efforts of his opponents to block many of his programs and policy initiatives. Nevertheless, Vicente Fox will continue to occupy his seminal role in Mexican politics for having been the first opposition president of postrevolutionary Mexico.

Hidalgo y Costilla, Miguel (1753–1811). Creole priest who led a grassroots independence movement in 1810. With the proclamation of his famous *grito de Dolores* issued on September 16, 1810, the march toward independence from Spain was irrevocably initiated. His movement, which appealed to disenfranchised lower and middle classes, was resisted by Mexico's privileged classes. Hidalgo was ultimately captured, defrocked, sentenced to death, and executed by the combined forces of creole and peninsular elites who feared the social transformations attendant to his independence movement.

Juárez, Benito (1806–1872). First and only Indian president of Mexico. A full-blooded Zapotec Indian, Benito Juárez was born on March 21, 1806, in the state of Oaxaca. Orphaned at the age of three, Juárez was raised by an uncle until the age of 12, at which time, knowing hardly any Spanish words, Juárez left his indigenous village for the state capital, where an older sister introduced him to a Franciscan lay brother who took Juárez under his charge, gave him a job in his bookbinding business, and provided for his general welfare and his education. Juárez eventually worked his way through law school and obtained his attorney's license in 1831. At this point, Juárez also began his career in public service as a politician, serving first as an alderman in the local Oaxaca city council and eventually receiving a provisional appointment as governor of the state of Oaxaca during the U.S.-Mexican War, and then winning popular election outright to this post in 1848. As a liberal critic of the autocratic governments of Antonio López de Santa Anna of the early 1850s, Juárez spent some time exiled abroad in the 1850s, during which he forged important and lasting relationships with like-minded liberal intellectuals and statesmen who would later become the architects of the liberal reform movement. From his exile in New Orleans, Louisiana, Benito Juárez participated directly in the crafting of the Plan de Ayutla, which called for the ouster of Santa Anna and the establishment of a liberal government. The Plan de Ayutla bore fruit in a revolution of the same name, which succeeded in deposing Santa Anna and inaugurating the liberal reform project. Juárez returned to Mexico in late 1855 as the secretary of Justice in the new provisional government and immediately set to work with his colleagues in realizing the liberal reform program. One such reform measure instituted by Juárez in his capacity as the secretary of Justice restricted the scope and function of ecclesiastical and military privileges, particularly circumscribing the reach of the ecclesiastical and military courts.

This reform measure, known appropriately as the Ley Juárez, required members of the clergy and the military to stand trial in civil courts, as opposed to the special ecclesiastical or military courts, for civil offenses. In 1857, Juárez became chief justice of the Supreme Court, which, according to the new liberal Constitution of 1857, made him second in line to the presidency. When a conservative rebellion broke out in December 1857, forcing the resignation of then-President Ignacio Comonfort, Juárez assumed the presidency under the terms of the 1857 Constitution. He governed Mexico from 1858 to 1870, during which time he fought against the conservatives in the War of the Reforms (1858–1861) and later led the struggle against the conservative-supported French occupation (1862–1867) and the resulting French-backed empire of Ferdinand Maximilian of Habsburg (1864–1867). Benito Juárez was a liberal purist in his staunch commitment to the more radical elements of liberal ideology of the time. However, Juárez was also a political pragmatist who realized that governing sometimes demanded accommodation with and openness toward alternative ideas. He died of a heart attack in 1872 while serving in his fourth term of office.

Kahlo, Frida (1907–1954). Another of Mexico's famous postrevolutionary artists, whose surrealist and visually graphic paintings reflected her appreciation of Mexico's indigenous culture and the painful circumstances of her personal life, particularly her physical disability. Along with her husband, Diego Rivera, and other muralists of the time, she formed part of a cadre of activist artists inspired by the socialist underpinnings of the Mexican Revolution. Frida Kahlo was born on July 6, 1907, in the family house in the Coyoacan suburb of Mexico City. Her father was a German immigrant to Mexico, and her mother was mestizo with strong indigenous roots. When she was 19 years old and still in school, Frida Kahlo was involved in a terrible trolley car accident that nearly cost her her life. She suffered multiple serious bone fractures throughout her body, but the most horrific injury came from being impaled by an iron handrail from the trolley car, which lanced both her abdomen and her uterus. She suffered the rest of her life from this injury, undergoing dozens of operations during her relatively short life; her reproductive organs were irreparably damaged, although she tried multiple times unsuccessfully to carry a conceived fetus to term, experiencing painful and bloody miscarriages each time. Her artistic production graphically mirrored the pain of her personal physical condition and also captured her fascination with indigenous folk culture as it interacted with modernity. She was an active social-ist/communist, and she participated regularly in marches and political manifestations. Kahlo's artwork, as well as her enigmatic life, has etched her image squarely into the national and artistic consciousness of modern Mexico. She died on July 13, 1954, at only 47 years of age.

López Obrador, Andrés Manuel (1953–present). A charismatic former mayor of Mexico City and ex-governor of the state of Tabasco who ran for president of Mexico as the left-leaning Democratic Revolutionary Party (PRD) candidate in the national elections of July 2006. López Obrador was officially defeated in the election by a slim margin, but he refused to accept the results of the election, claiming substantive voting irregularities. Supporters of López Obrador, with his approval and support, organized a massive protest movement challenging the official results of the election using the slogan "Voto por Voto" (or Vote by Vote) and demanding a full, nationwide recount of every individual ballot cast in the election. As part of this protest strategy, López Obrador supporters staged massive rallies in the *zocalo,* or the central plaza, of Mexico City throughout the months of July and August 2006 and forcefully occupied major thoroughfares in the downtown areas of Mexico City for much of this time as well. Having failed in his efforts to win a national recount of each individual ballot, López Obrador declared his intention to operate, from the streets, an alternative government to the officially sanctioned one.

Madero, Francisco (1873–1913). Mexico's first postrevolutionary president, his agitation against the dictatorship of Porfirio Díaz created the initial sparks that ignited the Mexican Revolution. An educated professional from the ranks of the upper classes, Francisco Madero represented the frustrations of Mexico's more politically liberal-minded elite who were kept at an arm's distance from the halls of power. His inability or unwillingness to address the underlying social inequities that bubbled out of the reform movement he initiated prevented him from consolidating his power. Soon after assuming the presidency following the fall of the dictatorship and the exile of Porfirio Díaz, Madero fell victim to a reactionary coup and was assassinated in 1911 along with his vice–president, Pino Suárez.

Malinche. Mexico's earliest and most infamous female personality. An Aztec woman sold into slavery to a Mayan indigenous community, Malinche (also known as Doña Marina) served as Hernán Cortés's translator and mistress. She was critical to the success of the Spaniards in defeating the Aztecs and dethroning Montezuma II, and she also was the mother of Cortés's son, who is considered symbolically to be the first true Mexican—a mestizo born of the violent union of a Spaniard and a person native to the region.

Maximilian von Habsburg (1832–1867). Archduke of Austria from the house of the Habsburgs who accepted an invitation from Mexican conservatives to preside over a monarchy in Mexico. With the backing of Napoleon III of France and the French military, and with the support of Mexico's conservatives, Maximilian ruled the country from

1864 to 1867. His short-lived regime ended in 1867 with his capture and execution by forces led by liberal Benito Juárez.

Maya. A highly developed group of indigenous peoples located primarily in the southern parts of Mexico, particularly in the Yucatan Peninsula. The origins of the Maya are hotly debated among historians and archaeologists, but it is certain that a flourishing and highly cultured Mayan civilization existed in the Mesoamerican region as early as AD 250. Some of the elements of Mayan culture and life include the construction of magnificent temples, palaces, and ball courts in the jungles of the Yucatan and the establishment of a highly complex social and political organization. Some scholars divide the Maya into two distinct civilizations: the classic (from about AD 250 to about 900) and the postclassic (from about 1250 to the arrival of the Spaniards in the early 1500s). Given the existence of multiple and linguistically distinct languages spoken among the Maya peoples throughout the region, it is impossible to pinpoint a single language that one might call Maya. There is considerable debate over whether the pre-Columbian Maya civilizations engaged in human sacrifice to the same extent as the Aztecs, but there is general consensus that some ritual human sacrifice did take place. There is also debate over whether the Maya social and political systems were decentralized around mini city-states or whether they were organized around major capital cities and subject to a centralized imperial authority. Regardless, the scientific accomplishments of the Maya are uncontested. The early pre-Columbian Maya were arguably the most advanced astronomers and mathematicians of their day.

Mexican Constitution of 1917. Mexico's governing document, produced out of the Mexican Revolution of 1910. It is subdivided under nine main sections, or titles, and contains 136 articles. It also contains an official addendum of 16 transitory articles. The original text was signed on October 31, 1917, but the original document has been officially and legally modified and amended numerous times since then. Not only is it a statement of political rights and principles addressing fundamental attributes of citizenship and the structure and mechanics of government, but it also contains significant social and economic provisions.

Mexican independence. Mexico's independence day is celebrated officially each year on September 16, which was the date that the criollo priest Miguel Hidalgo y Costilla issued his famous *grito de Dolores* in 1810, calling for Mexican independence from Spain. It is traditional that on this day, every executive authority, from the president of the country to state governors to city mayors, declare the *grito* in the public square. In Mexico City, the president reenacts Hidalgo's cry for independence from the balcony of the National Palace in the Mexico City *zocalo,* or central plaza, at 11:00 p.m. precisely, to the cheering and festive crowds gathered in the square.

Mexican Revolution. A violent and chaotic civil war that began in 1910 with the armed uprisings against the dictatorship of Porfirio Díaz and provoked by Francisco Madero in his Plan de San Luís Potosí. The violent phase of the Mexican Revolution lasted 10 years, from 1910 to 1920, and was institutionalized by the late 1920s and early 1930s. The Mexican Revolution produced some of Mexico's most famous national icons and heroes, including Francisco "Pancho" Villa, Emiliano Zapata, Venustiano Carranza, and Alvaro Obregón. Some estimates indicate that as much as 10 percent of the Mexican population died during this tempestuous period. The Mexican Revolution was perhaps the first significant social revolution in the world in the 20th century, and it continues to define Mexican nationalism today.

Montezuma II (16th century). Aztec emperor at the time of the arrival of the Spaniards to Mexico. His reluctance to challenge and confront the Spanish conquistadors led by Hernán Cortés contributed to his downfall and the defeat of the Aztec empire. Montezuma II lost his prestige and his people's allegiance when he permitted himself to be held under house arrest by Cortés. He died an ignominious death, with some reports indicating that he was stoned by his own people while attempting to appease them on behalf of the Spaniards from his captivity.

Morelos, José María (1765–1815). A creole priest who succeeded Hidalgo in the leadership of the mass independence movement. Morelos advanced the popular cause of the independence movement and even presided over Mexico's first effort at developing a national constitution. However, like his predecessor, Morelos was eventually captured, defrocked, and executed by Spanish colonial authorities. Morelos is hailed as a much more competent military tactician than Hidalgo, as well as a statesman who recognized the need to legitimize the military struggle for independence by codifying its underlying principles in a guiding document. Some might justifiably argue that Morelos was the first of Mexico's various independence leaders to attempt the formulation of a written constitution.

La Noche Triste. Infamous night during the conquest of Mexico during which Hernán Cortés and his party of Spanish soldiers and indigenous allies had to fight their way out of the center of Tenochtitlán in the middle of Lake Texcoco against the Aztecs. The date of La Noche Triste (also known as the Sad Night or the Night of Sorrows) is most commonly given as July 1, 1520. It is certainly the low point of the conquest for the Spaniards, who were disheartened by reports of significant casualties among the Spaniards and their indigenous allies. Hernán Cortés and some of his men managed to cross Lake Texcoco and to fight their way to safety. However, some chronicles report that the losses were so numerous and the despair so palpable that Cortés himself, utterly exhausted and stunned, wept bitterly in the immediate aftermath of the event.

Paz, Octavio (1914–1998). Nobel laureate and one of Mexico's leading intellectuals of the 20th century. At one time an ambassador of the Mexican government in India, Octavio Paz wrote numerous essays, poems, and pieces of fiction about all aspects of Mexican life. His most famous treatise, *The Labyrinth of Solitude,* remains an enduring portrait of the Mexican psyche and national identity. In 1968, Paz made a very public break with the authoritarian single-party state when he renounced his appointment as Mexico's ambassador to India because of the government's repression of student protestors in Tlatelolco plaza in 1968.

Plan de Agua Prieta. A formal pronouncement of rebellion against Venustiano Carranza formulated by revolutionary generals Alvaro Obregón, Adolfo de la Huerta, and Plutarco Elias Calles. This plan rejected the authority of the Carranza government and protested Carranza's intent to appoint his successor as well as Carranza's failures to implement more fully the provisions of the Constitution.

Plan de Ayutla. A plan of governing principles constructed by a group of liberal Mexican exiles in 1854 and pronounced officially on March 1 of that year. The plan conveyed a list of grievances against the autocratic government of Antonio López de Santa Anna and served as the ideological basis for a movement of rebellion against the Santa Anna government. The Plan de Ayutla served as the guiding document for what would become the Revolution of Ayutla, and the numerous rebellions that proclaimed their adherence to the Plan de Ayutla throughout 1854 eventually forced Santa

Anna from office. The Plan de Ayutla also called for the convocation of a junta guided by liberal principles to replace the ousted dictator and the eventual creation of a new national constitution based on the governing principles outlined in the document. The Plan de Ayutla ushered in the period known as The Reform (*La Reforma*) in Mexico, and the 1857 Constitution that emerged out of that period served as the basis for many of the guiding principles of the Mexican revolutionary Constitution of 1917. In fact, the date of March 1 is set aside as a national holiday in Mexico today in celebration of this event.

Plan de Casa Mata. An agreement reached by insurgent general Guadalupe Victoria and disaffected general Antonio López de Santa Anna in 1823 to challenge the empire of Agustín Iturbide. The plan represented an effort to coordinate and consolidate opposition movements against the Iturbide empire and called for a constituent congress to establish a constitutional republic to replace the empire.

Plan de Iguala. A plan formulated between conservative criollo General Agustín Iturbide and his liberal rivals to secure Mexico's independence from Spain in 1821. The plan outlined three guarantees that would form the cornerstones of an independent Mexico: the Catholic Church as the official state religion, the maintenance of the corporate rights and privileges of the Catholic Church in Mexico, and state-recognized equality of status between criollos and *peninsulares.*

Plan de San Luís Potosí. Francisco Madero's detailed pronouncement against the dictatorship of Porfirio Díaz. Issued in October 1910, the Plan de San Luís Potosí called for Mexicans to rise up in arms against the dictator and fixed the date of November 20 for this uprising. The plan concentrated on issues related to elite power transitions and did not emphasize the radical restructuring of Mexican society and economic life that the Mexican Revolution, which the Plan de San Luís Potosí initiated, would later come to represent.

PRI. The Partido Revolucionario Institucional, or the Institutional Revolutionary Party, was the ruling political party of Mexico, in one form or another, from 1929 until 2000. The origins of the PRI can be traced directly back to the formation of the Partido Nacional Revolucionario, or National Revolutionary Party (PNR) by Plutarco Elias Calles. Calles created the PNR following the assassination of Alvaro Obregón as a vehicle to manage the process of presidential succession without the inherent splintering and degeneration into the kind of unpredictable violence that had cost Obregón his life. The primary goal of the PNR was to provide an official imprimatur of consensus agreement among the revolutionary family in support of Calles's hand-selected successor. Essentially, the PNR was nothing more than an organizational vehicle subordinate to the personal authority of Calles. In 1938, Lázaro Cárdenas reformed the ruling party apparatus to be more broadly inclusive of the corporatist interest groups that constituted the pillars of the revolutionary family. The new party, the Partido Revolucionario Mexicano, or Mexican Revolutionary Party (PMR), brought together organized labor, peasant organizations, the popular sector (urban professionals, students, state functionaries, etc.), and the military as formal branches of the ruling coalition. Toward the end of the administration of Manuel Ávila Camacho, Cárdenas's successor, the PRM was converted to the PRI in recognition that the violent phase of the Revolution had become a rather distant memory and that the radical thrust of the revolutionary impulse had been tempered and had given way to an institutionalized normalcy. The PRI, appropriating all the symbols of the revolution and the national identity, would dominate Mexican politics for the remainder of the 20th century.

The Reform. Known in Spanish as *La Reforma,* The Reform was a movement led by liberals in the 1850s to transform Mexican state and society along liberal political, social, and economic principles. These principles included the restriction and limitation of corporate privileges, especially for the church and the military (the Ley Juárez); the secularization of the state and the dismantling of Catholic Church power (the Ley Lerdo and the Ley Iglesias), and the implementation of free market principles to guide Mexico's economic development. The controversial elements of the reform program provoked a civil war in Mexico between liberal reformers and conservative traditionalists. This civil war is known as the War of the Reforms.

Rivera, Diego (1886–1957). One of Mexico's most famous painters of the 20th century. Diego Rivera is best known for his massive murals that depict Mexico's indigenous past and its national history in the context of revolutionary ideals. He, along with David Alfaro Siqueiros and José Clemente Orozco, led the influential muralist movement in Mexican art that continues to exercise a profound influence over Mexico's postrevolutionary visual art traditions.

Salinas de Gortari, Carlos (1948–present). Mexican president from 1988 to 1994. Born in Mexico City in 1948 to a well-established political family, Salinas had an extensive career in government within a multitude of federal executive agencies before his election to the presidency in 1988. A lifelong member of the Institutional Revolutionary Party (PRI), Mexico's long-standing ruling party, Salinas worked his way up the ranks of the party bureaucracy to become the campaign manager for the PRI's 1982 presidential candidate, Miguel de la Madrid Hurtado, in whose administration he also served from 1982 to 1988 as the head of the powerful Planning and Budget Secretariat. Having earned a PhD from Harvard University in the United States in political economy and government, Salinas was the architect of Mexico's insertion in the global economy as a major player through his commitment to neoliberal economic reform. During his administration, Mexico signed the North American Free Trade Agreement (NAFTA) with the United States and Canada and underwent perhaps the largest privatization program of state-run enterprises in the nation's history. However, his administration was plagued with corruption and malfeasance, and Salinas, facing the prospect of criminal prosecution on a variety of charges, sought exile in Ireland soon after his term of office expired in 1994.

Santa Anna, Antonio López de (1794–1876). Antonio López de Santa Anna was a Mexican president, dictator, and military general during the early mid-19th century. Santa Anna was an enigmatic and charismatic leader who vacillated between supporting conservative and liberal factions in Mexico's early postindependence struggles to shape a national identity. He served as president, either elected or through military coup, a total of 11 times over the years 1833–1856. From 1824 to 1833, prior to his formal assumption of the presidency, Santa Anna was essentially the power behind the presidency. He is infamous for directing the Mexican troops in the bloody battle at the Alamo in 1836 following the secession of Texas from Mexico and its declaration of independence. Eventually captured and released by U.S. armed forces, Santa Anna returned to Mexico in disgrace, where he retired quietly for a while to his hacienda, Manga de Clavo, in his home state of Vera Cruz. However, when France blockaded the port of Vera Cruz and threatened to invade Mexico in 1838 as part of an effort to collect outstanding debts owed to French interests, Santa Anna sensed an opportunity to rehabilitate his damaged reputation and reestablish himself as the patriotic leader of a beleaguered and besieged nation. With the blessing of the hapless government in Mexico City, Santa Anna assumed leadership of the country's military response to the French aggression and personally led the successful armed resistance against the French forces. In the course of the fighting on the streets of Vera Cruz, Santa Anna suffered a battle injury to his left leg, the severity of which ultimately required its amputation below the knee. His reputation renewed, and his physical sacrifice to the nation duly noted, Santa Anna once again assumed his place as Mexico's preeminent leader for the next seven years. In early 1845, faced with popular discontent and armed uprisings against his increasingly autocratic tendencies, Santa Anna stepped down from power and was ultimately exiled to Cuba. But fate and circumstance would once again resuscitate Santa Anna in the Mexican national consciousness, for when the United States declared its annexation of Texas just a few short months after Santa Anna's exile to Cuba, Mexico once again found itself on the brink of war and desperate for seasoned military leadership to defend the national interest against the pretensions of a hostile foreign power. Santa Anna, who boasted a record of having chalked up impressive military victories on the fields of battle with the Spanish in 1829, with the Texans at the Alamo in 1836, and with the French in Vera Cruz in 1838, returned to attempt another military victory against the forces of the United States in 1846. Santa Anna was not so successful this time, as the forces of the United States eventually defeated the Mexicans and occupied Mexico City. Thus, Santa Anna also is infamous for being the Mexican leader responsible for surrendering the country to U.S. troops and for subsequently negotiating the terms of peace with the United States in the Treaty of Guadalupe

Hidalgo, a negotiation that essentially forced Mexico to cede to the United States nearly 525,000 square miles of the country's national territory in exchange for a paltry cash settlement of $15 million (about $28 per square mile of territory). Santa Anna managed to keep himself at the center of Mexico's political life for the next seven years following the U.S.-Mexican War. During his final presidency, Santa Anna secured his ignominy in Mexico's history by negotiating another sale of Mexican territory in 1853 to the United States in what is known as the Treaty of the Mesilla in Mexico, or the Gadsden Purchase in the United States. The Gadsden Purchase gave the United States, for its $10 million payment, about 30,000 square miles of territory in what is today southern New Mexico and Arizona. Santa Anna was finally and permanently ousted from power in 1855, spending the next 20 years of his life in exile. In 1876, Santa Anna returned to Mexico as part of a general amnesty, and he died a few years later in Mexico, ignored and penniless. However, Santa Anna left an indelible mark on Mexico and, for better or for worse, embodied and personified the cult of the charismatic caudillo, or military strongman.

Sor Juana. Sor Juana Inéz de la Cruz was a nun in 17th-century Mexico of extraordinary intellect and poetic talent. Instead of resigning her fate to the confinements of marriage and the limitations of advanced study that faced women of means in her day, Sor Juana chose a monastic religious life so as to be able to engage her intellectual pursuits. Sor Juana is perhaps most famous for her essay in response to public criticism of her life levied by the archbishop of Mexico in an essay published by him under a pseudonym. This "Answer to Sor Filotea" gave testament not only to the accomplished and rich intellectual life of Sor Juana but also highlighted the injustices and oppressions faced by women that served to subdue female creativity and limit their roles as contributors to the intellectual efforts of the time.

Tenochtitlán. The famous capital city of the Aztec empire. Built on an island in the middle of Lake Texcoco, Tenochtitlán was connected to the mainland by a series of bridges or causeways, and residents and visitors of the lake city navigated the city environs in canoes through a network of canals. The Aztecs founded Tenochtitlán in 1325. Legend has it that when the Aztecs arrived in the central valley and were searching for a place to settle in the region, they saw in the middle of Lake Texcoco an eagle perched on a cactus with a snake in its talons. According to an ancient prophecy, it was in just such a place where the Aztecs were to establish their new city. Upon the arrival of the Spaniards in November 1519, Tenochtitlán was a bustling center of commerce and activity, home to approximately 200,000 inhabitants. The great Aztec palaces, temples, and markets that characterized the city and added to its magnificence were nearly completely destroyed in the wars of conquest. In its place, the victorious Spaniards erected what is today Mexico City, which continues to be one of the largest and most populous metropolitan areas in the world.

Tlatelolco. Prior to the Spanish conquest, Tlatelolco was essentially a borough of the Aztec capital city, Tenochtitlán, even though it was nominally considered a distinct city in its own right. It was the Aztec empire's most important center for commerce and home to perhaps the largest and most vibrant market throughout the Western Hemisphere at the time. By the time the Spanish had arrived, Tlatelolco had been absorbed by the Aztecs and its management fell under the jurisdiction of the Aztec emperor. It was the last Aztec holdout in the wars of conquest, and its capture represented the final defeat of the Aztec empire, with some historians estimating that upwards of 40,000 native men, women, and children perished in the final battle of August 13, 1521. The Aztec emperor of the time, Cuauhtémoc, led the final stand against the Spanish at Tlatelolco, and his capture, torture, and execution soon after the end of this battle represented the last of the Aztec imperial authority. Today, Tlatelolco is home to the Plaza of the Three Cultures, where the intersections of pre-Columbian, colonial, and modern influences in Mexico are clearly on display. Today, a visitor to Tlatelolco plaza can see within the span of a single city block excavated ruins of the pre-Columbian architecture, a magnificent colonial church and convent built out of the stones that pre-Columbian peoples had used to construct their buildings and temples there, and the towering modern structure that was until very recently home to the Secretariat of Foreign Relations. Tlatelolco plaza is also significant to Mexico's modern history, as it was the site of the infamous 1968 government repression of university students and antigovernment activists who had gathered to rally in protest against the government's economic policies and the closed political system just prior to the 1968 Mexico City Olympic Games.

Villa, Francisco "Pancho" (1878–1923). Born as Doroteo Arambo Arámbula, Francisco "Pancho" Villa is one of Mexico's infamous and enigmatic revolutionary military leaders. From his base of operations in the northern state of Chihuahua, Pancho Villa commanded a large fighting force originating in the northern ranching region of the country. His military force, known as the Division of the North, represented the largest and best organized fighting contingents in the early years of the Revolution. Pancho Villa was known for his brashness, his fearlessness, and his vanity. Pancho Villa encapsulated the image of the Mexican revolutionary as a tough, mustachioed cowboy with the carbine belts (ammunition clips) criss-crossed along the chest. One of his most infamous moments involved the United States and occurred in January 1916. Pancho Villa, angry and disappointed with the United States for siding with his rival, Venustiano Carranza, ordered an attack on the U.S. city of

Columbus, New Mexico. In that attack, a number of U.S. soldiers and resident citizens of Columbus were killed. As a consequence, U.S. President Woodrow Wilson authorized General John Pershing to invade Mexico in search of Pancho Villa in order to capture him and bring him to justice for his attack on Columbus. For almost a year Pershing unsuccessfully hunted Villa. However, Villa's attack on the United States did not help his cause within the context of Mexico's internal political dynamic. Partly because of this, but also partly because of his continued hostility toward the Carranzistas and Obregonistas, Pancho Villa was eventually marginalized in the revolutionary struggle, went into a negotiated semiretirement from his revolutionary and military activities in 1920, and was himself eventually assassinated in northern Mexico in 1923. The details surrounding his death are not fully known, but there is considerable speculation that his political rivals at the local and national levels were complicit.

Virgin of Guadalupe. Also referred to as Our Lady of Guadalupe, the Virgin of Guadalupe is an indigenous representation of the Virgin Mary who has become a symbol of Mexico's Catholic and indigenous heritage. According to legend, the Virgin Mary, herself retaining indigenous features and characteristics, reportedly appeared to the native Mexican Juan Diego in 1531 on the hills of Tepeyac, located in the northern part of today's Mexico City. According to the story of the apparition, the image of the Virgin was miraculously imprinted on Juan Diego's *tilma,* a kind of cloak or apron worn by Aztec men as an outer-garment, and revealed to the archbishop of Mexico as proof of her appearance. There is much controversy over the authenticity of both the apparition and the image imprinted on the *tilma,* but there is no question that the Virgin of Guadalupe has served as an important manifestation of Mexican nationalism, having been used numerous times in the course of Mexican history as a rallying point for protest against abusive authority. Perhaps the most notable use of the Virgin of Guadalupe in this was during the 1810 independence movement led by Mexican criollo priest Miguel Hidalgo y Costilla and his successor, José María Morelos. Her image was repeatedly invoked by these early independence leaders as inspiration for the movement and as the patroness of the nation. Her feast day is celebrated on December 12, when thousands of devoted pilgrims come from all over the country to her shrine, many approaching on their knees to give her thanks and to invoke her blessings. Some consider the Virgin of Guadalupe to be a Christianized version of the Aztec goddess Tonantzin, especially since the shrine to the Virgin of Guadalupe is apparently constructed on the site that supposedly once hosted the Tonantzin temple. Pope John Paul II named the Virgin of Guadalupe as the Patroness of the Americas during his official papal visit to Mexico in 1999.

Zapata, Emiliano (1879–1919). One of Mexico's more important revolutionary leaders. Emiliano Zapata became the leader and the voice of Mexico's dispossessed peasantry during the turbulent and violent early years of the Mexican Revolution (1910–1914). He led a movement whose principle goal was agrarian land reform, and his efforts on behalf of the rural, largely indigenous, poor in the Mexican countryside resulted in the first meaningful representation of the rural peasantry in the formal political structure of the country. He was assassinated by his rivals among the different revolutionary factions in 1914.

Zapatistas. The EZLN, or the Zapatista Army of National Liberation. More commonly known as the Zapatistas, this group is a peasant-based resistance movement that initiated an armed uprising against the government in the southern Mexican state of Chiapas on January 1, 1994. Appropriating the name of one of Mexico's famous revolutionary leaders, this contemporary social and human rights movement advocates on behalf of indigenous rights and for a greater inclusion of indigenous voices in the national government.

MEXICAN PRESIDENTS SINCE INDEPENDENCE

Agustín de Iturbide (emperor) (1822–1823)
Guadalupe Victoria (1824–1829)
Vicente Guerrero (1829)
José María Bocanegra (interim, 1829)
Pedro Vélez, Luis Quintanar, and Lucas Alamán, triumvirate (1829)
Anastasio Bustamante (1830–1832, 1837–1839, and 1842)
Melchor Múzquiz (interim, 1832)
Manuel Gómez Pedraza (1833)
Antonio López de Santa Anna (variously from 1833 to 1855)
Valentín Gómez Farías (1833, 1834, and 1847)
Miguel Barragán (1835–1836)
José Justo Corro (1836–1837)
Nicolás Bravo (variously from 1839 to 1846)
Javier Echeverría (1841)
Valentín Canalizo (1844)
José Joaquín Herrera (interim, 1844, 1845, and 1848–1851)
Mariano Paredes Arrillaga (1846)
Mariano Salas (1846)
Pedro María Anaya (1847 and 1848)
Manuel de la Peña y Peña (1847 and 1848)
Mariano Arista (1851–1853)
Juan Bautista Ceballos (interim, 1853)
Manuel María Lombardini (1853)
Martín Carrera (interim, 1855)
Rómulo Díaz de la Vega (1855)
Juan Alvarez (1855)
Ignacio Comonfort (1855–1858)

Benito Juárez (1855–1872, liberal government)
Félix Zuloaga (1858 and 1859, conservative government)
Manuel Robles Pezuela (1858, conservative government)
Miguel Miramón (1859–1860, conservative government)
Ignacio Pavón (1860, conservative government)
Conservative Junta (1860–1864, conservative government)
Maximilian von Habsburg (emperor) (1864–1867, conservative government)
Sebastián Lerdo de Tejada (1872–1876)
Porfirio Díaz (1876–1880 and 1884–1911)
Juan M. Méndez (1876)
Manuel González (1880–1884)
Francisco León de la Barra (interim, 1911)
Francisco I. Madero (1911–1913)
Pedro Lascuraín (interim, 1913)
Victoriano Huerta (interim, 1913–1914)
Francisco S. Carbajal (interim, 1914)
Venustiano Carranza (1914 and 1915–1920)
Eulalio Gutiérrez (interim, named by convention, 1914)
Roque González Garza (1914)
Francisco Lagos Cházaro (1915)
Adolfo de la Huerta (interim, 1920)
Alvaro Obregón (1920–1924)
Plutarco Elías Calles (1924–1928)
Emilio Portes Gil (interim, 1928–1930)
Pascual Ortiz Rubio (1930–1932)
Abelardo L. Rodríguez (interim 1932–1934)
Lázaro Cárdenas (1934–1940)
Manuel Ávila Camacho (1940–1946)
Miguél Alemán Valdés (1946–1952)
Adolfo Ruiz Cortines (1952–1958)
Adolfo López Mateos (1958–1964)
Gustavo Díaz Ordaz (1964–1970)
Luís Echererría Alvarez (1970–1976)
José López Portillo y Pacheco (1976–1982)

Miguel de la Madrid Hurtado (1982–1988)
Carlos Salinas de Gortari (1988–1994)
Ernesto Zedillo Ponce de León (1994–2000)
Vicente Fox Quesada (2000–2006)
Felipe de Jesús Calderón Hinojosa (2006–present)

Source: Meyer, Michael C., William L. Sherman, and Susan E. Deeds. *The Course of Mexican History*, 8th ed. New York: Oxford University Press, 2007.

Mexican Language, Food, Etiquette, and Holidays

LANGUAGE AND COMMON EXPRESSIONS

Nearly all Mexicans speak Spanish, or *Español,* which is the official language of Mexico. In fact, as an individual country, with its national population totaling above 100 million inhabitants, Mexico contains by far the largest contingent of Spanish-speaking citizens in the world. Spanish is a romance language originating in the Iberian Peninsula of Europe. As a romance language, it is rooted in the classical Latin language and uses the basic Latin alphabet and grammatical structure, with only very minor variations.

Formally, the Spanish alphabet contains 30 characters: *a, b, c, ch, d, e, f, g, h, i, j, k, l, ll, m, n, ñ, o, p, q, r, rr, s, t, u, v, w, x, y, z.*

The letters "ch," "ll," and "rr" are considered as separate, individual letters within the Spanish alphabet, though they are each formed by the combination of two single-character letters that exist independently in the alphabet. Only the letter "ñ" with its required tilde may perhaps be considered a unique symbolic addition to the standard Latin alphabet within the Spanish linguistic tradition.

With the singular exception of the letter "h," which is silent, every letter of the Spanish alphabet has at least one distinct sound and pronunciation. The letters "c," "g," and "x" have two possible distinct pronunciations. The letter "c" can carry either a soft pronunciation, equivalent to that of the letter "s," or it can carry a hard pronunciation, equivalent to that of the letter "k." The letter "g" also has an aspirated pronunciation when immediately followed by the vowels "e" or "i" that would be the phonetic equivalent of the English pronunciation of the letter "h" sound. Conversely, the "g" in Spanish can also be pronounced with a hard, guttural sound that would be phonetically similar to the sound normally associated with the pronunciation of the letter "g" in English. The letter "x" can be pronounced either as the equivalent to the English diphthong "sh" or alternatively as the phonetic equivalent of the English letter "h" sound. These phonetic variations of the Spanish alphabet notwithstanding, a basic rule of thumb in speaking Spanish that applies almost universally is that nearly every letter and every syllable of the Spanish vocabulary is pronounced clearly and distinctly according to its unique sounds. In other words, Spanish is spoken as it is written. This rule represents the oral tradition of the Spanish language, setting it apart from other languages that make use of the Latin alphabet. If one has mastered the phonetic pronunciations of the Spanish alphabet, vocalizing the language from the written word is a relatively easy and simple process, as is writing the language from the spoken word. With the exception of the letter "h," there are no silent consonants or vowels. And the concept of blended diphthongs, which, in the English language, can create new sounds or which can swallow up individual pronunciations of single letters in multiple letter combinations, basically does not exist in the Spanish language.

However, even though Spanish is the dominant and official language throughout Mexico, a significant number of indigenous languages are still spoken in parts of the country that remain predominantly indigenous. When the Spaniards arrived in Mexico, the language spoken by the governing Aztecs was Nahuatl, while a Maya dialect was spoken in the Yucatan region. Other indigenous communities throughout the country still maintain elements of their native languages, and one can still hear native languages such as Mixtec and Zapotec, for example, just to name two, being spoken with some regularity in some areas of the country.

The persistence of functional and operational native indigenous languages in Mexico in the context of the imposition and development of Castilian Spanish as the predominant national discourse language has created a unique linguistic hybrid of sorts in which native words unique to Mexico have become assimilated in the Spanish language lexicon in Mexico. For instance, Spanish words such as *chocolate, guacamole, coyote,* and *tomate* are all derived directly from the Nahuatl language: *chocolatl, ahuaca-mulli, coyotl,* and *tomatl,* respectively. In fact, not only do these particular Nahuatl-derived words now garner universal acceptance as part of the official Spanish language lexicon, but they also have entered the standard lexicon of English. In the Yucatan region of southern Mexico, the same process can be noticed with regard to the blending of the Yucatecan Maya language and the Spanish language.

Common Spanish Words or Phrases

Buenos días   Good morning
Buenas noches   Good night
¡Hola! Cómo estás?   Hello! How are you?
Muchas gracias   Thank you very much
De nada   You're welcome
Discúlpame   Pardon me
Por favor   Please
¿Cómo te llamas? Me llamo . . .   What is your name? My name is . . .

Spanish Slang Particular to Mexico

¡Ándale, pues!   Well, get going!
¡Híjole!   My goodness!
¡Que padre!   How cool!

Órale Sounds great
Güey Dude
Cuate Buddy
Güero/a Light-haired, light-skinned person
Gringo A North American/U.S. citizen
El Otro Lado The United States

FOOD, HOLIDAYS, FESTIVITIES, AND FOLK CULTURAL PRACTICES

Avocado This fruit is unique to Mexico. Its Spanish name is *aguacate,* and its rich, creamy texture forms the basis for many of Mexico's popular dishes. It is sliced and used as a sandwich spread, and it is also mashed and mixed with tomatoes and spices to create a paste that is best known as guacamole.

Chile In Mexico, the chile refers to a wide variety of peppers. Most often the chile is associated with a hot, spicy taste, but only a selection of chiles actually have this effect. Many chiles have a mild taste and are used for a wide variety of dishes, including the very popular chile relleno, which consists of a mild chile that is stuffed with cheese and sometimes breaded. Chiles can range from the mild bell pepper all the way to the spicy jalapeño pepper and are used either to flavor certain dishes as a spice or to serve as a main dish itself. The chile pepper originates in the Americas. Certain chiles are dried and ground up into a powder, which is used as a spice that is placed on many different foods as seasoning.

Elote Roasted corn sold by street vendors in Mexico. It is served roasted directly on the corn cob and covered with any combination of condiments, such as mayonnaise, chili powder, grated cheese, or lime juice; or the roasted corned is cut from the cob and placed in a cup or bowl mixed together with the condiments and eaten with a fork or a spoon. Elote functions in Mexican popular cuisine and street food vending like the hot dog does in the United States.

Enchiladas   This typical Mexican dish consists of lightly fried corn tortillas that are basted in a particular sauce, usually one containing some measure of chile seasoning (hence the name en*chil*ada), and stuffed with a particular filling, covered with more sauce, and baked. Common stuffings include chicken, cheese, and beef.

Maíz   Maize, or Corn. It is the most important grain food in the Mexican diet. It forms the basis of tortillas and is often added to soups. In fact, corn can be obtained on the cob as a snack (see "Elote" above). Although maize is central to the Mexican diet throughout the entire country, in many areas, particularly among Mexico's indigenous communities in the south, corn is also central to religious beliefs, customs, and social life.

Nopal   The nopal is a vegetable plant derived from what are essentially the leaves of the prickly pear cactus. These flat, oval-shaped leaves, which are carefully plucked from the cactus plant, are covered with spines, which are removed from the tough skins of the leaves before cooking and consumption. Usually, the nopal leaf is cut into thin slices and is canned in water. The flesh of the nopal has a thick, viscous texture. It can be eaten raw, pickled, or sautéed. Usually it is served as part of a salad mixture; it can also be used as a garnish for tacos or other meat dishes. It has a tart, sometimes bitter flavor.

Pulque   An alcoholic beverage that is made from the fermented juice of the maguey plant. It has an opaque and milky consistency, and is mostly consumed by working and peasant classes in Mexico. Its origins are unknown, but pulque clearly appears in pre-Columbian pictorial manuscripts and artifacts as an important beverage imbued with special social and religious ritualistic meaning. Pulque is often mixed with fruit juices for a more pleasant taste.

Taco Perhaps the most common and most popular Mexican dish, the taco is a soft round corn tortilla whose edges are often dipped in cooking oil or grease and warmed on a grill or frying pan and filled with a variety of cooked meats. Sometimes seafood is used as a filling in tacos, but in Mexico, ground beef is almost never used. Very few condiments are put on top of taco meats. The most common toppings are chopped onion and cilantro, along with a variety of salsas. It is also usual for Mexicans to squeeze lime juice on tacos. Tacos are eaten with the fingers and involve folding the soft corn tortillas in half around the meat. Eating tacos is as much a social event as it is a meal, as Mexicans will gather outdoors around sidewalk taco stands during lunchtime and eat tacos while visiting with family, friends, or coworkers.

Tamale A Mexican dish made of a ground cornmeal mixture that is spread out over corn husks or banana leaves and filled with pieces of cooked meat or vegetables. The corn husk or banana leaf wrapping is folded so that the cornmeal mixture is completely contained, and the wrapped tamales are then cooked, usually by a steaming process. Tamales are quick and easy to make and are quite filling.

Tequila An alcoholic beverage made from the fermented and distilled juice of the blue agave cactus. Its production is strictly regulated by the government, and only certain regions of the country are legally licensed to farm the blue agave and to make tequila from it. Tequila is perhaps Mexico's most famous alcoholic beverage throughout the world. It can be drunk straight or it can be mixed with fruit juices and other liquors to produce a margarita, another well-known beverage associated with Mexico. Tequila comes in three main types: blanco (white), reposado (rested), and añejo (aged). Each type is determined by whether and for how long the tequila is stored in wooden casks before bottling and distribution. Blanco tequila is bottled immediately following the distillation process. Reposado tequila sits in wooden casks for 2 to 12 months. Añejo tequila must be aged for at least one year.

Tortilla   A flat, round, and thin pancake traditionally made out of corn kernels that have been soaked in a lime water mixture, ground into a pasty dough (or *maza*), and cooked over either a stone or a metal stove or griddle. In Mexico, the tortilla is much thinner than the tortillas made in other parts of Mesoamerica. Tortillas are a staple at nearly all Mexican meals. They can be eaten plain or can be used to make a variety of tasty dishes such as tacos, enchiladas, or fajitas.

Recipes of Traditional Mexican Dishes

Sopa de Tortilla.   This traditional Mexican dish makes use of a number of ingredients unique to Mexico's culinary culture: corn tortillas, tomatoes, cilantro, and chiles. In fact, a variety of chiles can be used, according to one's preference for taste and spiciness. Without the many garnishes or the tortillas, the soup is a relatively simple tomato vegetable base with a strong chile flavor. However, the garnishes and the fried tortilla strips are what make the soup particularly rich and tasty.

Ingredients
Soup
2 fresh ancho chiles
3 medium tomatoes, peeled (or one 15-oz can of whole tomatoes)
1 large onion, diced
5 cloves garlic
6 cups stock (usually chicken, but vegetable works just as well)
3 tbsp corn oil
1 tbsp finely chopped fresh cilantro

Salt
Corn tortillas
Garnish
Farmer's cheese
Avocado
Fried pork rinds (crumbled)
Crème fraîche (or sour cream)
Dried ancho chile (crumbled)

Cooking Instructions
First, cut off the stem of the chiles. Then remove the seeds from the chiles, slice the chiles into strips, and wash the chile strips. Place one-quarter of the chile strips aside. Lightly fry the remaining three-quarters of the chile strips, diced onions, and garlic in a large saucepan with the corn oil (3 tbsp) until they begin to soften. Place the lightly fried mixture into a food processor along with the remaining chiles and the fresh cilantro, and puree. Pour the mixture back into the saucepan along with the stock and bring to a boil. Then reduce heat and simmer for 30 minutes, stirring occasionally.

While the soup is simmering, prepare the tortillas and the garnish. First, cut the farmer's cheese and avocado into small cubes. Then place the cheese cubes, avocado cubes, crumbled pork rinds, crumbled dried ancho chiles, and crème fraîche in small bowls. Cover and set aside until soup is served. Next, slice corn tortillas into strips and fry the strips on both sides in corn oil (enough oil to cover the bottom of the frying pan) until crispy. Once crispy, remove from frying pan and drain.

When soup is ready to serve, place a portion of the fried tortillas in the bottom of the soup bowls and then ladle in the soup. Top off the soup with garnish according to preference and taste, and enjoy.

Mole Poblano. This dish is a peculiarly Mexican creation that combines unsweetened chocolate with other Mexican foods such as chiles and typical nuts and spices. The mole (chocolate) sauce is poured on top of cooked enchiladas, chicken, or turkey. It is an acquired taste, but one that really represents the unique role of chocolate in Mexican culinary traditions.

Ingredients
6 dried ancho chiles
4 dried pasilla chiles
4 dried mulato chiles
1 drained canned chipotle chile, seeded and chopped
    (optional)
2 onions, chopped
2 garlic cloves, chopped
1 lb tomatoes, peeled and chopped
1 stale tortilla, torn into pieces
1/3 cup seedless raisins
1 cup ground almonds
3 tbsp sesame seeds, ground
1/2 tsp coriander seeds, ground
1 tsp ground cinnamon
1/2 tsp ground anise
1/4 tsp ground black peppercorns
6 tbsp corn oil
1.5 oz unsweetened (bitter) chocolate, broken into
    quarters
1 tbsp sugar
2 cups turkey stock (chicken or vegetable stock may
    substitute)
Salt and freshly ground pepper

Cooking Instructions
Put the ancho, pasilla, and mulato chiles in a dry frying pan over gentle heat and roast them for a few minutes, shaking the pan frequently. Remove the stems and shake out the seeds. Tear the pods into pieces and put these into a small

bowl. Add sufficient warm water to just cover and soak, turning from time to time, for 30 minutes until soft.

Tip the chiles, with the water in which they have been soaked, into a food processor. Add the chipotle chile, if using, with the onions, garlic, tomatoes, tortilla, raisins, ground almonds, cinnamon, anise, and ground peppercorns. Process to a puree. Do this in batches if necessary. Then heat the oil in a large frying pan or a sauce pan that can accommodate both the puree mixture and the remaining ingredients, including the 2 cups of stock. After heating the oil for about a minute, stir in the puree mixture and continue stirring and cooking the mixture for 7–10 minutes on medium-high heat.

Stir in 2 cups of the turkey stock (part water may be used to make up the liquid content). Add the chocolate, and season with salt and pepper. Cook over low heat until the chocolate has melted. Stir in the sugar. Add more stock if needed. Cover the pan and simmer very gently for 30 minutes. The end of this process produces the mole sauce, which is then usually served over baked chicken or turkey or enchiladas, garnished with fresh coriander, and sprinkled with the sesame seeds.

Source: 101 Cooking Recipes.com, www.101cookingrecipes .com/mexican-recipes/mole-poblano-de-guajolote.php

Chicken and Chile Tamales. This relatively simple dish is basically ground cornmeal made into a dough, called *masa,* which is then filled with shredded rotisserie grilled chicken and chiles, wrapped tightly in a corn husk, and steam cooked. Though this particular recipe uses a chicken and chile filling, the corn dough can be steam cooked in the corn husk without any filling or with any precooked meat, poultry, fish, or vegetable filling of your preference.

Ingredients
6 cups corn masa mix for tamales
6 cups chicken broth

1 cup corn oil
2 tsp salt
1 tsp baking powder
1 1/2 large rotisserie chicken
4 poblano chile peppers
2 cans green salsa (salsa verde)
1 bag corn husks

Cooking Instructions
1. Soak the corn husks in warm water until soft.
2. Remove the stems, deseed, and dice the poblano chile peppers into small pieces. Sautee diced chile pieces in a little corn oil until soft.
3. Blend corn masa mix for tamales, corn oil, salt, baking powder, and chicken broth in an electric mixer until you obtain a consistent mixture.
4. Shred the chicken, mix in the sautéed chiles, and marinate mixture in the green salsa or tomatillo sauce.
5. Spread masa evenly over corn husks, and spread a spoonful of marinated chicken on top of the masa.
6. Fold the sides of the corn husk to center over the masa so that they overlap to make a long package.
7. Fold the empty part of the husk under so that it rests against the side of the tamale with a seam.
8. Place the tamales in tamale steamer and cook tamales for 35–40 minutes. Check every 20 minutes. The tamales are cooked when they separate easily from the corn husk.

Holidays

Day of the Dead Also known as Día de los Muertos, the celebration of this holiday is unique to Mexico. The Day of the Dead corresponds somewhat to the Catholic Christian traditions of All Saints' Day and All Souls' Day. It is celebrated over the days of October 31–November 2. However, in Mexico, the celebration is also rooted in pre-Columbian Aztec traditions in which participants celebrate and commune with the dead. During this holiday, Mexicans construct altars in honor of their deceased relatives and friends. Often, Mexicans will do so at the graveyards where their relatives and friends are buried. In blending ancient pre-Columbian indigenous traditions with Catholic Christian traditions, Mexicans both celebrate and mock death during these days, and they commemorate the deceased in a unique way.

Retablos   Traditionally, retablos are small paintings, generally on flat surfaces such as pieces of wood or tin, which depict religious devotional scenes. Retablos are a form of art that blends popular devotion with Catholic iconography. While retablo production concentrated on religious altar pieces and depicted Christian saints and holy scenes, retablos have been embraced by the public as a means to express graphically thanks for prayers answered or for divine protection rendered.

Día de los Reyes   Celebrated on January 6 in commemoration of the Christian event marking the visit of the Three Wise Men, or the three Magi, to the stable where Jesus Christ was born. On this day, children awake to find presents left for them by the Magi, and the day is usually celebrated with a lively family meal that includes the traditional *rosca de reyes,* or king cake. Tiny figurines of babies are hidden in the cake dough before baking, and whoever receives that piece of the king cake containing the baby is traditionally supposed to host the next party before the formal end of the Christmas season, which is Candlemas on February 2.

Posadas Navideñas (Christmas Posadas)   Lasting nine days, from December 16 to Christmas Eve (December 24), the Posadas festivities take place all throughout Mexican neighborhoods and commemorate the journey of Mary and Joseph to Bethlehem and their search for a place to stay. Usually, the festivities are for children, who dress in costume each day as Christmas *peregrinos* (pilgrims) reenacting the journey. Children will dress as shepherds, the Three Wise Men, and Mary and Joseph themselves. The group of young pilgrims, led by the little Virgin Mary, sometimes even riding a live donkey, stop at the door of three houses as part of the ritual. At each house, the children pilgrims and the homeowners will sing the traditional posada song that requests shelter for the holy family. The first two homes turn the pilgrims away, but the last home invites the pilgrims to stay in the stable, at which time the doors to the home are opened and everyone enters for a grand party. For the children, this means being able to break the traditional piñata filled with Christmas sweets and treats.

Mexican Independence Day   September 16 is Mexico's national independence day. This is the day when Mexican priest Miguel Hidalgo y Costilla issued his famous *grito* (shout) for independence in 1810. Although Mexico's legal independence would not be achieved until 11 years later with Spanish Viceroy Juan O'Donojú's recognition of the principles of General Agustín Iturbide's Plan de Iguala, September 16, 1810, is popularly recognized as the birth of Mexican independence. Every September 15, the day before Mexico's independence day, executive authorities all throughout the country, from the Mexican president to municipal mayors, gather in the place of executive authority and reissue Hidalgo's *grito* as part of a ceremonial remembrance of the country's independence.

Feast Day of the Virgin of Guadalupe   The feast day of the Virgin of Guadalupe is December 12. On this day, thousands of Mexicans gather at the Basilica of the Virgin of Guadalupe, which contains the *tilma,* or cloak, of Juan Diego upon which the Virgin's image was supposedly miraculously imprinted some 475 years ago. During this feast day, pilgrims to the Basilica will come to worship and pray to the Patroness of the Americas for her continued protection and intercession.

Civic holiday calendar   In addition to the cultural traditions and festivities that Mexicans celebrate, Mexicans observe a number of civic holidays in honor of the important moments and people in the political history of Mexico. Some of the most prominent of these civic holidays are as follows:

February 5: Anniversary of the Promulgation of the
    Mexican Constitution
February 19: National Army Day
February 24: National Flag Day
March 1: Anniversary of the Proclamation of the Plan de
    Ayutla
March 21: Birthday of Benito Juárez
March 26: Anniversary of the Proclamation of the Plan de
    Guadalupe
May 5: Anniversary of the Mexican Victory over the
    French Army
May 8: Birthday of Miguel Hidalgo y Costilla
June 1: National Navy Day
September 16: Independence Day
September 30: Birthday of José María Morelos
October 12: Columbus Day/Day of *La Raza* (the race)
November 20: Anniversary of the Start of the Mexican
    Revolution

Mexico–Related Organizations

BUSINESS ORGANIZATIONS

Association of Banks of Mexico
(*Asociación de Bancos de México,* or ABM)
Av. 16 de Septiembre No. 27, 3er Piso
Centro Histórico
C.P. 06000, México, D.F.
www.abm.org.mx/
    This organization is composed of 31 of the largest banking institutions in Mexico. It was originally established in 1928 to represent the interests of the banking community. In addition to promoting the interests of its member institutions, it functions as an advisory body to the Mexican government on matters of finance and credit.

Business Coordinating Council
(*Consejo Coordinador Empresarial,* or CCE)
Lancaster 15
Col. Juárez
C.P. 06600, México, D.F.
www.cce.org.mx/cce/home.htm
    Organized in 1976 as a coordinating body that represents the largest and most important business groups in Mexico, its goals are to promote economic stability, respect for private property, and the rights of business. Additionally, it functions as a lobbying group whose purpose is to represent its members' interests in front of national political authorities.

Confederation of National Chambers of Commerce,
  Services, and Tourism
(*Confederación de las Camaras Nacionales de Comercio,
  Servicios, y Tourismo,* or CONCANACO-SERVYTUR)
Balderas No. 144
Col. Centro C.P. 06079, México, D.F.
www.concanacored.com/
This organization traces its origins back to the earliest
days of the Mexican Revolution. Founded in 1917, its mis-
sion is to represent the interests of the various chambers of
commerce that exist throughout Mexico.

Confederation of Industrial Chambers of the United
  Mexican States
(*Confederación de las Cámaras Industriales de los
  Estados Unidos Mexicanos,* or CONCAMIN)
Manuel Ma. Contreras 133
Col. Cuauhtémoc
Delegación Cuauhtémoc
C.P. 06500, México, D.F.
www.concamin.org.mx/
Founded in 1918, the Confederation of Industrial Cham-
bers represents the major industrial, construction, trans-
portation, and manufacturing companies throughout Mexico.

Employers' Confederation of the Mexican Republic
(*Confederación Patronal de la República Mexicana,* or
  COPARMEX)
www.coparmex.org.mx/index.php
Founded in 1929, this is a voluntary association of businesses whose purpose is to promote employer rights, to
struggle against unjust labor demands, and to promote respect for private property and private industry. It has historically been a group hostile to the statist economic
development model and opposes state ownership of business.

National Chamber of the Industry of Transformation
(*Camara Nacional de la Industria de Transformación,* or
    CANACINTRA)
Av. San Antonio No. 256
Col. Ampliación Nápoles
Delegación Benito Juárez
C.P. 03849, México, D.F.
info@canacintra-digital.com.mx
www.canacintra.org.mx/

This organization was founded by a group of industrialists in 1941 to promote the development of small- to medium-size national industrial enterprises. It was created in the context of the beginning of Mexico's state-led import-substituting industrialization economic development model to facilitate business ties to the federal, state, and local governments. It has been closely associated with the Institutional Revolutionary Party (PRI) government and, under the banner of forming a nationalist industrial capacity that serves the domestic market, generally supports governmental efforts to protect small- to medium-size Mexican-owned industrial enterprises from larger and better-capitalized national and international competitors.

National Livestock and Agricultural Council
(*Consejo Nacional Agropecuario,* or CNA)
Xola No. 914 esquina con Juan Sánchez Azcona
Col. Narvarte
Delegación Benito Juárez
C.P. 03020, México, D.F.
E-mail: cna@prodigy.net.mx
www.cna.org.mx/index.htm

This organization was formed in 1984 to represent the interests of the private agricultural and livestock industry. Its goals are to encourage modernization and innovation in the agrarian sector of the Mexican economy with the intent to create an agrarian sector that serves as the main engine for national economic growth and to meet the basic alimentary needs of the Mexican people through sustainable, market-led rural development.

Mexican Association of Insurance Institutions
(*Asociación Mexicana de Instituciones de Seguros,* or AMIS)
Francisco I. Madero, No. 21
Col. Tlacopac
Delegación San Angel
C.P. 01040, México, D.F.
E-mail: amis@mail.internet.com.mx
www.amis.com.mx

Initially founded in 1897 as an association of fire insurance agents, the organization went through many modifications throughout its evolution. Originally, its members were constituted primarily by foreign insurance companies until 1935, when the Cárdenas administration effectively nationalized the insurance industry. The organization represents its affiliated members in front of local, state, and federal authorities.

CULTURAL ORGANIZATIONS

National Institute of Anthropology and History
(*Institúto Nacional de Antropología y Historia,* or INAH)
Córdoba No. 45
Col. Roma
Delegación Cuauhtémoc
C.P. 06700, México, D.F.
www.inah.gob.mx/

This government-run agency is responsible for the care, maintenance, preservation, and promotion of Mexico's cultural and archaeological patrimony. It manages more than 110,000 national monuments as well as approximately 29,000 registered archaeological zones across the country, including the pyramids of Teotihuacan, the Templo Mayor, and the well-known Maya sites in the Yucatan Peninsula such as Chichén-Itzá and Tulum. Additionally, the INAH supports and maintains a number of important national museums, among them the world-famous National Museum of Anthropology. It also oversees the operations of the many regional state museums across the country.

National Council for Culture and the Arts
(*Consejo Nacional para la Cultura y las Artes,* or
   CONACULTA)
Arenal No. 40
Col. Chimalistac
Delegación Álvaro Obregón
C.P. 01050, México, D.F.
www.conaculta.gob.mx/
   Another government-run agency responsible for the preservation and dissemination of Mexican culture and the arts, its mission is broader than that of the INAH in that it coordinates the full range of state-supported visual and creative arts throughout the country. As a division of the Secretariat of Public Education, its mission also includes arts education and training.

Mexican Federation of Soccer Association
(*Federación Mexicana de Fútbol Asociación,* or
   FEMEXFUT)
Colima #373
Col. Roma Norte
Delegación Cuauhtémoc
C.P. 06700, México, D.F.
www.femexfut.org.mx/
   The Mexican Federation of Soccer Association is the governing body for the sport of soccer in Mexico. It fields the Mexican national soccer team for international competition,

it maintains a professional soccer league within Mexico, and it guides and promotes the sport of soccer at all other levels within Mexican society. It adheres to the International Federation of Soccer Association, better known by its acronym, FIFA, which governs the sport of soccer at the international level.

MEDIA

Grupo Televisa
Avenida Vasco de Quiroga 2000
C.P. 01210, Mexico, D.F.
www.televisa.com

This organization is one of Mexico's prominent media giants. It provides television programming as well as other media services not only to Mexicans but also throughout the world.

TV Azteca, SA de CV
Periférico Sur #4121
Col. Fuentes del Pedregal
Delegación Tlalpan
C.P. 14141, México, D.F.
www.tvazteca.com/corporativo/directorio.shtml

TV Azteca is Mexico's second-largest media outlet. Like its main competitor, Grupo Televisa, TV Azteca provides various television and other media programming throughout Mexico and the world.

News Agency of the Mexican State
(*Agencia de Noticias del Estado Mexicano,* or NOTIMEX)
Morena 110
Col. Del Valle

Delegación Benito Juárez
C.P. 03310, México, D.F.
www.notimex.com.mx

An organization that serves as the official vehicle of disseminating news relative to the functioning of the state and its various public agencies, it functions loosely as a kind of official news wire service, but it lacks the managerial and organizational independence from the Mexican government that other independent news wire services such as the Associated Press or Reuters enjoy.

Reforma Newspaper
Av. México Coyoacán
40 Col. Santa Cruz Atoyac
Delegación Benito Juárez
C.P. 03310, México, D.F.
Telephone: +52 (55) 5628 7100
www.reforma.com

Established in 1993 as an alternative to the traditional print news sources, the *Reforma* newspaper has evolved into one of Mexico's most influential print media outlets with an impressive national circulation. It has ties to the reform-minded elites of Monterrey, in the northern region of the country, who saw this newspaper as a way to democratize the print media from its semidependent relationship with the state. The *Reforma* newspaper is often characterized as a right-leaning source, though it regularly publishes columnists from all political perspectives. Its use of color printing, its particular sectional divisions, and its emphasis on keeping its stories short and contained to one page whenever possible transformed the method of news presentation within Mexico into a more corporate and commercialized process.

La Jornada Newspaper
Ave. Cuauhtémoc
1236 Col. Santa Cruz Atoyac
C.P. 03310, México, D.F.
Telephone: +52 (55) 9183 0300
www.jornada.unam.mx/
    Mexico's traditionally left-leaning, progressive newspaper, *La Jornada,* holds perhaps the best reputation for independent, critical investigative journalism in Mexico. In keeping with its progressive orientation and its commitment to the democratization of news dissemination, *La Jornada* makes its entire reporting available free of charge on the Internet. Its Web site is hosted out of the National Autonomous University, Mexico's preeminent public institution of higher education.

TOURISM

Mexican Secretariat of Tourism
Av. Presidente Masaryk No. 172
Col. Chapultepec Morales
C.P. 11587, México, D.F.
Telephone: +52 (55) 3002 6300
www.sectur.gob.mex
    This governmental cabinet-level agency sets and implements policy regarding Mexico's tourism industry. It also regulates the tourism industry and coordinates the government's interactions with the private sector. Additionally, part of this agency's mission is to make Mexico attractive to potential foreign tourists and visitors. As such, it involves itself in the tourism industry's marketing and advertisement campaigns.

HUMAN RIGHTS AND NONGOVERNMENTAL ORGANIZATIONS

Civic Alliance
(*Alianza Cívica*)
Benjamin Franklin 186
Col. Escandon
C.P. 11800, México, D.F.
www.sol-com.com/clientes/alianza-civica/

This organization is a national nongovernmental organization (NGO) whose mission is to foster citizen interest and engagement in public policy matters. It conducts workshops, meetings, and seminars that address issues concerning independent civic life; it also emphasizes leadership training among Mexican politicians.

Transparency Mexico
(*Transparencia Mexicana*)
Dulce Olivia 73
Col. Villa Coyoacan
C.P. 04000, México, D.F.
www.transparenciamexicana.org.mx/

An affiliate of Transparency International, Transparency Mexico is an independent NGO committed to fighting institutionalized corruption and to creating vehicles for greater public access to information relative to the functioning and the operations of the Mexican government. One of its main goals is to hold government accountable and, in so doing, preserve the fundamental civil rights of individual citizens relative to the government.

National Commission of Human Rights
(*Comisión Nacional de Derechos Humanos*)
Periférico Sur 3469
Col. San Jerónimo Lídice
Delegación Magdalena Contreras
C.P. 10200, México, D.F.
www.cndh.org.mx/

This organization, sanctioned by the state and supported by constitutional mandate, is responsible for investigating any human rights violations complaints. It supposedly functions independently of the state. In addition to investigating and acting upon human rights violations complaints, it also educates the Mexican population on human rights issues and serves in an advisory capacity to the state with regard to national and international accords that treat human rights.

Friar Bartolome de las Casas Center of Human Rights
(*Centro de Derechos Humanos Fray Bartolomé de las Casas*)
Calle Brasil
No. 14 Barrio de Méxicanos
C.P. 29240, San Cristóbal de Las Casas
Chiapas, México
www.frayba.org.mx/

This organization specifically monitors the human rights situation of the indigenous people of Chiapas. In addition to publishing and exposing human rights abuses against the indigenous people of Chiapas, the organization also seeks to preserve the historical memory of the struggle of the indigenous people of Chiapas against abuses.

GOVERNMENT AND POLITICAL ORGANIZATIONS

Presidency of the Republic
(*Presidencia de la República*)

Residencia Oficial de los Pinos Casa Miguel Alemán
Col. San Miguel Chapultepec
C.P. 11850, México, D.F.
www.presidencia.gob.mx/en/

The office of the Presidency of the Republic is responsible for coordinating the activities and the agenda of the Mexican president, as well as the management of his cabinet. The office also serves as a conduit for the articulation of public sentiments to the national executive. Conversely, the office of the presidency, through its public relations and public information divisions, communicates executive policy and the president's strategic vision for the country to the public and to the international community.

Secretariat of Foreign Relations
(*Secretaría de Relaciones Exteriores*)
Plaza Juárez No. 20
Col. Centro
Delegación Cuauhtémoc
C.P. 06010, México, D.F.
www.sre.gob.mx/

This government ministry is responsible for maintaining and promoting Mexico's interests and its image beyond the country's borders. Mexican foreign policy is channeled through this cabinet agency. The Mexican Secretariat of Foreign Relations is also charged with protecting and defending the rights of Mexican citizens abroad. Because it is the agency of the Mexican state responsible for directing relations with the United States, U.S. citizens interested in any kind of exchange with Mexico are well advised to familiarize themselves with this particular government agency's services and functions.

National Trust Fund for Tourism Development
(*Fondo Nacional de Fomento al Turismo,* or FONATUR)
Tecoyotitla No. 100

Col. Florida
C.P. 01030, México, D.F.
www.fonatur.gob.mx/

As the Mexican economy becomes ever more dependent on revenues generated through the tourism industry, the need for the state to become increasingly involved in its continued financial success also becomes more urgent. The National Trust Fund for Tourism Development is a parastatal agency whose mission is to coordinate and facilitate the sustainable growth and development of this vital sector of the Mexican economy, especially as it relates to the development of other sectors of the Mexican economy, such as manufacturing, energy, and industrial production.

Federal Electoral Institute
(*Instituto Federal Electoral,* or IFE)
Viaducto Tlalpan No. 100
Col. Arenal Tepepan
Delegación Tlalpan
C.P. 14610, México, D.F.
www.ife.org.mx/

The Federal Electoral Institute is an autonomous organization responsible for conducting national elections to the presidency and to the Mexican federal legislature. It was established in 1990 as part of a sweeping electoral reform program intended to address the issue of electoral fraud and to sanction the fairness and independence of the electoral process at the national level. Not only does the IFE implement the electoral process at the national level but it also assumes responsibility for voter registration as well as the formal registration and regulation of Mexico's political parties.

Annotated Bibliography of Recommended Works on Mexico

The literature on Mexico is plentiful and varied. For students interested in texts that focus on Mexico's history in a comprehensive, but readable, way, perhaps the best place to start is Michael C. Meyer, William L. Sherman, and Susan E. Deeds's *The Course of Mexican History*, 8th edition (New York: Oxford University Press, 2007). This classic textbook, now in its eighth edition, covers the entire range of Mexico's history from the earliest civilizations in the region to the contemporary period. The book is divided into clear and standard historical periods, with chapters covering the basic institutional and political history of each period as well as the culture and society of the times. As an added bonus, instead of the comprehensive bibliography at the end of the full text, each brief chapter ends with a selected list of about 15 to 20 additional readings specifically on the subject of the chapter. It is perhaps the best general source written in English on the full range of Mexican history. Supplementing this work is Brian R. Hamnett's *A Concise History of Mexico*, 2nd edition (New York: Cambridge University Press, 2006), which is a bit more dense and a bit less comprehensive, but still a very useful source in English, which covers the full range of Mexico's history. Not to be forgotten is Lesley B. Simpson's classic work *Many Mexicos*, 4th edition revised (Berkeley: University of California Press, 1966). Simpson's book amounts to a series of essays on various individuals and events throughout Mexico's history up through the Mexican Revolution. Its purpose, I believe, is not to chart every moment of Mexico's history but to give a sense of the overall environment and context in Mexico in which these people existed or these events took place. Simpson offers a very spirited and animated account of the stories from Mexico's history he chooses to tell. His history is simply a joy to read, and his chapter on Santa Anna is one of the most expressive and humorous tellings of this story that I have experienced.

The literature on specific periods in Mexico's history is even more rich and plentiful. Excellent treatments of Mexico's pre-Columbian civilizations include Michael D. Coe's *Mexico: From the Olmecs to the Aztecs* (London: Thames and Hudson, 1994); Eric Wolf's *Sons of the Shaking Earth: The People of Mexico and Guatemala—Their Land, History, and Culture* (Chicago: University of Chicago Press, 1974); Richard F. Townsend's *The Aztecs,* revised edition (London: Thames and Hudson, 2000); Michael D. Coe's *The Maya,* 7th edition (London: Thames and Hudson, 2005); and Alan Knight's *Mexico: From the Beginning to the Spanish Conquest* (Cambridge, UK: Cambridge University Press, 2002). Among these five books, Knight's is perhaps the most readable and concise summary of Mexico's pre-Columbian history.

With regard to the literature on the Spanish Conquest of Mexico, nothing compares with the works of the chroniclers who witnessed the events and wrote contemporary accounts of them. Bernal Díaz del Castillo, a Spanish soldier in Hernán Cortés's army, is the author of perhaps the most famous of such accounts, *The Conquest of New Spain,* translated by John Cohen (New York: Penguin Publishers, 1963). An engaging retelling of the story, based on painstaking research into many of these primary documents, is Hugh Thomas's *Conquest: Montezuma, Cortés, and the Fall of Old Mexico* (New York: Simon & Schuster, 1995). Although his scholarship is sound, Thomas's approach to relating history is less that of the dispassionate academic and more that of a narrative storyteller; Thomas makes the story of the

Conquest of Mexico vibrant and lively. Of course, this story would not be complete without at least some reference to the indigenous account of the events. Scholars continue to give more attention and study to uncovering the native version of this controversial history, but the standard and still excellent contribution to this avenue of scholarship is Miguel León-Portillo's *The Broken Spears: The Aztec Account of the Conquest of Mexico*, expanded and updated edition (Boston: Beacon Press, 2007).

Alan Knight's *Mexico: The Colonial Era* (London: Cambridge University Press, 2002), is perhaps the best general treatment of Mexico's particular place in Spain's imperial project in the Americas. However, other works that look at the Spanish colonial system overall give a very good grounding in the dynamics that explain the political, economic, and social life of colonial Mexico. Although it is a bit dated, Clarence H. Haring's *The Spanish Empire in America* (New York: Harcourt, 1985), explains in great detail the structure and functioning of the Spanish colonial political and administrative apparatus. It is an excellent source for understanding how various actors such as the viceroy, the *audiencia,* the Council of the Indies, and so forth, interacted and evolved in the Spanish colonial empire. Works that treat in some detail important economic and social institutions of colonial Mexico include François Chevalier's *Land and Society in Colonial Mexico: The Great Hacienda* (Berkeley: University of California Press, 1963); Lesley B. Simpson's *The Encomienda in New Spain* (Berkeley: University of California Press, 1960); and Robert Ricard's *The Spiritual Conquest of Mexico* (Berkeley: University of California Press, 1966).

Some works that provide concise accounts of Mexico's modern history, from the period of independence in 1810 until the present, include the volume on modern Mexico edited by Leslie Bethell as part of the excellent Cambridge History of Latin America series. The particular volume on modern Mexico is *Mexico since Independence* (Cambridge: Cambridge University Press, 1991). This book is a thorough study of Mexican history from 1821 through the 1988 presidential elections. It comprises six essays written by prominent scholars of Mexican history, with each essay taking up a clearly defined period in Mexico's modern history. Perhaps the best aspect of this book is the inclusion of a comprehensive bibliographic essay. Colin H. MacLachlan and William H. Beezley's *El Gran Pueblo: A History of Greater Mexico* also provides an engaging account of Mexico's modern, postindependence history. MacLachlan and Beezley's book is of special interest for two reasons: the detail given to the late 19th century, or the period known as the Porfiriato, in Mexico's modern history, and the unique approach to understanding how the borderlands region factored decisively in the general course of Mexico's history. Although many scholars have spilled much ink in studying that phenomenon known as the Mexican Revolution, Alan Knight's painstakingly researched treatise on the event, a study so detailed and lengthy that it required two volumes, is unsurpassed in telling the complex story of the Mexican Revolution. The first volume is titled *The Mexican Revolution, Volume I: Porfirian Liberals and Peasants* (Cambridge: Cambridge University Press, 1990) and the second is *The Mexican Revolution, Volume 2: Counter-revolution and Reconstruction* (Cambridge: Cambridge University Press, 1990). Another very engaging study of Mexico's modern history since independence is Enrique Krauze's *Mexico: Biography of Power: A History of Modern Mexico, 1810–1996,* translated by Hank Heifetz (New York: HarperCollins, 1997). Krauze writes for a more popular audience. As such, his book reads easily and well but does not stray too far from standard institutional history organized around the different personalities of Mexico's political leaders. Krauze's book starts with a brief section of the highlights of Mexico's pre-Columbian and colonial history, which is immediately followed by another section that basically covers the entire 19th century. The remainder of the book, which constitutes the bulk of the writing, is focused on the 20th century and makes perhaps the strongest contribution to the study of modern Mexican history. Krauze was able to obtain access to documents and individuals previously inaccessible to scholars, and his work thus provides a unique glimpse into contemporary Mexican history.

Turning our attention to the nature and evolution of Mexico's economic system over the contemporary period, some general works that provide a readable overview of how this system evolved and transformed over the course of the 20th century include Nora Lustig's *Mexico: The Remaking of an Economy* (Washington, D.C.: Brookings Institution, 1992) and Judith A. Teichman's *Privatization and Political Change in Mexico* (Pittsburgh: University of Pittsburgh Press, 1995). Lustig's book surveys the transition of the Mexican economic model from the statism of the postrevolutionary period in 20th-century Mexico to the more open, free market–oriented, neoliberal model following the economic crises of the late 1970s and early 1980s. While touching on themes similar to Lustig, Teichman's book emphasizes how Mexico's transition between economic models influenced and was influenced by the nature of Mexico's social and political system.

In the realm of politics and government, perhaps the best and most succinct, but comprehensive, survey is Roderic Camp's *Politics in Mexico: The Democratic Consolidation,* 5th edition (New York: Oxford University Press, 2006). Camp's textbook covers all the basics of modern Mexican politics. Chapters in this text explore general political culture and values, the party and electoral system, political institutions and governing bodies, leadership elites and recruitment, nonstate actors and other interest groups who participate in the political process, U.S.-Mexican relations, and a summary of Mexico's current political reality focusing on the most pressing issues facing Mexican political elites today. Supplementing and expanding upon many of the subjects introduced by Camp is Daniel C. Levy and Kathleen Bruhn, with Emilio Zebadúa, *Mexico: The Struggle for Democratic Development,* 2nd edition (Berkeley: University of California Press, 2006). For another perspective on modern Mexico's social and political reality, Julia Preston and Samuel Dillon, journalists and former correspondents for the *New York Times* in Mexico, have written a book entitled *Opening Mexico: The Making of a Democracy* (New York: Farrar, Straus and Giroux, 2005), that compiles their observations of and reflections on the dramatic and unprecedented political transformation from semiauthoritarianism to democracy that is occurring in Mexico today.

One important subset of this political science literature focuses on Mexico's international relations, and particularly its relationship with the United States. Because Mexico has had such a complex and troubled relationship with the United States, and because the contrasts between these two bordering countries are so stark, the study of this relationship deserves special mention. Sifting through this literature, I would point to Clint E. Smith's *Inevitable Partnership: Understanding Mexico-U.S. Relations* (Boulder, CO: Lynne Rienner, 2000) as a good introduction to U.S.-Mexico relations. Another very interesting and illustrative book dealing with U.S.-Mexican relations is the volume co-authored by Robert A. Pastor and Jorge G. Castañeda, *Limits to Friendship: The United States and Mexico* (New York: Knopf, 1989). Although it is a bit dated, it is still a very valuable source because it presents a dialogue between individuals from each country over particular issues affecting the relationship. This dialogue highlights some of the ways that the United States and Mexico talk past one another and is a direct example of how the relationship between the countries functions even today.

Other works that discuss elements of Mexican society and popular culture include Patrick Oster's *The Mexicans: A Personal Portrait of a People,* 2nd edition (New York: HarperCollins, 2002), which imagines modern Mexico by looking at and describing various personality types among the Mexican population. These personality types presented by Oster, on the surface, seem to reinforce traditional stereotypes of the Mexican people, but Oster is careful to put such images in proper context and does not allow the reader to leave the book without confronting and challenging the accuracy or veracity of such stock images. Alan Riding's book *Distant Neighbors: A Portrait of the Mexicans* (New York: Knopf, 1989), although somewhat dated, is another outsider's perspective of modern Mexico that I consider still to be a valuable and worthwhile read, especially his chapter on U.S.-Mexican relations. In contrast to Oster and Riding, who both look at Mexico from a foreigner's viewpoint, the Mexican writer and intellectual Octavio Paz provides us with an interpretation of the Mexican character and psyche from within the culture. His classic and enduring work, *The Labyrinth of Solitude: The Other Mexico, Return to the Labyrinth of Solitude, Mexico and the United States, the Philanthropic Ogre* (New York: Grove Press, 1985), although philosophically and conceptually dense at points, should be required reading for anyone interested in understanding some of the roots of Mexican identity—or at least a compelling perspective on this identity. For an engaging set of stories that offer a view of what I call "modern Mexico on the margins," Sam Quinones, a North American journalist, has written a wonderful account of his impressions of a part of the Mexican identity that is often overlooked in academic scholarship in his *True Tales from Another Mexico* (Albuquerque: University of New Mexico Press, 2001).

Other general works on Mexico include William Canak and Laura Swanson's *Modern Mexico* (Boston: McGraw-Hill,

1998). This textbook, which was published as part of Mc-Graw-Hill's Comparative Society Series (Harold R. Kerbo, editor), offers a survey of modern Mexico mostly from an anthropological and sociological perspective. What sets this book apart from other social science surveys of modern Mexico is its inclusion of subjects such as family structure, educational systems, demographic trends, and social stratification that tend to be overlooked in most other social science introductory surveys of Mexico, which typically concentrate on history, politics, economics, and institutions.

ELECTRONIC AND INTERNET RESOURCES

The following is a list of electronic references that are invaluable to any study of Mexico. The Internet is a powerful resource for learning and for the dissemination of knowledge; but it is also fraught with misinformation and misleading polemics. The list I have compiled below represents electronic and Internet resources that are regularly updated, meticulously managed, and very reliable for providing excellent and quality coverage of Mexico.

Embassy of Mexico in the United States
portal.sre.gob.mx/usa/
    This link will bring you to the Mexican Secretariat of Foreign Relation's Web site for this embassy in the United States. Here you can get updated information on current events in Mexico as well as information that can help you plan a visit or travel to Mexico. From this Web site, you can also find information on the location of Mexico's many consulates spread out across the United States and a listing of services that these consulates and the embassy provide, both to Mexican nationals residing in the United States and to United States nationals interested in commerce with or travel to Mexico.

Latin America Network Information Center (LANIC)
lanic.utexas.edu/

This information Web portal on Latin America is managed by the University of Texas at Austin, under the auspices of its well-respected Institute for Latin American Studies. The staff of LANIC are very vigilant in monitoring both the content and the utility of the sources included in its listings. It is an excellent resource for the entire Latin American region and has sections specifically dedicated to each country within the region. Anyone interested in accurate and up-to-date information on Mexico can rely on LANIC as a resource.

Political Database of the Americas
pdba.georgetown.edu/

This database, managed by Georgetown University's Center for Latin American Studies, is especially useful for acquiring information on the governments and political systems of any Latin American country. At this site, one can readily find information on the electoral cycle, current elected officials, political parties, constitutions, and a variety of other topics related to the political life of the countries of Latin America.

The *World Factbook*
https://www.cia.gov/library/publications/the-world-factbook/index.html

The Central Intelligence Agency's *World Factbook* offers some consistent basic data on the countries of the region. Its research is very current and can give a snapshot of the current political, economic, and social conditions of almost any country in the world. Of course, any content or analysis published at this site is influenced by official U.S. policy considerations regarding the country in question, but it remains an invaluable resource for basic information on the countries of the world.

Mexico Connect
www.mexconnect.com/

This Web site is an excellent resource for individuals considering travel to Mexico. It is less relevant for scholarly research on the country, but it provides links to an extensive network of agencies, news outlets, arts and cultural forums, and many other interesting points of reference regarding Mexico that you will not often find at the more academically oriented Web portals and sites.

Mexico Online
www.mexonline.com/

Mexico Online is another site, like Mexico Connect, whose primary purpose is to reach an audience interested in basic information on the country that would be useful to students planning to study abroad in Mexico or tourists planning a short-term visit to the country. What is particularly interesting about this site is that it publishes brief content articles on Mexico's history, culture, and arts that are generally well informed and more deeply researched than many other popular content Internet sources on the country.

Index

About the Author

James D. Huck, Jr., is assistant director of Graduate Programs at the Center for Latin American Studies at Tulane University. He earned a BS in Foreign Service with a Certificate in Latin American Studies (1990) from Georgetown University, and both his MA (1993) and his PhD (1997) in Latin American Studies from Tulane. He served as the founding director of the Johnson Center for Latin American Studies at Albright College in Reading, Pennsylvania (1998–2000).